THE ECONOMIC AND SOCIAL IMPACT OF ELECTRONIC COMMERCE

Preliminary Findings and Research Agenda

ORGANISATION FOR ECONOMIC CO-OPERATION AND DEVELOPMENT

ORGANISATION FOR ECONOMIC CO-OPERATION AND DEVELOPMENT

Pursuant to Article 1 of the Convention signed in Paris on 14th December 1960, and which came into force on 30th September 1961, the Organisation for Economic Co-operation and Development (OECD) shall promote policies designed:

- to achieve the highest sustainable economic growth and employment and a rising standard of living in Member countries, while maintaining financial stability, and thus to contribute to the development of the world economy;
- to contribute to sound economic expansion in Member as well as non-member countries in the process of economic development; and
- to contribute to the expansion of world trade on a multilateral, non-discriminatory basis in accordance with international obligations.

The original Member countries of the OECD are Austria, Belgium, Canada, Denmark, France, Germany, Greece, Iceland, Ireland, Italy, Luxembourg, the Netherlands, Norway, Portugal, Spain, Sweden, Switzerland, Turkey, the United Kingdom and the United States. The following countries became Members subsequently through accession at the dates indicated hereafter: Japan (28th April 1964), Finland (28th January 1969), Australia (7th June 1971), New Zealand (29th May 1973), Mexico (18th May 1994), the Czech Republic (21st December 1995), Hungary (7th May 1996), Poland (22nd November 1996) and Korea (12th December 1996). The Commission of the European Communities takes part in the work of the OECD (Article 13 of the OECD Convention).

Publié en français sous le titre :

LES INCIDENCES ÉCONOMIQUES ET SOCIALES DU COMMERCE ÉLECTRONIQUE

Foreword

This book was prepared as a background document for the OECD Ministerial Conference on "A Borderless World: Realising the Potential of Global Electronic Commerce", held in Ottawa, Canada, in October 1998. It represents one of the very first analyses of the role of electronic commerce in the broader economy, and addresses such issues as the impact of e-commerce on employment and on society as a whole, as well as its contribution to economic growth and efficiency. The book presents a significant amount of data to provide policy makers with a picture of the current state and likely future direction of electronic commerce. The preliminary findings and broad policy implications constitute an initial analytical basis for understanding electronic commerce, how it may evolve and how it may transform our economies and societies. As with any analytical report which examines a phenomenon as young and complex as electronic commerce, it generates as many questions as it answers. These questions form the basis of a potential future research agenda which is outlined in the book. The book is divided into chapters organised according to major areas of impact – economic growth, economic efficiency, organisational change, employment, and broader social issues.

The OECD has been studying issues associated with the "Information Society" for nearly two decades. This book builds on that work, but represents a significant departure from those earlier studies as the focus has broadened to embrace an economy-wide perspective. To support this extension, advisory groups were created, and the book has benefited from significant review, both internally within the OECD, in Member countries, and from a group of private experts who attended a workshop where the book was discussed (Ottawa, 28-30 June 1998). In particular, the OECD would like to thank the following experts for their valuable contributions:

Dr. Richard Hawkins
Fellow – Information,
Networks & Knowledge (INK)
Science Policy Research Unit (SPRU)
University of Sussex, United Kingdom

Johan Helsingius
Director of Product Development
and Marketing
EUnet International BV

Prof. Jiro Kokuryo
Associate Professor
Keio University Graduate School of Business
Administration, Japan

Prof. Robin Mansell
Director – Information,
Networks & Knowledge (INK)
Science Policy Research Unit (SPRU)
University of Sussex, United Kingdom

Lynn Margherio
Business strategy consultant, United States

Michael McCracken
Chairman and CEO
Informetrica Limited, Canada

Professor Dr. Luc L.G. Soete
Director MERIT, Faculty of Economics
and Business Administration
University of Maastricht, The Netherlands

Philip Swan
Director of Economics
IBM Corporation, United States

The book, written by Andrew Wyckoff and Alessandra Colecchia of the Information, Computer and Communications Policy Division at the OECD, has also benefited from both substantive and financial contributions made by the Government of Canada. Canada's Electronic Commerce Task Force assisted in the drafting of some portions, particularly the chapter on the societal implications, hosted and financed the workshop where the book was discussed, and provided the French translation. The OECD would like to express its appreciation to Richard Simpson, Director General for Policy Coordination, and his team for their efforts in support of this work. At the OECD, substantive contributions by Anthony Rottier of the Secretary-General's Private Office, Dirk Pilat of the Science and Technology Policy Division, Muriel Faverie, consultant, Doranne Lecercle for the editing, and Pierre Montagnier for statistical assistance, are gratefully acknowledged.

Nevertheless, none of these individuals or organisations are accountable for the findings and conclusions of the book.

The book is published on my responsibility as Secretary-General of the OECD.

Table of contents

List of tables

List of figures

List of boxes

EXECUTIVE SUMMARY

Introduction

Electronic commerce over the Internet is a new way of conducting business. Though only three years old, it has the potential to radically alter economic activities and the social environment. Already, it affects such large sectors as communications, finance and retail trade (altogether, about 30 per cent of GDP). It holds promise in areas such as education, health and government (about 20 per cent of GDP). The largest effects may be associated not with many of the impacts that command the most attention (*e.g.* customised products, the elimination of middlemen) but with less visible, but potentially more pervasive, effects on routine business activities (*e.g.* ordering office supplies, paying bills, and estimating demand), that is, on the way businesses interact.[1]

Electronic commerce has the potential to radically alter some economic activities and the surrounding social environment.

Figure 1. **Growth in Internet host computers and major e-commerce developments**

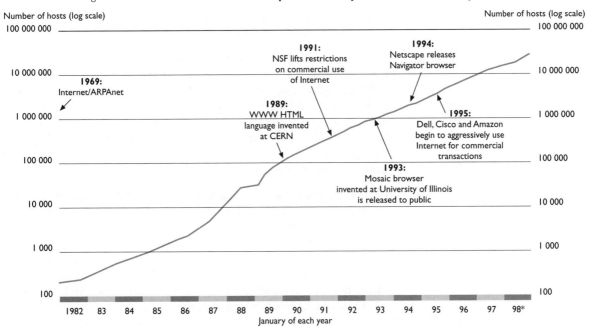

* New methodology used in January 1998.
Source: Network Wizards.

It emerged in the wake of regulatory reform and various technological innovations...

A combination of regulatory reform and technological innovation enabled e-commerce to evolve as it has. Although the precursor of the Internet appeared in the late 1960s, Internet e-commerce took off with the arrival of the World Wide Web and browsers in the early 1990s and the liberalisation of the telecommunications sector and innovations that greatly expanded the volume and capacity of communications (optic fibre, digital subscriber line technologies, satellites).

... and barriers to entry have fallen.

As a result, barriers to engage in electronic commerce have progressively fallen for both buyers and sellers. Earlier forms of e-commerce were mostly custom-made, complex, expensive and the province of large firms. Today, for a few thousand dollars, anyone can become a merchant and reach millions of consumers world-wide. What used to be business-to-business transactions between known parties has become a complex web of commercial activities which can involve vast numbers of individuals who may never meet. In this sense, the Internet has done for electronic commerce what Henry Ford did for the automobile – converted a luxury for the few into a relatively simple and inexpensive device for the many.

It is important to begin to explore these impacts and provide some analytical foundation for further work.

This book begins to explore these impacts and provides a preliminary analytical foundation for further work. It does not present an exhaustive analysis – it is too early for that – but musters as much information as possible so as to provide policy makers with a quantitative picture, albeit blurry, of the current state and likely future direction of electronic commerce. On this basis, policy makers can begin to outline the parameters of its impact and identify areas in need of future research.

Economic drivers of e-commerce

Five broad themes have emerged as important for understanding the economic and social impact of electronic commerce:

The effect on the marketplace...

Electronic commerce transforms the marketplace. E-commerce will change the way business is conducted: traditional intermediary functions will be replaced, new products and markets will be developed, new and far closer relationships will be created between business and consumers. It will change the organisation of work: new channels of knowledge diffusion and human interactivity in the workplace will be opened, more flexibility and adaptability will be needed, and workers' functions and skills will be redefined.

... the catalytic role...

Electronic commerce has a catalytic effect. E-commerce will serve to accelerate and diffuse more widely changes that are already under way in the economy, such as the reform of regulations, the establishment of electronic links between businesses (EDI), the globalisation of economic activity, and the demand for higher-skilled workers. Likewise, many sectoral trends already under way, such as electronic banking, direct booking of travel, and one-to-one marketing, will be accelerated because of electronic commerce.

... the impact on interactivity...

E-commerce over the Internet vastly increases interactivity in the economy. These linkages now extend down to small businesses and households and reach out to the world at large. Access will shift away from relatively expensive personal computers to cheap and easy-to-use TVs and telephones to devices yet to be invented. People will increasingly have the ability to communicate and transact business anywhere, anytime. This will have a profound impact, not the least of which will be the erosion of economic and geographic boundaries.

Openness is an underlying technical and philosophical tenet of the expansion of electronic commerce. The widespread adoption of the Internet as a platform for business is due to its non-proprietary standards and open nature as well as to the huge industry that has evolved to support it. The economic power that stems from joining a large network will help to ensure that new standards remain open. More importantly, openness has emerged as a strategy, with many of the most successful e-commerce ventures granting business partners and consumers unparalleled access to their inner workings, databases, and personnel. This has led to a shift in the role of consumers, who are increasingly implicated as partners in product design and creation. An expectation of openness is building on the part of consumers/citizens, which will cause transformations, for better (*e.g.* increased transparency, competition) or for worse (*e.g.* potential invasion of privacy), in the economy and society.

... and openness...

Electronic commerce alters the relative importance of time. Many of the routines that help define the "look and feel" of the economy and society are a function of time: mass production is the fastest way of producing at the lowest cost; one's community tends to be geographically determined because time is a determinant of proximity. E-commerce is reducing the importance of time by speeding up production cycles, allowing firms to operate in close co-ordination and enabling consumers to conduct transactions around the clock. As the role of time changes, so will the structure of business and social activities, causing potentially large impacts.

... and the relative importance of time are fundamental to understanding the economic and social impact of electronic commerce.

Main findings and future research agenda

The force that drive e-commerce will require a re-examination of the framework for conducting business and a questioning both of the efficacy of government policies pertaining to commerce and of traditional commercial practices and procedures, most of which were formed with a much different image of commerce in mind. Beyond these narrower considerations, electronic commerce is seen by many as having important implications for consumer protection, tax collection and trade and competition policies. These changes have helped to elevate electronic commerce to a high position on many Member countries' policy agendas and constitute the basis of much of the policy work, including the OECD's, on e-commerce issues. To better understand the importance, interaction and nature of these policies, it is necessary to understand the economic and social implications of e-commerce.

Changes brought about by e-commerce require new frameworks for conducting business and a re-examination of government policies relating to commerce.

The growth of electronic commerce

Given the embryonic state of electronic commerce, policies should be crafted with care and with due recognition of its fragile and evolving nature.

At present, electronic commerce over the Internet is relatively small (some $26 billion) but is growing very rapidly and may approach a trillion dollars by 2003-05. Even at that level, it would be less than current sales by direct marketing in the United States using mail, telephone and newspapers (Table 1). Clearly, electronic commerce is in an embryonic stage, and technology and market dynamics are still casting its basic shape. This is especially true for the business-to-consumer segment (which is only a small fraction of the business-to-business segment), where concerns about security of payment, potentially fraudulent merchants, privacy of personal data, and difficulty and expense in accessing e-commerce merchants affect its growth potential. These issues represent significant policy challenges. While the appeal of convenience and mass customisation may promote business-to-consumer e-commerce, its success is not assured. It may become no more than another channel for retailers, like mail order, rather than a new dominant mode of commerce. Policy decisions will have a major impact on the kind of environment in which e-commerce will develop and should therefore be crafted with care and with due recognition of its fragile and evolving nature.

Table 1. **Estimates of e-commerce sales compared to various benchmarks**

	Estimated revenue from e-commerce (US$ billion)	As a percentage of: US catalogue sales	As a percentage of: US credit card purchases	As a percentage of: direct marketing	As a percentage of: OECD-7 total retail sales
Current (1996/97)	26	37	3	2	0.5
Near-term (2001/02)	330	309	24	18	5
Future (2003/05)	1 000	780	54	42	15

Source: See notes to Table 1.3.

The business-to-consumer segment is potentially very important...

... but further examination of business-to-business e-commerce is warranted, given that it dominates overall e-commerce activity.

The near-term (2001/02) and future (2003/05) growth of e-commerce is much more likely to be determined by the business-to-business segment, which currently accounts for at least 80 per cent of total e-commerce activity. Three factors will contribute: i) a reduction in transaction costs and improvement of product quality/ customer service; ii) a defensive reaction to competitors engaging in e-commerce; and iii) insistence by large businesses that all of their suppliers link into their e-commerce system as a condition of doing business. The first factor, reduced transaction costs, drives the second and third. It is likely that the largest impact of business-to-business e-commerce will be on small and medium-sized enterprises (SMEs), because many large businesses already have EDI systems in place. The accessibility of the Internet makes electronic commerce a realistic possibility for SMEs and is likely to lead to its widespread diffusion. The fierce competition that surrounds use of e-commerce among businesses means that information about its impact is closely guarded; as a result, not enough is known about this important segment, making it a prime area for future research.

The United States accounts for about 80 per cent of the global total of electronic commerce. While its share will probably decrease, it does not face some of the constraints that confront Europe and Asia, such as high cost and the lack of sufficient bandwidth and the slow pace of planned liberalisation of the telecommunications sector. Experience with mail order sales suggests that European consumers are less inclined to use this mode of shopping than Americans, with per capita sales less than half of those in the United States. Although some Asian economies, especially Singapore and Hong Kong (China), have embraced electronic commerce, the impact has been uneven, especially across large countries like Japan and Korea. Countries will dismantle barriers to global electronic commerce at different speeds, and this may raise competitive concerns and pose possible risks to the efficient development of global electronic commerce.

Countries will dismantle barriers to global electronic commerce at different speeds...

... and this may raise competitive concerns and pose possible risks to the efficient development of global electronic commerce.

E-commerce's most significant impact will be on sectors that primarily transmit information (postal service, communications, radio and TV) and those that produce it (finance, entertainment, travel agents or stock brokers). Electronically delivered products such as software, travel services, entertainment and finance are leading products in both the business-to-business and business-to-consumer markets. Because of the intangible nature of such products, existing rules and practices will have to be re-examined.

Electronically delivered products in particular require a re-evaluation of existing rules and practices.

Statistics that measure the level, growth, and composition of e-commerce are lacking, as is a consistent definition of e-commerce. Both are needed to help focus the policy debate.

A better definition of e-commerce and better statistics are needed.

E-commerce and economic efficiency

A key reason why electronic commerce, especially the business-to-business segment, is growing so quickly is its significant impact on business costs and productivity. Because many of these applications are relatively simple, they may be expected to be widely adopted and have a large economic impact.

It is the impact on costs ranging from...

Even though some Web sites cost hundreds of millions of dollars, simpler sites can be designed and constructed for tens of thousands. In general, it is less expensive to maintain a cyber-storefront than a physical one because it is always "open", has a global market, and has fewer variable costs. For exclusively e-commerce merchants who maintain one "store" instead of many, duplicate inventory costs are eliminated.

... the cost of owning and operating a physical establishment...

A key factor in reducing inventory costs is adopting a "just-in-time" inventory system and improving the ability to forecast demand more accurately. Both of these can be accomplished through the adoption of electronic commerce, which strengthens the links between firms. Improved demand forecasting and replenishment of stocks is estimated to lead to a reduction in overall inventories of $250-$350 billion, or about a 20 to 25 per cent reduction in current US inventory levels. While this estimate is probably optimistic, pilot

... to carrying an inventory...

... to conducting a sale...

studies on the US auto market obtained a 20 per cent savings, and even a 5 per cent reduction would have a significant economic impact.

... to placing an order...

By placing the necessary information online in an accessible format, electronic commerce merchants greatly increase the efficiency of the sales process. As a result, even when customers complete a transaction in a traditional way (off-line), over the phone or in a showroom, they frequently arrive knowing which product they want and ready to buy. This can improve the productivity of sales people by a factor of ten (although in some cases it simply shifts the costs to consumers).

... to customer support and after-sales service...

The electronic interface allows e-commerce merchants to check that an order is internally consistent and that the order, receipt, and invoice match. While this simple process may seem trivial, both General Electric (GE) and Cisco report that one-quarter of their orders (1.25 million in the case of GE) had to be reworked because of errors. E-commerce has reduced Cisco's error rate to 2 per cent.

... to simple purchase orders and...

In what are increasingly knowledge-based economies dominated by sophisticated products, customer service and after-sales service are a major cost for many firms, accounting for more than 10 per cent of operating costs. Through electronic commerce, firms are able to move much of this support online so that customers can access databases or "smart" manuals directly; this significantly cuts costs while generally improving the quality of service.

... product distribution that is expected to fuel strong growth in the business-to-business segment of e-commerce.

Internet-based e-commerce procedures now make it possible to apply EDI-type systems to relatively small purchases, thereby drastically reducing errors, ensuring compliance with organisational norms, and speeding the process. Estimates of the savings gained range from 10 to 50 per cent, although in many cases the time reductions are as important as the monetary savings: firms report cutting the time needed to process purchase orders by 50 to 96 per cent.

Although shipping costs can increase the cost of many products purchased via electronic commerce and add substantially to the final price, distribution costs are significantly reduced (by 50 to 90 per cent) for electronically delivered products such as financial services, software, and travel (Table 2).

Table 2. **E-commerce impact on various distribution costs**

US$ per transaction

	Airline tickets	Banking	Bill payment	Term life insurance policy	Software distribution
Traditional system	8.0	1.08	2.22 to 3.32	400-700	15.00
Telephone-based		0.54			5.00
Internet-based	1.0	0.13	0.65 to 1.10	200-350	0.20 to 0.50
Savings (%)	87	89	71 to 67	50	97 to 99

Source: See notes to Table 2.4.

E-commerce over the Internet exploits a group of technologies – information and communication technologies (ICTs), software that links ICTs into a network regardless of the brand of hardware or software (Internet protocol), and relatively easy to use, universal, graphical interfaces (WWW and browsers) – with an application with broad appeal, commerce. This combination has the potential to provide the productivity gains that "prove" the worth of ICTs and unravel the "productivity paradox". An OECD estimate of the potential impact of cost reductions generated by retail (business-to-consumer) e-commerce in five OECD countries is of the order of one-half to two-thirds of a percentage point. This is a considerable gain, since a reduction in these costs is a rough proxy for productivity gains (total factor productivity – TFP) which has only averaged an annual increase of 0.8 per cent across the G7 economies in the recent past (1979-97). Given that the cost savings due to business-to-business e-commerce are significant and that the business-to-business segment represents a much larger portion of the overall total, these estimates can be considered conservative.

E-commerce has the potential to be the application that ushers in large productivity gains that prove the worth of ICTs.

Achieving these gains is contingent on a number of factors, including access to e-commerce systems and the requisite skills. However, what is unique about e-commerce over the Internet and the efficiency gains it promises is the premium placed on openness. To reap the potential cost savings fully, firms must be willing to open up their internal systems to suppliers and customers. This raises policy issues concerning security and potential anti-competitive effects as firms integrate their operations more closely. Another source of efficiency associated with e-commerce is the opportunity for "boundary crossing" as new entrants, business models, and changes in technology erode the barriers that used to separate one industry from another. This leads to increased competition and innovation, which are likely to boost overall economic efficiency. More generally, e-commerce highlights differences and similarities that may exist between products and industries, and suggests the need for a consistent regulatory environment.

However, as this segment of e-commerce grows and firms integrate their operations more closely, policy issues arise concerning security and potential anti-competitive effects.

While e-commerce can dramatically reduce some production costs, it does not really offer a "friction-free" environment. Rather, owing to new costs associated with establishing trust and reducing the risks inherent in this type of activity, it requires new intermediaries. Widespread "disintermediation" (producers selling directly to consumers without the aid of intermediaries) is unlikely to be any more pronounced than what has already occurred through direct mail, telephone, newspapers, TV and radio. A potentially larger impact involves the ease of access to information that to date has been possessed by intermediaries such as travel agents, insurance agents, stockbrokers and real estate agents. Rather than eliminating intermediaries, it is more likely that their role will be restructured and redefined.

E-commerce is unlikely to eliminate intermediaries, although their role is likely to change.

To date, e-commerce has not caused widespread price reductions, but lower costs associated with e-commerce should lead to lower prices as competition is felt, especially in services.

The translation of cost reductions into price reductions is not automatic. It is contingent on sufficient competition. Currently, price reductions attributable to e-commerce have only been evident in a few sectors (*e.g.* retail stock trading). However, the lower costs associated with e-commerce should lead to greater product, market and international competition, especially in services, and thus to greater price competition.

However, various factors might have a negative impact on competition in electronic markets.

Even if the growth of markets for services on electronic networks is increasing competition, it is not clear that there is a direct relation between the adoption of open links and open market structures. A number of factors could have a negative impact on competition in electronic markets, notably sector-specific transaction structures, first-mover advantages or differences in regulatory environments.

Electronic commerce will change the structure, if not the level, of pricing...

It is clear that electronic commerce will change the structure, if not the level, of pricing, as more and more products are subject to the differential pricing associated with customised products, fine market segmentation and auctions, and as the ease of changing prices increases. While these changes will generally improve economic efficiency, they may raise some consumer concerns. Consumers are accustomed to paying different prices for products such as cars, but they may be less comfortable with differentiated pricing for smaller, common purchases. In addition, the more widespread use of variable pricing, the advent of greater price competition, and the ability to change prices quickly may affect expectations about price movements. Changes in the structure of price setting will affect the ability to measure changes in prices and inflation accurately.

... and this will affect the ability to measure accurately changes in prices and inflation.

Business models, sectoral organisation and market structure

E-commerce is playing a catalytic role in transforming the marketplace.

While cyber-traders may not yet be representative of a new commercial paradigm, electronic commerce is playing a catalytic role in organisational change by opening up the possibility of new models for organising production and transacting business, thereby forcing existing firms to re-examine their cost structure and competition strategies.

E-commerce favours flatter organisational forms and a flexible work force.

E-commerce encourages streamlined business processes, flatter organisational hierarchies, continuous training, and inter-firm collaboration. Firms' ability to reorganise in the new electronic environment will crucially depend on the flexibility and adaptability of workers and on firms' continuing efforts to innovate.

E-commerce entails new ways of competing in domestic and international markets.

The Internet opens up certain proprietary relationships, extends relations between sectors, makes the electronic market accessible to smaller businesses and allows them to address international markets. The nature of competition as well as firms' strategies and competitive advantages in domestic and international markets also change. Increasingly, new entrants compete in setting standards and providing the interface, and Web-based alliances will play a strategic role in the emerging standard. Online firms also compete to capture customer information, and virtual communities could play a role in striking the balance of market power among consumers and suppliers. Work can be performed from a variety of locations and firms are increasingly being exposed to global competition.

Smaller firms may in fact benefit from the opportunities offered by electronic commerce as they are unencumbered by existing relationships with traditional retail outlets or a large sales force. They may adopt a business model that forces larger, established competitors to restructure their existing relationships or be seen as non-competitive. The Internet can level the competitive playing field by allowing small companies to extend their geographical reach and secure new customers in ways formerly restricted to much larger firms.

Smaller companies can benefit disproportionately from the opportunities offered by information technologies and electronic commerce.

Nonetheless, it is also possible that conditions of access to networks and connectivity, technical standards, institutional arrangements and the market power of well-known brands could pose barriers to entry that might impede SME involvement. This means that both governments and the business community must remain attentive to developments in the electronic marketplace in order to prevent or remove barriers to full SME participation.

Jobs and skills

There is concern that some of the efficiencies associated with electronic commerce will result in widespread dislocation of jobs. The preliminary analysis contained in this book, studies conducted by other researchers, and an examination of somewhat analogous activities (such as France's Minitel) do not support this concern at this stage. It seems more likely that, in the short term, there may be net employment creation as firms experiment with both modes of commerce, that, in the medium term, there may be some losses, especially in certain sectors, but that, in the longer term, the combination of new products, extended market reach, and income gains and lower prices derived from productivity increases will lead to net employment gains as increased sales of software, online services, audio-visual, music, publishing and yet-to-be invented products offset losses due to displacement of other products. These effects are likely to differ across countries, depending on the size and structure of e-commerce. These observations are necessarily speculative because, as a share of all economic activity, e-commerce is currently very small and its potential has not been fully realised.

Indirect, long-term employment effects due to demand for new or existing products are likely to offset shorter-term adjustments, although effects are likely to differ across countries.

Table 3. **IT jobs unfilled owing to skill shortages**

	Current estimate of unfilled jobs
World	600 000
United States	346 000
Germany	60 000
Canada	20 000/30 000
United Kingdom	20 000

Source: See notes to Annex Table 4.13.

E-commerce is likely to accelerate upskilling/multi-skilling trends in the OECD area work force.

What is clearer is the fact that electronic commerce will cause changes in the mix of skills required, driving demand for information technology (IT) professionals. This may exacerbate a supply shortage, which has received great attention in the United States, although it is not peculiar to that country (Table 3). For electronic commerce, IT expertise also needs to be coupled with strong business applications skills, and therefore requires a flexible, multi-skilled work force. Apart from contingent skills needed to support electronic commerce transactions and applications, there will be a more structural and long-term shift in the skills required to perform economic activities on line. In general, e-commerce is likely to accelerate existing upskilling/multi-skilling trends in the OECD work force.

These skill requirements place new demands on schools and vocational training facilities.

These skill requirements place new demands on schools and vocational training facilities. Becoming computer-literate can be a significant additional cost, one which is likely to vary as a function of age and educational background. A system of education that familiarises young students with the technology of the Internet can greatly reduce skills acquisition costs and decrease differences in participation rates in electronic commerce in the various segments of a society's population.

Changes in the labour force caused by e-commerce underscore the need for flexible labour markets and active labour policies that help workers adjust.

These changes in the labour force caused by e-commerce underscore the need for flexible labour markets and active labour policies that help workers adjust to changes in these markets. This will be particularly important for those service sector jobs, such as those in retailing, that have not yet been exposed to significant technological change or international competition.

Social implications

Societal factors merit policy attention in order to establish the social conditions that will allow electronic commerce to reach its full economic potential and to ensure that its benefits are realised by society as a whole.

Although primarily an economic phenomenon, electronic commerce is part of a broader process of social change, characterised by the globalisation of markets, the shift towards an economy based on knowledge and information, and the growing prominence of all forms of technology in everyday life. These major societal transformations are now under way and will probably continue far into the foreseeable future. As both a product and manifestation of such transformations, electronic commerce is being shaped by, and increasingly will help to shape, modern society as a whole especially in the areas of education, health and government services. Societal factors will merit attention from a public policy standpoint, both to establish the social conditions that allow electronic commerce to reach its full economic potential and to ensure that its benefits are realised by society as a whole. Two such elements are first, access and its determinants (*e.g.* income) and constraints (*e.g.* time) and, second, confidence and trust.

Policies that promote the development and availability of information technologies and access to advanced networks may be required.

Access to the physical network will affect the adoption of e-commerce, particularly among consumers and SMEs located outside the urban centres of the developed world. One consistent finding across many countries is that there is a strong positive correlation between the use of information technology (PC ownership, access to the Internet) and household income: for every

$10 000 increase in household income, the percentage of homes owning a computer increases by seven points (Figure 2). Governments might well look at ways to promote the development and availability of information technologies and access to advanced networks, either by means of conventional telecommunications policy measures or through other appropriate policy instruments.

Internet penetration rates show a similar pattern. As a consequence, households with higher incomes have more opportunity to benefit from electronic commerce than those with lower incomes. While this phenomenon is common to the introduction of most new technologies (*e.g.* electricity, telephone, TV), it may warrant the attention of policy makers since e-commerce could provide access to a market with special properties, such as lower prices, that could particularly benefit the disadvantaged. This fuels concerns about greater inequality due to information "haves" and "have nots". There is reason to believe that the correlation between income levels and Internet usage may weaken, as lower-cost and simpler alternatives to the traditional personal computer become available, although recent work carried out in the United States between 1994 and 1997 reveals a widening gap in PC ownership between upper and lower income groups. Governments may wish to consider what policies, if any, might encourage the trend towards lower prices and thus accelerate connectivity.

The correlation between income and access to the Internet means that policies to ensure access for lower income groups may be needed.

Figure 2.   ***Computer penetration rates, by household income, in Australia, Canada, Japan and the United States***

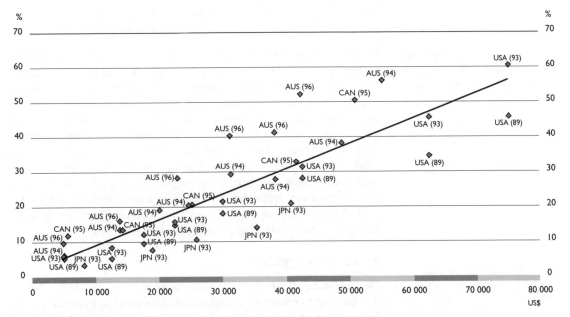

1.   Household incomes were converted to US$ using PPPs. Income values were obtained by taking the midpoint of each income bracket except for the upper open-ended ranges where the lower bounds were used.
Source: OECD, 1997c.

Where teledensities are low, public access sites located in schools, post offices, community centres, public libraries or even franchised shops are likely to be a potential alternative.

Visions of a global knowledge-based economy and universal electronic commerce characterised by the "death of distance" must be tempered by the reality that half the world's population has never made a telephone call, much less accessed the Internet. In countries with extremely low teledensities, universal access must be defined in some way other than access from every home; the alternative is access at the level of community or institutions. Public access sites located in schools, post offices, community centres, public libraries or even franchised shops are potential alternatives to home-based access.

A better understanding of the impact of e-commerce on time use is needed because availability of free time is a driver of demand for e-commerce, since many of its products are interactive.

E-commerce and other information and communication technologies reduce the importance of time as a factor that dictates the structure of economic and social activity. It raises the potential for saving time as consumers shop more efficiently, but could also reduce leisure, as the technology can provide a continuous electronic link to work. A better understanding of the impact of e-commerce and ICTs on time use is needed because the availability of free time is an essential factor in driving demand for e-commerce, since many e-commerce products (*e.g.* entertainment) are interactive and require immediate consumption.

More generally, it is necessary to better understand the impact of faster and more interlinked exchanges on individuals, organisations, governments and communities.

Whereas technological development is taking place at an astounding and accelerating speed, reaching understanding and consensus, especially on social issues, is typically time-consuming. The nature of the Internet forces a reconsideration of the most effective way to govern and of whether centralised decision making can keep up with the speed and fluidity of the Internet. This suggests the need to consider decentralised modes of decision making, such as self-regulatory mechanisms. Another option may be to consider methods of controlling speed by "throwing sand into the wheels". This points to the need to develop a deeper understanding of the impact of faster and more interlinked exchanges on individuals, organisations, governments and communities.

A fuller understanding of what is needed to foster confidence in electronic markets, particularly among consumers, must be sought.

One of the hallmarks of electronic commerce is that, by drastically reducing transaction and search costs, it reduces the distance between buyer and seller, enabling businesses to target very small niches, develop individual customer profiles, and essentially provide a means of marketing on a one-to-one basis. The ability to realise this goal will largely hinge on the climate of confidence and trust that businesses are able to create in their relations with their business partners and customers. Assurances about protection of privacy and personal information play an important role in building that confidence. Both the public and private sectors need a fuller understanding of the requirements for fostering confidence in electronic markets, particularly among consumers.

Broad policy implications

These findings have many implications for policy. While the intent of this book is to establish a preliminary analytical foundation on which further work can be developed and to suggest a research agenda, the potential policy implications have a direct bearing on this agenda. Many of the narrower policy implications have been identified, while others (*e.g.* privacy, consumer protection, access to the infrastructure, taxation) are analysed in depth elsewhere by the OECD and other organisations (*e.g.* WTO on trade issues). Nevertheless, the horizontal, potentially pervasive impact of electronic commerce has implications for broader economic and social policies as well.

Technology policy

One of the key features of electronic commerce is the potential system-wide gains in efficiency to be reaped when firms are linked across industries. Fostering such system-wide improvements requires rethinking technology and innovation policies, such as technology diffusion programmes, which tend to focus on one industry, such as manufacturing, while in fact the largest contributions to system-wide gains may come from services, such as wholesale trade, transportation and retail trade. This suggests the need to widen the notion of "innovation" from a focus on high technology in manufacturing to include consumer goods and services and to adopt a more systemic perspective.

The focus of technology policy should be broadened to give greater attention to consumer goods and services and systemic objectives.

Trade policy

Issues of how to accommodate products bought and sold by electronic commerce in existing trade rules are being analysed at the WTO. E-commerce will increase international trade, particularly in electronically delivered products, many of which are services which have not yet been exposed to significant international trade but have been "traded" through foreign direct investment or have operated on a global level only for large corporate clients. This change may come as a shock to sectors that have been sheltered by logistical or regulatory barriers. In addition, it will generate pressures to reduce differences in regulatory standards – accreditation, licensing, restrictions on activity – for newly tradable products.

E-commerce will generate pressures to reduce differences in regulatory standards for newly tradable products.

Competition policies

As the ease of forming business networks increases, as traditional market boundaries blur, and as technology undermines the rationale for the monopoly privileges granted to many service activities, competition policy will have to address new types of anticompetitive practices. Many e-commerce products benefit from non-rivalry (one person's consumption does not limit or reduce the value of the product to other consumers), network externalities (each additional user of a product increases its value to other users), and increasing returns to scale (unit costs decrease as sales increase). These factors create an environment where producers may seek to engage in practices that permit them to establish themselves as the, or part of the, de facto standard. This can hinder innovation and competition.

Competition policy will have to address new types of anti-competitive practices.

Regulatory reform

Current policies pertaining to commercial transactions should be looked at in terms of their applicability to electronic commerce.

Electronic commerce raises many issues regarding the application of existing regulations and issues such as tax law, commercial codes and consumer protection which have received a lot of attention. However, it also calls into question the applicability of retail regulations designed for a "bricks and mortar" world, such as restrictions on the size of stores and opening hours, limitations on pricing and promotions, granting of monopolies for the sale of certain products (*e.g.* liquor) and permit and licensing requirements. In many cases, these regulations need to be re-examined in light of the realities of electronic commerce. In addition to these regulations are those that continue to apply to communications. For e-commerce to function properly, cheap and easy access to information and communication technologies is needed; conditions that increase their cost will slow the diffusion of e-commerce and place industries that use information technologies at a disadvantage.

Social policies

Social policies need to support an entrepreneurial culture that promotes cross-fertilisation, risk taking and boundary crossing.

While small, e-commerce has the potential to grow quickly and may be symptomatic of other applications that have been enabled by advances in information and communication technologies that create demand for new skills, new organisational structures, and new businesses models and generally increase the speed and geographic reach of economic and social activity. To many, these changes appear to be occurring more quickly than in the past and this may create a sense of insecurity. While it is unclear whether the pace of change is faster than in the past, insecurity may be lessened by social policies that match the fluidity of the economy: *e.g.* pensions that are portable between employers, education that occurs over a lifetime, health services that are not tied to a particular job.

Business-government policies

The experience of the last three decades suggests that governments should not intervene unduly in e-commerce, nor should they simply be spectators.

Nearly all parties agree that the Internet and e-commerce will be led by business, with government playing a minimalist role. The dynamism of the e-commerce market as described in this book would support this view. Nonetheless, it is important to recall that governments have played, and continue to play, a critical role in developing technology for these activities, and that they have an obligation to pursue broad societal goals. Conventional economic theory would suggest that governments should only subsidise basic research into ICT technologies. However, the experience of the past three decades shows that most of the major ICT innovations [*e.g.* timesharing, networking, routers, workstations, optic fibres, semiconductors (RISC, VLSI), parallel computing], many of which are more applied or developmental in nature, are the result of government-funded research or government programmes. This is also true of e-commerce. The Internet's forerunner (ARPAnet), the World Wide Web (CERN), and the browser (government centre at the University of Illinois) were developed with government support. Government procurement and demonstration projects also play an important part. While governments should not intervene excessively in this area, neither should they simply be spectators. Governments will need to work closely with business to maximise the potential of this activity.

Productivity and growth

A key economic impact of e-commerce today is its beneficial impact on reducing firms' production costs. This is identified as a factor that will spur the use of e-commerce within and between businesses. Although there are measurement problems associated with capturing the quality changes inherent in many of these activities, it is assumed that e-commerce will result in productivity gains. Given that e-commerce is more a way of doing business than a sector, these gains could be distributed widely across OECD economies – including in the services sector, which has not enjoyed significant, measurable productivity gains in the past – and could help to enable long-term growth. As e-commerce evolves, it is likely to follow the "reverse product cycle", in which process efficiency gains are followed by quality improvements to existing products and then the creation of new products. Typically, it is in this final stage that significant economic growth occurs. E-commerce has the potential to be a platform from which significant new products emerge, many of which will be digital and delivered online. New products have a tendency to beget more new products and processes in a virtuous spiral, just as Edison's electric lamp led to the development of power generation and delivery, which led to other electrical products.

E-commerce is expected to result in productivity gains and growth and to be a source of many new products as well.

CONCLUSION

Still small in economic terms, e-commerce has the potential to accelerate existing trends and introduce new ways of conducting business, organising work and interacting in society. As with the advent of any new technology that may be widely diffused, there are overly optimistic and pessimistic predictions, which are generally inaccurate (mail order has not displaced traditional retail trade and the VCR has not displaced teachers). Nor is this the first time that our societies have been exposed to the broad diffusion of information and communication technologies: over the 20-year period from 1874 to 1895, the typewriter, telephone, phonograph, electric light, punch card, hydro-electric plant, automated switchboard, cinema and radio were all invented. At this point, research is needed in order to see more clearly the problems and the potential.

These preliminary findings and broad policy implications constitute an initial analytical basis for identifying areas of future research. The following conclusions are offered for discussion with the aim of establishing research priorities concerning the economic and social impact of electronic commerce.

Fundamental to any analytical work on electronic commerce is the ability to measure it accurately. To focus the policy debate, statistics that measure the level, growth, and composition of e-commerce are badly needed. Today, while nearly all sources indicate that business-to-business e-commerce dominates the market, most existing analysis and available data focus on the business-to-consumer segment.

- *A statistical methodology and apparatus for measuring electronic commerce should be developed. Key areas for future research are the business-to-business segment; electronically delivered products such as software, travel services, entertainment and finance; and country-specific differences in the size and growth potential of electronic transactions.*

A main reason for the rapid growth of electronic commerce, especially the business-to-business segment, is its significant impact on costs associated with inventories, sales execution, procurement and distribution, and with intangibles like banking. To reap the potential cost savings fully, firms must be willing to open up their internal systems to suppliers and customers. As firms integrate their operations more closely, issues of security and potential anti-competitive effects arise. More generally, e-commerce illuminates differences that may exist between products, industries and countries, thereby highlighting the need to reform inconsistent regulations.

- *The economy-wide and sector-specific impact of e-commerce on productivity should be assessed, and the notion that this application may lead to a sustained higher level of economic efficiency should be explored.*

E-commerce can dramatically reduce some production costs, but it does not offer a "friction-free" environment. Rather, owing to new costs associated with establishing trust and reducing inherent risks, it requires new intermediaries. Widespread "disintermediation" (producers selling directly to consumers without aid of intermediaries) is unlikely, but the nature of intermediary functions is likely to change.

- *Monitoring of the restructuring of intermediary functions is needed.*

Cost reductions are not automatically translated into price reductions. They are contingent on sufficient competition. Electronic commerce will certainly change the structure, if not the level, of pricing as more products are subject to the differential pricing associated with customised products, fine market segmentation and auctions, and as the ease of changing prices increases.

- *While a general assessment of the impact of e-commerce on prices may be premature, sectoral studies on a variety of consumer and business products should be undertaken to measure the impact and identify factors that encourage and inhibit price competition, including the use of intelligent agents. The impact of the structure of price setting and of the frequency of price changes on markets and on measurement also requires study.*

Electronic commerce is transforming the marketplace by changing firms' business models, by shaping relations among market actors, and by contributing to changes in market structure. Electronic commerce also changes firms' competitive advantages and the nature of firms' competition. Given the dynamic nature of these processes, the impact of electronic commerce will be firm-, sector-, and time-specific.

- *The electronic marketplace needs to be continuously monitored. Case studies should address the sectoral and market specificity of organisational impacts. Ongoing assessment of potential new barriers to market entry is also needed.*

Research on the evolving nature of the commercial environment will help policy makers address issues of commercial governance, which are critical to the development of electronic commerce. Asymmetries in firms' ability to control access to the electronic marketplace should also be investigated. This research will help policy makers to address competition issues, as well as to formulate policies targeted to SMEs.

The overall impact of electronic commerce on employment is the net result of the countervailing forces of job displacement in one industry and job creation in another. Electronic commerce will also create new markets or extend market reach beyond traditional borders. The final effect on jobs will depend crucially on development of demand for electronic activities.

● *Case studies can help to better understand impacts on sectoral employment. As the employment potential of electronic commerce differs among countries, differences in their production of Web-related hardware and software content, which seems to be driving employment gains from electronic commerce, should be explored. Also, the impact on employment in the distribution sector, which will depend on countries' regulatory and organisational differences, should be investigated. Given the crucial role played by demand, trends in demand for new activities should be monitored and policy makers should be made aware of the factors underlying country-specific differences.*

Electronic commerce generates demand for a flexible, multi-skilled work force and is likely to accelerate existing upskilling trends in the OECD labour force.

● *It is important to identify specific skill needs for e-commerce and opportunities for worker requalification. Policies to cope with skill mismatches will have to be reinforced as the volume of electronic transactions increases. Better methodologies and data are needed for tracking rapidly changing skill requirements and monitoring labour market responses and adjustment mechanisms given the swiftly changing demand for different categories of ICT workers.*

Fundamental changes are taking place at virtually every level of society, prompted by the growth of the Internet, electronic commerce and other applications of information networks.

● *Since gaining access to the network is crucial for participating in the "Information Society", the factors that help and hinder access to the Internet, such as cost, language and skills, should be analysed to learn whether they can explain differences observed across countries.*

Many efficiency gains in the electronic marketplace will hinge on the climate of confidence businesses can create in their relations with their business partners and customers. Assurances of protection of privacy and personal information play an important role in building that confidence. Both the public and private sectors need a fuller understanding of the requirements for fostering confidence in electronic markets, particularly among consumers.

● *It is necessary to better understand the economics associated with the use and protection of private information, and the means to evaluate the costs and benefits of various proposals to protect or reveal private information. These may include firm- and industry-level benefits, and costs of assuring the confidentiality and integrity of personal data; the relative impact of firm-based, sectoral-based and economy-wide standards for safeguarding personal information; and the effects on trade and investment of divergent levels of privacy protection across economies and jurisdictions.*

NOTE

1. The analysis focuses disproportionately on the United States, owing to the availability of material. Because of the size of that country and its cultural and regulatory characteristics, the relevance of its experience to other countries may be limited. However, information and communication technologies (ICTs) are closely linked to the emergence of electronic commerce, and as ICT diffusion rates in other countries begin to approach those of the United States (or of countries such as Finland), their experience may be similar. If so, the demographic and industrial diversity of the United States may provide a useful indication of what can be expected in other countries that openly embrace ICTs. Lastly, the Internet is less country-specific and more international in nature than earlier ICTs, so that its impact in any given country is likely to be more generalisable than that of earlier ICTs (*i.e.* France's Minitel). While this book tries to rely on scholarly work and solid statistical data as much as possible, to gain insight into the macroeconomic impact of a phenomenon that is changing as quickly as e-commerce requires relying on private data sources, expert opinion, the popular press and anecdotal statistics as well.

Chapter 1

GROWTH OF ELECTRONIC COMMERCE: PRESENT AND POTENTIAL

The promise of significant economic growth places electronic commerce (see Box 1.1) high on many public and private sector agendas. And to date, the growth has been impressive. Starting from basically zero in 1995, total electronic commerce is estimated at some $26 billion for 1997; it is predicted to reach $330 billion in 2001-02 (near term) and $1 trillion in 2003-05 (future). These estimates are very speculative and rank among the highest of the dozen estimates generated by various management consultancy or market research firms (Table 1.1). They are adopted so as to ensure complete geographical (world) and product (business-to-business and business-to-consumer) coverage and because recent reports of sales by leading e-commerce merchants (Table 1.2) suggest that the growth rate may be faster than expected.

To put these estimates into a broader context, four benchmarks are selected for comparison: US catalogue sales, purchases made on credit cards in the United States, total sales generated by direct marketing in the United States, and retail sales summed across seven OECD countries.[1] Electronic commerce in 1995-97 is the equivalent of 37 per cent of US mail order catalogue shopping, 3 per cent of US purchases using credit/debit cards, and 0.5 per cent of the retail sales of the seven OECD economies (Table 1.3). The near-term estimate suggests that e-commerce will quickly overwhelm US catalogue shopping. If the optimistic future forecast (2003-05) is realised, OECD-wide e-commerce will be the equivalent of 15 per cent of the total retail sales of seven OECD countries. While significant, this level of activity is less than current sales generated by direct marketing in the United States through mail, telephone and newspapers (Direct Marketing Association, 1998).

Table 1.1. **Comparison of various total e-commerce estimates**

US$ million

Activity	1995-97	2000-02
Total		
IDC	1 000	117 000
INPUT	70	165 000
VeriFone	350	65 000
ActivMedia	24/400	1 522 000
Data Analysis	2 800	217 900
Yankee	850	144 000
E-land	450	10 000
EITO	475	262 000
AEA/AU	200	45 000
Hambrecht & Quest	1 170	23 200
Forrester	8 000	327 000
Morgan Stanley	600	375 000
Median value	725	154 500

Sources: Girishankar, 1998a; http://www.tpn.geis.com (10 May 1997); Morishita, 1997; Borland, 1997b; Morgan Stanley Dean Witter, 1997; Direct Newsline, Media Daily Archive, 1998; Strassel, 1997b; Margherio *et al.*, 1998; "PC Week's Top-10 E-commerce Sites", http://www.pcweek.com (14 January 1997); "Lawsuite Aside, Amazon.com Racks Up Sales", www.techweb.com (16 February 1998); "Barnes and Noble Sees $100M in Online Sales", www.techweb.com (19 January 1998); Jackson, 1997b; "The Once and Future Mall", *The Economist* (1 November 1997); Margolis, 1998; "CyberSex", *The Economist* (4 January 1997); Weber, 1997; Sussman, 1997; Macavinta, 1998; Schwartz, 1995; Brunker, 1997; "Competition on the Rise as Net Music Sales Take Off", www.internetnews.com (13 February 1998). Detailed sources available on request.

Box 1.1. Defining electronic commerce

In order to explore and estimate the socio-economic impacts of electronic commerce, it is essential to define electronic commerce. As with many new services, this is not a simple matter, as definitions given by various sources differ significantly. Some include all financial and commercial transactions that take place electronically, including electronic data interchange (EDI), electronic funds transfers (EFT), and all credit/debit card activity. Others limit electronic commerce to retail sales to consumers for which the transaction and payment take place on open networks like the Internet. The first type refers to forms of electronic commerce that have existed for decades and result in trillions of dollars worth of activity every day. The second type has existed for about three years and is barely measurable.

Enter the Internet

This study takes a view somewhere between these two extremes. It is concerned specifically with business occurring over networks which use non-proprietary protocols that are established through an open standard setting process such as the Internet. As used here, the term "business" broadly means all activity that generates value both within a firm (internally) and with suppliers and customers (externally). In this sense it would include internal networks (*e.g.* intranets) as well as networks that extend to a limited number of participants (*e.g.* extranets). Some of this activity may result in a monetary transaction and some will not. To assess the economic impact of e-commerce more fully, that portion of the infrastructure which is primarily dedicated to such activity is also included.

The focus on networks that use non-proprietary protocols, which are a relatively new phenomenon, is central. Earlier forms of e-commerce required pre-existing relationships, expensive and complex custom software, and dedicated communication links. In many cases, the system required strictly compatible equipment. Consequently, the main users of early e-commerce (EDI and EFT) were large businesses and their first-tier suppliers. These links created two-way markets between specific parties. While such forms of e-commerce will continue, recent attention to e-commerce is due to the Internet and its open, non-proprietary protocol (Transport Control Protocol/Internet Protocol – TCP/IP), to the development of the World Wide Web (WWW) which uses a standard coding system (hypertext markup language – HTML) for representing data, and to the development and diffusion of browsers that provide a standard interface for accessing WWW sites. All of these technologies use existing communication systems to create a network that is independent of any one platform. In fact, one of the drivers of the Internet is the fact that it exploits all of the existing ICT infrastructure, so that it can be used with a minimal amount of new investment. Telephone systems, computer systems, and cable TV systems can be interconnected, largely thanks to the widespread regulatory reform of communications systems, which has eroded the boundaries that previously separated the different systems and led to competition and innovation, thereby lowering costs and vastly increasing options.

This new information infrastructure has certain properties which make it attractive to users and help to propel its exponential growth:

– The cost of accessing the Internet is very low compared with networks that adhere to proprietary systems. This has reduced users' fears that the technology may quickly become obsolete or be abandoned and has encouraged many to adopt it and build to the current standard. Inclusiveness is a hallmark of open networks like the Internet, and the widespread adoption of these standards has created a virtuous circle: a significant industry is innovating and producing to these standards, with the result that they are being extended to a wide range of data, including voice, audio and video.

– The combination of technologies – Internet, WWW and browser – enable interactive media that allows one-to-many communication. It accommodates customer feedback and interaction (Wigand, 1997) and presents a significant advantage over other e-commerce technologies such as EDI, TV, and telephone. In a sense, EDI is a market, while e-commerce over open networks is a marketplace in which all types of buyers and sellers can interact (Richard Hawkins, SPRU, personal communication).

Because each of these technologies is evolving, today's "Internet" may very well become a different set of technologies and standards in the future. Yet the appeal of universal connectivity keeps most of these fundamental technologies (*e.g.* a new TCP/IP version, new mark-up text language) open and non-proprietary (*e.g.* Java, Netscape Communicator code). This both generates and encourages a large industry that supports and develops the Internet; it also explains why the current interest in and enthusiasm for e-commerce is focused on Internet-enabled e-commerce. Thanks to these technologies and to institutional reforms, the cost and difficulty of electronic commerce have decreased, so that average consumers can routinely engage in it from their homes.

Box 1.1. Defining electronic commerce (*cont.*)

A policy-driven definition of e-commerce

By focusing on e-commerce over networks which use an open, non-proprietary standard, the definition adopted here can be narrowed to an *application* that operates across an information and communication infrastructure like the Internet. Viewed in this way, electronic commerce is one of many applications and components of the broader Internet and the ICT sector. This book does not attempt to synthesise the extensive work that has been conducted on the impact of ICT on OECD economies, but it draws upon that work when it provides insight into how e-commerce may affect our economies. The division is not always clear and presents many conceptual problems. Why does the migration of commercial activity from a proprietary EDI system to an Internet EDI system not count as e-commerce one day but count as e-commerce the next? Do other internal business production processes, such as the "publication" of company phone directories on an intranet, constitute e-commerce? Like any definition of cross-cutting activities (*e.g.* tourism), it is difficult to make sharp distinctions, and further analysis and refinement are needed. However, the Internet protocol makes such a difference in terms of its potential reach, that it makes a useful demarcation point. Moreover, adopting too broad a definition would dilute the utility of an impact analysis and the policy implications that may be drawn from it. Nevertheless, there are important lessons to be learned from other, non-Internet based, forms of electronic commerce, especially in terms of identifying some of the broader social impacts. Where appropriate, allusions to these other types of electronic commerce will be made.

Future research agenda

Future work analysing electronic commerce would clearly benefit from the adoption of a definition that would provide some consistency across studies and a reference point for the collection of data. Work to develop a definition should be undertaken at the national and international level in consultation with business, labour and consumer representatives. Because of inherent differences in policy interests, a flexible definition based on a core concept which can then be expanded to include other aspects of electronic commerce may be the most practical.

This chapter analyses the geographic distribution, product mix and sectoral penetration, and likely growth of electronic commerce now (1995-97), in the near-term (2000-02), and in the future (2003-05). It does this by marshalling as many estimates as possible, for two main reasons:

– first, to reveal the huge variance that exists across various estimates, a fact that underscores the lack of empirical rigour that plagues measurement of this activity (see Box 1.2) and should raise cautionary flags about the use of any one set of estimates (including those presented above);

– second, by drawing together such disparate data, it may be possible to construct a mosaic which provides a clearer quantitative picture of the current structure and future direction of e-commerce.

Electronic commerce in the United States, Europe and Asia

At present, the United States is typically credited with about four-fifths of world-wide e-commerce activity (Table 1.5). Again, the figures are very rough (see Box 1.2). They suggest that Western Europe represents about 10 per cent and Asia about 5 per cent of the world total. In Europe, the United Kingdom and the Nordic countries are the current leaders, although some estimates attribute significant activity to Germany (Table 1.5). A supporting indicator is the location of the top 100 Web sites for consumer (retail) activity (Table 1.6). For each of the major categories of e-commerce activities – live audio, shopping, finance, and content (news, sports, adult) – the United States typically has 67 to 85 of the top 100 sites. Canada comes in second for five out of the six categories. Another proxy is the number of adults who access the Internet (Figure 1.1); the United States accounts for more than half of the OECD total.

Over the near term, the United States' lead is expected to decline to about two-thirds to three-quarters of world total e-commerce activity,[2] particularly because France's Minitel and Germany's T-Online services have accustomed their citizens to online buying; as these services migrate to the Internet, e-commerce should expand. Also, Europe may see a user-led demand pull, in contrast to the technology push thought to characterise the US situation (Hawkins, 1998).

Table 1.2. **Selected individual firm e-commerce revenues by activity**

US$ million

Activity	1995-97
E-commerce: business-to-business	
CSX	3 000
GE	1 000
NEC	16 528
Cisco (e-commerce sales)	2 496
Computers: Dell	730
Computers: Gateway	150
Computers: NECX	35
Images: Photodisc	4
Total business-to-business	**23 943**
E-commerce: business-to-consumer	
Autos: Auto-By-Tel	14
Flowers: 1-800-Flowers	48
Books: Amazon	148
Books: Barnes & Noble	14
Groceries: Peapod	60
Groceries: NetGrocer	78
Gardening: Garden Escape	1
Misc.merchandise: AoL	464
Misc.merchandise: Onsale.com	100
Misc. merchandise: NetMarket.com (Cendant (CUC))	1 000
Misc. merchandise: Internet Shopping Network	15
Misc. merchandise: eBay	100
Toys: eToys	10
Newspapers: Wall Street Journal	7
Travel: Expedia	104
Travel: Preview	12
Travel: EasySABRE and Travelocity	100
Ticket sales by Ticketmaster	60
Pornography: Virtual Dreams	8
Pornography: Internet Entertainment Group	20
Pornography: Persian Kitty	1
Pornography: CyberErotica	9
Pornography: Playboy	4
On-line gambling: Sports International	6
On-line gambling: Interactive Gambling and Communications	58
Music: CDnow	15
Music: Tower Records	8
Music: N2K	12
Consumer stock brokerage: E*Trade	148
Total business-to-consumer	**2 624**
Total	**26 567**

Source: See Table 3.1.

Table 1.3. **Estimates of e-commerce sales compared to various benchmarks**

	E-commerce estimates (US$ billion)	US catalogue sales (percentage)	US credit card purchases (percentage)	Direct marketing (percentage)	OECD-7 total retail sales (percentage)
Current (1996/97)	26	37	3	2	0.5
Near-term (2001/02)	330	309	24	18	5
Future (2003/05)	1 000	780	54	42	15

Source: OECD estimates; US catalogue sales ($78.6 billion) and direct marketing sales ($1 226.0 billion) data and growth rates (6.3 and 8.7 respectively) are from Direct Marketing Association (1998), ''Economic Impact: US Direct Marketing'', April; credit card activity is based on VISA and MasterCard US charges in 1997 ($870 billion) and the 1996 to 1997 growth rate of 10 per cent; OECD-7 retail sales ($5 328 billion) are for Canada (1997), France (1996), Finland (1997), Germany (1995), Japan (1994), United Kingdom (1994) and the United States (1997).

Box 1.2.   Data and measurement issues for e-commerce

For many reasons – its recent emergence, its fast growth from a small base, entry and exit by a wide variety of firms (often small and not publicly traded), and the multitude of business models being tested – traditional sources of economic data such as public statistical offices have not yet compiled data on electronic commerce (see Box 3.2). Consequently, the only readily available data come from firms engaging in e-commerce or from market research firms or management consulting firms that conduct surveys of electronic commerce.

This can pose problems. Some firms may seek to "talk themselves up" prior to an initial public stock offering. Many are suppliers of e-commerce infrastructure and may want to build momentum for the activity. Market research firms or management consulting firms, for their part, provide advice and data about the current state and future direction of electronic commerce. Since they will presumably expand along with the electronic commerce market, they are likely to have an incentive to suggest that the e-commerce market is large and growing rapidly (Franson, 1997). Neither of these sources of data is immune from the statistical problems that plague the public statistical agencies. However, they rarely make available information on their collection methods or definition of e-commerce, or provide reports describing the statistical robustness of the data. Some estimates vary by over a factor of 100, presumably because of differences in coverage, definition and methodology.

While this situation is problematic for businesses thinking about engaging in electronic commerce, they are usually seasoned consumers of such data. They also benefit from their own internal data collection exercises, which can act as a check on these estimates, an advantage not enjoyed by most public policy makers and analysts.

Moreover, most estimates are based on sales or revenue. The problem here is three-fold. First, these figures include costs of doing business; this results in double-counting as the output of one e-commerce industry (*e.g.* Internet advertising or e-payment services) is counted in the "sales" figures of other e-commerce businesses, especially for business-to-business electronic commerce. Second, they give no indication of whether or not electronic commerce is simply displacing sales from more traditional channels. Third, they do not reveal whether firms engaging in electronic commerce are making a profit. In fact, most business-to-consumer electronic commerce firms are not. This severely limits an analysis of the economic impact of electronic commerce in terms of contribution to gross domestic product (GDP) (value added). Nonetheless, sales or revenues are typically the only indicator of activity available, and, although crude, they do give an idea of market size.

Lastly, most e-commerce estimates and anecdotes come from the United States. This is natural, to some degree, given that the United States generates a large share of e-commerce. While many aspects of the United States' culture and regulations may limit generalisation of that experience to the rest of the OECD, the size and diversity of the US market and fact that the United States is relatively advanced in the adoption of e-commerce, make it a useful case study of what may happen more broadly.

Factors which might limit growth in Europe are the continued high costs and the lack of good intra-Europe bandwidth (KPMG, 1998), the slow pace of planned liberalisation of the telecommunications sector (Forrester Research, 1998*a*), and a lack of awareness of the potential benefits (European Commission, 1997*a*). In general, European consumers appear to be less inclined to engage in "distance" retail than Americans, with per capita mail order sales that are less than half those of the United States (Federation of European Direct Marketing and NTC Research Ltd., 1997). Although Asia, especially Singapore and Hong Kong (China), have been keen adopters of electronic commerce, take-up has been more sporadic in the larger Asian economies of Japan and Korea. In general, the high cost of communications, the difficulty of engaging in new investment during the current economic turbulence, and the transition associated with regulatory reform may limit near-term growth (Ministry of International Trade and Industry, 1997). Even so, Japan has seen the number of its "cyberstores" increase from 214 in September of 1995 to 6 500 in February of 1998, with nearly $700 million in revenues (Ministry of Post and Telecommunications, 1998).

The infrastructure for e-commerce

Like traditional commerce, electronic commerce requires a substantial infrastructure composed of intermediaries that allow sellers to transact business with buyers. As in the US gold rush of the 1800s, the real winners may not be the miners but the suppliers that outfitted them with food, clothes and pickaxes. In 1995-97, in fact, expenditures on Internet-related infrastructure are estimated to reach some $40 billion, far more than

Box 1.3. **Recent efforts by national statistical offices**

One reflection of the importance of electronic commerce is the fact that it has begun to be evaluated by public statistical offices, many of which have started preliminary surveys or are in the planning stages.

Australia: Questions asking the extent and value of online e-commerce activities were incorporated into the most recent surveys on business and household use of IT.

Canada: In 1997, Canada conducted a survey on communications and electronic banking services conducted by telephone, PC dial up and the World Wide Web as well as e-commerce-related questions in its innovation survey and its survey of advanced technology in manufacturing in 1998.

France: The main focus to date has been on business-to-business use of networks and the impact on organisational structure and productivity. It is envisioned that the annual survey on company structure will increasingly ask questions about the share of investment dedicated to ICT and the portion of sales made through networks.

Nordic countries: The five Nordic countries (Denmark, Finland, Iceland, Norway and Sweden) collectively contribute to a project which develops methods for measuring ICT usage. Out of 18 ICT issue areas, electronic commerce has been identified as having the highest priority and members such as Finland plan to survey enterprises in 1999. Sweden started to survey this activity in 1997.

United States: The United States, in consultation with Canada and Mexico, is studying the creation of a new industry code to recognise electronic shopping establishments separately for inclusion in the North American Industry Classification System (NAICS) in 2002. Currently, e-commerce merchants are included in "nonstore retailers" (US SIC 596) (*e.g.* mail order).

A number of other countries, such as **Italy,** have work under way to explore various methodological issues associated with measuring electronic commerce activity. Others, such as the **United Kingdom** and the **Netherlands**, are using private consulting firms to survey electronic commerce activity.

OECD: An advisory statistical panel was established in 1996 in response to the adoption by Ministers of recommendations made by the ICCP Committee in "Global Information Infrastructure and Global Information Society" (GII-GIS) [OCDE/GD(96)93]. One of the primary tasks this group was charged with was the creation of internationally recognised definitions. Meeting in 1998, this group agreed upon a definition for information and communication technologies. Work has begun on defining the broader "information economy", and some Member countries have suggested that the group should define electronic commerce statistically.

the business-to-consumer segment and above most estimates of current business-to-business activity. Assuming that one-fifth of Cisco's $6.4 billion in router sales is attributable to demand linked to electronic commerce, this exceeds most estimates of total current electronic commerce.

The firms that were among the first to exploit the advantages of electronic commerce are those that are supplying the infrastructure for electronic commerce. Cisco's router sales and Dell's sales of personal computers (PCs) are two prominent examples. While their experience cannot be broadly generalised, their growth has been extraordinary: in the space of one year, Dell increased its online sales from $1 million a day

Table 1.4. **Geographic breakdown of e-commerce, various years**

	Booz-Allen & Hamilton (1997)	IDC (1997)	ActivMedia (1997)
United States/North America	76	87	86/93
Western Europe/Europe	24	8	5
Japan/Asia-Pacific		4	1
Rest of world		1	1
Total	**100**	**100**	**93/100**

Source: ActivMedia 1997 quoted by Margolis, 1998; March; Booz-Allen & Hamilton, 1997*a*; IDC, 1998.

Table 1.5. **Comparison of various e-commerce estimates by country**

US$ million

	1995-96	1996-97	2000-01	2001-02
Europe				
Benelux	13		4 800	
France	0	4	6 100	8 367
Germany	0	73	9 700	16 090
Italy	0	1	3 900	
Netherlands		2		
Nordic	13		6 800	
Sweden		3		
Scandanavia				6 436
Spain	0	1	1 500	
United Kingdom	26	9	11 000	12 872
Rest of EU	13	3	500	20 595
EU total	**65**	**96**	**44 300**	**64 360**
Asia				
Australia		28		
Japan		682		

Source: EITO, 1997; Strassel, 1997*a*; Forrester Research, 1998*b*; IDC, 1997*c*; "Internet Commerce to Top $30 Billion in Western Europe in 2001", http://www.internetnews.com (20 February 1998); MPT, 1998; Parliament of the Commonwealth of Australia, 1998.

to $5 million a day today and expects that online sales will soon represent half of its total sales[3] Cisco first allowed customers to purchase equipment over its Web site in 1996 and generated $100 million in sales; sales reached over $1 billion in 1997 and are expected to reach $4 billion in 1998 (Margherio *et al.*, 1998).

As Internet technology forces convergence across what were once considered separate areas (*e.g.* broadcasting, communications and computing), it becomes more difficult to identify clearly what constitutes the infrastructure supporting e-commerce. Under a very narrow and conservative definition, the e-commerce infrastructure has four parts: *i*) *hardware* (PCs, routers, servers, etc.); *ii*) *network service providers* (*e.g.* Internet access); *iii*) *software* to run the hardware and e-commerce packages; and *iv*) *enabling services* (*e.g.* e-payment, authentication/certification services, advertising, delivery). Of the four categories, hardware is estimated to have the largest sales at present, at roughly $10 billion to $30 billion (Table 1.7). In most cases, however, estimates of hardware expenditures cover all Internet-related hardware, not just that portion of Internet use dedicated to electronic commerce. The software for running PCs, servers, routers and support networks is a smaller but not insignificant part of the market, ranging from $300 million to $900 million in 1996; specific software, such as "turnkey" packages that allow merchants to set up a storefront on line, are estimated by Forrester Research to have earned revenues of about $20 million in 1996.[4] Providers of Internet service (ISPs) currently generate about $125 million in revenues but this could drop as prices fall; in the past year, the OECD average for 20 hours of Internet access has fallen from $68 to $20 (OECD, 1997*a*).

Table 1.6. **Location of top 100 WWW sites by category, June 1997**

	Live audio	Shopping	Finance	News	Sport	Adult
United States	78	85	75	67	79	79
Canada	4	6	6	5	8	10
United Kingdom	3	2	5	6	8	2
Germany	4	1	1	2	2	1
France	–	–	2	1	3	–
Japan	2	–	1	–	–	2
Other						

Source: OECD, 1997*d*; http://www.allwhois.com.

Figure 1.1. ***Adults accessing the Internet, selected OECD countries***[1]

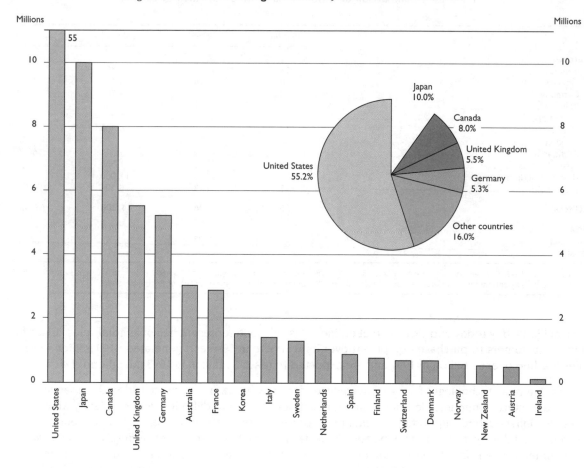

1. Methodologies vary across countries. Data are provided as an indicator of the diffusion of Internet's use within countries. The numbers were measured between December 1997 and June 1998.
Source: OECD, based on data from http://www.headcount.com.

Lastly, new intermediaries that help buyers and sellers conduct business are emerging. They provide services such as directories, advertising, e-payment, insurance, network diagnostics, authentication and certification. To date, advertising remains the dominant business model for business-to-consumer e-commerce: give away your product but charge for placing advertisements on or near it. Jupiter estimates 1996 Web-based advertising revenue at $310 million [reasonably close to the $266 million reported by the Internet Advertising Bureau (http://www.jup.com, 12 March 1997)]. Of this sum, ten sites – most of them providing some type of intermediary service (browser, search engines) – represent about half of the total.

In general, the information infrastructure that supports electronic commerce is a significant and growing part of the overall OECD economy, especially in the United States. A recent report by the US Department of Commerce estimates that while ICTs only represent about 8 per cent of GDP, they have contributed nearly double that to recent GDP growth (Figure 1.2). By 1998, the US ICT sector contributed a larger share to GDP than the automobile and aerospace sector combined.

Business-to-business electronic commerce

In business-to-business electronic commerce, businesses use the Internet to integrate the value-added chain which can extend from the supplier of raw materials to the final consumer. Business-to-business

Table 1.7. **E-commerce broken down into major segments and products**
Comparison of various estimates

US$ million

Activity	1995-97	2000-02
Infrastructure		
Hardware		
Total[1]	10 950	43 000
Computer products	140	2 105
Network hardware	29 000	72 000
Network services		
Total[1]	300	5 000
ISP revenue	125	12 000
Internet services market (access, hosting, communication)	6 200	34 400
Software and comp. serv.		
Total[1]	900	5 100
E-comm apps	121	3 800
Enabling services		
Total[1]	500	10 000
Ads	32	2 800
Ads	74	4 800
Ads	906	
E-commerce: business-to-business		
Retailer	10 000	
Auto manuf.	7 000	
Computers/consumer electronics	767	8 200
Software	212	3 498
Software	250	4 600
Internet telephony		9 000
E-commerce: business-to-consumer		
Apparel	46	322
Gifts/flowers	45	658
Books	109	2 200
Travel	276	8 600
Travel	457	10 000
Groceries	767	6 600
Food/drink	39	336
Clothing	18	1 900
Entertainment	298	1 920
Ticketing	52	1 700
On-line subscription	120	966
On-line subscriptions	22	158
On-line magazines	1	15
Pornography	137	296
Music	13	1 200
Music	46	1 600
On-line games	127	1 013
On-line games	165	1 260
On-line gambling	160	8 600
On-line gambling	2 245	9 911
Consumer stock brokerage	628	2 200
Consumer insurance (auto, term, homeowner)	39	1 110
Financial services	1 200	5 000
E-commerce total		
Forrester	518	6 579
Iconoclast	1 100	24 100

1. Estimate for the whole segment.
Sources: *Fortune*, "The Birth of Digital Commerce" (9 December 1996); Page, 1998; *Wall Street Journal* (3 March 1997, p. A12); ActivMedia, 1998; Data Analysis, 1997; Cerf, 1997; E-land, 1997; EITO, 1997; AEA/American University, 1996; http://www.cyberatlast.com (2 April 1997); http://www.forrester.com; Meeker, 1997; "Linking Up", *The Economist* (5 April 1997, p. 72); Meeker and DePuy, 1996; Lesk, 1997; Tchong, 1998; "Net Biz Software to Top $3B", http://www.techweb.com (13 May 1997); Internet Advertising Bureau, 1998; OECD, 1997e; Marsicano, 1998; Moad, 1997; SRI Consulting, 1998; http://www.jupiter.com, 1997; "Vanishing Breed", *The Economist* (10 January 1998); Franson, 1998; "Making Money on the Net", *Business Week* (23 September 1996); Margherio *et al.*, 1998; "Surf Music", *The Economist* (16 August 1997); Patrizio, 1997; Murphy, 1997; Crockett, 1997; Festa, 1997; Marable, 1997. Detailed sources available on request.

Figure 1.2. **US ICT industry share of GDP and contribution to growth**
Percentages

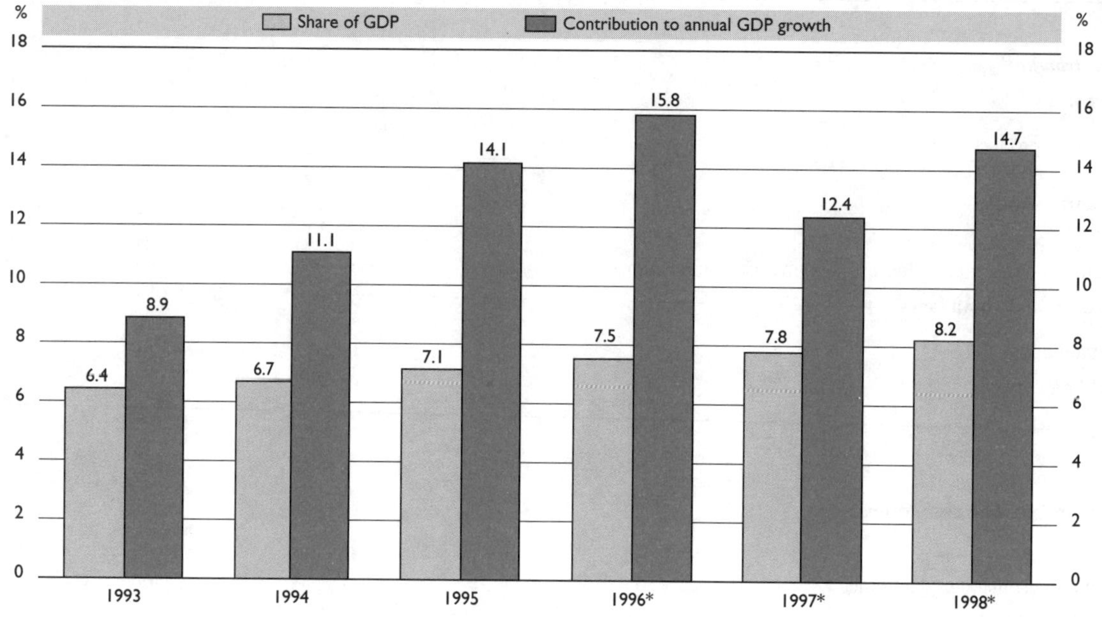

* Estimated.
Source: Margherio et al., 1998.

electronic commerce dominates the total value of e-commerce activity, accounting for about 80 per cent at present (Table 1.8). This share is probably conservative. As Table 1.2 shows, three firms – General Electric, CSX and NEC – report conducting over $20 billion in business-to-business electronic commerce. This exceeds all the business-to-consumer sales estimates for 1995-97 by a large margin as well as most estimated e-commerce totals. Because the economic factors affecting the adoption of e-commerce between businesses are much different from those affecting business-to-consumer e-commerce, business-to-business e-commerce is likely to maintain or enlarge its advantage for the foreseeable future.

Table 1.8. **E-commerce estimated to be business-to-business**

Firm (year)	Percentage
IDC (1997)[1]	61
Negroponte (1998)[2]	70
Forrester Research (1998)[3]	84
Forrester Research (2001)[4]	88
ActivMedia (1996)[5]	72
Lorentz (1997)[6]	80
Price Waterhouse (2002)[7]	78
Piper Jaffray (2001)[8]	90
Average	**78**

1. Meeker, 1997.
2. Moltzen, 1998.
3. Forrester Research, 1998b.
4. Forrester Research, 1998a.
5. ActivMedia, 1998.
6. Lorentz, 1998.
7. Price Waterhouse, 1998.
8. Cohen, 1998.

Electronic links between businesses are not new. They have existed for decades, in the form of electronic data interchange (EDI) supplied by value-added networks (VAN) operated over leased telephone lines. Large manufacturing firms are the main users of EDI. General Electric (GE), one of the largest EDI service suppliers, estimates that 80 per cent of suppliers are not connected to an EDI system but rely on fax, telephone or mail.[5] Currently, EDI accounts for some $150-$250 billion in sales (Margherio *et al.*, 1998).

Adoption of Internet protocols and use of the Internet infrastructure are expected to transform EDI from a set communication system, based on dedicated leased lines, between large firms with an established relationship to a flexible system that draws in a much wider range of firms, many of whom may not know each other. EDI over the Internet costs about one-tenth that of a VAN and greatly lowers the barriers to adoption.[6] Boeing, for example, saw a five-fold increase in customers participating in its parts-ordering system when it moved from a strictly EDI-VAN system to an EDI Internet system (Margherio *et al.*, 1998). For business-to-business electronic commerce, migration to the Internet is expected to result in a near doubling of EDI to $383 billion in the year 2000, a third of which will be used to connect second- and third-tier suppliers (OECD, 1998*a*).

In addition to EDI over the Internet, there are three other major forms of business-to-business e-commerce: *i*) use of the Internet, WWW pages and browsers; *ii*) deployment of "intranets" (networks internal to the firm that use the IP protocol), which streamline the firm's internal "business" functions; and *iii*) extension of a firm's intranet to select business partners ("extranets"). While all three are important aspects of business-to-business electronic commerce, estimating their impact on sales or economic growth is difficult. Furthermore, their greatest effect is often on transaction costs, firm organisation, employment, and product quality. Such impacts are only indirectly associated with economic growth and are analysed in later chapters of this book. Nevertheless, such networks may be large: Hitachi's extranet includes over 2 100 companies (Morishita, 1997), and Ford's intranet connects 120 000 workstations (Cronin, 1998). These are expected to have a ripple effect as firms or units now linked to these networks create their own extranet or intranet.

Not surprisingly, some of the largest business-to-business e-commerce players are firms involved in supplying the infrastructure for the Internet. Cisco, the dominant supplier of network routers, with over two-thirds of the market, reports that it will generate over $2 billion in revenue from its Web site this year (from orders to the Web site – payment is off-line) (Kerstetter, 1997). Dell, which makes PCs, uses electronic commerce to sell $3-$5 million worth of products daily and had over $1 billion in overall sales in 1997 (Oeler, 1998). Most of these transactions are business-to-business, although some fraction of PC sales are to households. Like hardware, much software is sold to businesses over the network, and as with PCs, a small portion of sales go to consumers. The Japanese Ministry of Posts and Telecommunications (1998) reports that about one-third of all purchases of goods and services on the Internet in Japan are for software. Similarly, e-commerce products thought to be primarily consumer items, such as books and travel, are now being aggressively promoted to businesses (Frook, 1998*a*).

Drivers and inhibitors of business-to-business electronic commerce

In business-to-business e-commerce, three factors are likely to lead to quick adoption of e-commerce: *i*) a reduction in transaction costs and improvement of product quality/customer service; *ii*) a defensive reaction to competitors engaging in e-commerce; and *iii*) insistence by large businesses that all of their suppliers link into their e-commerce system as a condition of doing business.[7] The first factor, reduced transaction costs, drives the second and third and will be explored in greater detail in the next chapter. However, electronic commerce clearly reduces these costs and thus drives its adoption.

It is expected that by 2001-02, many barriers, such as questions of security and reliability which now limit the extension of Internet EDI to unknown firms, will have been overcome. As a result, there will be a significant increase in business-to-business e-commerce as it draws in smaller second- and third-tier suppliers. For example, the US Automotive Network eXchange (ANX), developed by the Automotive Industry Action Group (AIAG), makes use of the Transport Control Protocol/Internet Protocol (TCP/IP) to link automotive suppliers to each other and to original equipment manufacturers (OEM) (*e.g.* GM, Ford and Chrysler). Dispensing with the multiple networks and protocols that now link first-tier suppliers to OEMs, the new system will provide a single common system that can be extended to include all suppliers.

Now in testing and pilot projects, it is expected to be operational by 2000.[8] Standard and Poor's and US Department of Commerce (1998) estimate that if a fifth of all US auto parts are sold by business-to-business electronic commerce in 2000, this will represent over $30 billion more than the total reported in Table 1.2. Likewise, many large firms are now experimenting with e-commerce. Once their system is operational, the level of activity should increase rapidly. For example, GE's use of the Internet for procurement currently stands at $1 billion, but GE has announced its intention to move $5 billion worth of procurement to this system in two years' time (Margherio *et al.*, 1998). As firms expand their experimentation with business-to-business e-commerce, the growth rate and resultant economic impact are likely to be large.

The largest impact of business-to-business e-commerce is likely to be on small and medium-sized enterprises (SMEs), because many large businesses already have EDI systems in place. The accessibility of the Internet makes electronic commerce a realistic possibility for SMEs and is likely to lead to its widespread diffusion. A recent survey conducted by International Data Corporation (IDC) found that the share of small firms (less than 100 employees) in the United States using the Internet had more than doubled between 1996 and 1998, from 19.7 per cent to over 40 per cent (Ohlson, 1998).

In addition to migrating existing activity to e-commerce, new business-to-business products are being created which did not, or could not, exist before electronic commerce over the Internet made them economically viable. For example, spot markets that match buyers and sellers for a wide variety of goods ranging from electronic components to agricultural commodities to transportation futures have sprung up; they represent only the beginning of what is expected to be a wide number of new business-to-business opportunities. Another example is the extension of EDI-type links via the Internet.

Parcel delivery, logistics and order fulfilment services, frequently by the same firm, are also experiencing growth as e-commerce increases. As businesses move to "build-to-order" processing and just-in-time inventories, a premium is placed on timely, accurate inbound and outbound logistics. In addition, there is greater demand by final consumers for fast order fulfilment and the ability to track an order as it is being processed and delivered. Given the complexity of these tasks, it is not surprising that a quarter of Web sellers are reported to outsource order fulfilment (Ernst & Young, 1998), letting firms like United Parcel Service, Federal Express, DHL, and Lufthansa provide not only shipping but also warehousing, packaging, customer support and, in some cases, new intermediary functions such as collection of taxes (KPMG, 1997). As e-commerce grows and as parcel volume increases, especially to small businesses, this intermediary business should experience significant growth. Federal Express estimates that 68 per cent of the 3 million packages it processes daily are now initiated through interactive networks. Federal Express started out using a software that linked firms to it via proprietary networks in 1983 and accumulated 50 000 clients over the next 12 years; between 1995 and 1998, as it moved to the Internet and as electronic commerce over the Internet began, the number of clients jumped to nearly a million.[9]

Business-to-consumer electronic commerce

The nature and scope of business-to-consumer electronic commerce

Although business-to-business electronic commerce represents the bulk of all electronic commerce, most attention and speculation about e-commerce has focused on the business-to-consumer segment. With household transactions typically accounting for over half of all domestic final demand,[10] this is not surprising. Moreover, as business PCs and networks are saturated, it is natural for the focus of attention to turn to the household.

The popular press has largely focused on e-commerce merchants that sell tangible products (*e.g.* books, wine, flowers, computers). However, with the possible exception of computers, the largest segments involve intangibles (*e.g.* entertainment, software) (Table 1.9). This confirms the experience of France Telecom's Minitel service, which has engaged in electronic commerce over a closed network for well over a decade and where the main beneficiaries have been intangibles (OECD, 1998a). This makes intuitive sense: when the product cannot be physically examined, traditional commerce has no advantage over the convenience of electronic commerce.

Table 1.9. **Top 10 retail shopping sites based on usage, February 1997**

Shopping site	Product
1. shareware.com	software
2. download.com	software
3. columbiahouse.com	music/video
4. Amazon.com	books
5. hotfiles.com	software
6. surplusdirect.com	computer hardware and software
7. freeride.com	coupon site
8. jumbo.com	software
9. gw2k.com	computers
10. bluemountainarts.com	greeting cards

Source: PC Meter data as reported by Meeker, 1997.

Intangible products

The largest segment of business-to-consumer e-commerce involves intangible products that can be delivered directly to the consumer's computer over the network. It is composed of five broad categories: entertainment, travel, newspapers/magazines, financial services, and e-mail.

Entertainment, which includes adult entertainment, online games, music and video, is the largest category of products sold to consumers. Forrester Research estimates that adult entertainment alone accounted for 10 per cent of all 1996 business-to-consumer e-commerce ($50 million) and would triple to $137 million in 1997, just behind computer products and travel.[11] Table 3.2 suggests that this figure is conservative, since five sites report revenues of roughly one-third of that total in 1995-97. Firms that track visits to Web pages and analyse the keywords typed into search engines confirm the popularity of adult material. One respected source of information on Web use reports that while adult sites account for 2 to 3 per cent of the 200 000 commercial Web sites, they account for 10 to 20 per cent of all searches by search engines.[12]

"Pay-for-play" online games and online distribution of music each generated revenues of roughly $50 million in 1996-97 (http://www.forrester.com, 12 April 1997). The interactivity of the Internet means that online game players, in some cases dozens of people, play against each other rather than against the computer as is the case for most current computer games. Many CD-ROM games now incorporate an online component. A limiting factor is the high-bandwidth requirement of some games that use realistic, moving graphics. While rapid growth is forecast for the music industry as well, current achievements have been more modest. Forrester Research predicts that online sales of CDs account for less than 1 per cent of all pre-recorded music sales (Lipton, 1997). Digital download represents a very small part of this segment and is mainly limited to unknown artists or those with a very small following. Jupiter Communications predicts that online downloads will represent only 2 per cent of music sales in 2002 (Lipton, 1998).

Online gambling is an entertainment area with large, but poorly understood, activity. Most of this activity is on sites located in off-shore havens such as Grenada, home of Sports International. According to one estimate, over $30 billion worth of gambling is conducted on line (Schwartz, 1995). If so, gambling would be the largest single electronic commerce activity. While this estimate seems high, one Internet gambling firm, Interactive Gambling and Communications Corp., had 1996 revenues of $58 million (Brunker, 1997).

Travel services, particularly airline reservations, are another major category of business-to-consumer e-commerce. A recent European Commission policy paper on electronic commerce credits travel services with over half of all electronic commerce (European Commission, 1997b). Jupiter estimates at $276 million in 1996 online revenues for travel (air, hotel, car rental, cruises, vacation packages, as well as advertising on travel-oriented sites).[13] Press accounts of individual firms such as Microsoft's Expedia and American

Airlines Travelocity suggest that this estimate may be conservative, as these firms are generating annual sales of roughly $100 million each (Table 1.2) (Anderson, 1997; Faiola and Ginsberg, 1998).

More than 2 700 US newspapers post an edition on line, and 60 per cent of them have a daily print circulation of less than 30 000 (Schavey, 1998). Estimated revenue for this segment is around $20 million, an indication that relatively few newspapers and magazines have begun to charge readers. Many of the early, high-profile entrants have had to significantly modify their strategies because readers balk at pay-ing.[14]

Financial services are an important business-to-consumer category. Because many firms engaged in online activity also provide traditional financial services, revenue estimates are difficult to obtain, but one stock brokerage, E*Trade, reported $148 million in revenues in 1996 from 50 000 active accounts and $2.8 billion in assets.[15] Another, Charles Schwab & Co., performs nearly two-fifths of all of its trades on line, has tripled the number of online accounts to 1.3 million in the last two years, and has doubled assets to $92 billion in one year (1997-98) (Girishankar, 1998*b*). By one estimate, online trading of stocks accounted for 17 per cent of all retail stock activity in 1997, double the 1996 share (Newsedge, 1998).

Banking is also enjoying significant e-commerce activity. A recent Ernst & Young survey of 130 financial services companies in 17 countries found that 13 per cent of the firms were using the Inter-net for transactions with customers in 1997 and that 60 per cent intended to do so by 1999 (Corrigan and Authers, 1997). Nearly a quarter of the 100 top US banks offer online access to accounts. Europe appears to be significantly ahead of the United States in this area; for example, nearly every major German bank is reportedly already on line and Finland has established an extensive network banking system (Strassel, 1997*a*).

Insurance, on the other hand, has taken advantage of the Internet more slowly. However, with the arrival of new entrants such as Quicken (a major US supplier of personal finance software) in this market segment, prospects for growth appear strong. Quicken's sales from its InsureMarket site doubled in 1997, and new product launches in the auto and home insurance segments are planned (Marable, 1997).

While e-mail receives less attention than many of the new e-commerce services appearing on the Internet, it is arguably one of the "killer apps" (an application which users find so useful that it is the rea-son for going on line and subsequently using other services). Nearly two-thirds of all US businesses with a computer have e-mail (IDC, 1997*a*). About 15 per cent of the US population has access to e-mail,[16] and as users become more accustomed to the Internet, use of e-mail increases on average to about 25 messages a day (ActivMedia, 1998). As a share of all messages (e-mail plus mail), e-mail has moved from less than a fifth in 1988 to almost half in 1994 (Meeker, 1997).

While e-mail is frequently a "free" service that comes bundled with Internet access, variations are becoming important electronic commerce services. Bill paying is one of the most important, as it repre-sents roughly half of the US Post Office's letter volume (Childs, 1998) and 40 per cent of all cheques writ-ten in the United States. E-commerce bill presentation and payment are growing quickly, largely because nearly 70 per cent of all bills are generated by 200 entities (utilities, credit card issuers, insurance com-panies, etc.) (Authers, 1998). This concentrated market, combined with significant savings in postage, paper and labour, has attracted a large number of participants.[17] It is estimated that 7 per cent of US bills were paid electronically in 1995 (Institute for the Future, 1996).

Tangible products

To date, the main tangible products sold electronically have been electronics (including computers), books, clothing and food/drink. Each currently generates $100-$200 million worth of business-to-consumer sales (Tables 3.2 and 3.7). Many of these categories are dominated by traditional retailers that have established electronic commerce operations (*e.g.* Dell in the United States, La Redoute in France, Marks & Spencer in the United Kingdom, and supermarkets in the Netherlands). Behind these broader categories are speciality-item merchants (books, flowers, and music CDs) that add value by providing a wider selection, more information about a product, or convenience. As Wal-Mart's decision to make 80 000 items available on line shows, however, a wide variety of products can be sold over the Internet (http://www.ft.com/hippocampus/4cfce.htm, 2 April 1997). Even some of the most tangible of all household items (groceries, houses, cars) are now sold electronically. Chrysler estimates that 1-2 per cent of all of its sales were done via online services in 1996;[18] and JD Power, a marketing firm specialising in the auto industry, estimates that 16 per cent of people buying a new car or truck in 1997 used the Internet as part of the purchasing process (Margherio *et al.*, 1998).

Recent and near-term growth rates

To comprehend how business-to-consumer electronic commerce may look over the near term, it is useful to look first at growth over the past few years. While it is easy to have fast growth rates from a small base, many start-ups have rapidly become important competitors in their industry. This suggests that e-commerce is more than a novelty item for select market niches.

- Amazon.com is now the fifth largest US bookseller, and book sales by electronic commerce now represent 20 per cent of all book sales in the United States.[19] Over six quarters, to mid-1997, the number of books sold grew by 3 066 per cent (Morgan Stanley Dean Witter, 1997).

- Ticketmaster reports that its online sales of tickets to events such as concerts or sporting events have increased to $19.8 million per quarter, up by 270 per cent from the first quarter of 1997 to the first quarter of 1998, and now account for 3 per cent of all its domestic ticket sales, up from 1 per cent in 1997.[20]

- Online retail trading of stocks accounts for 17 per cent of all US retail stock trading activity in 1997, double the 1996 share (Newsedge, 1998); 41 per cent of all stock trades made by Charles Schwab, the largest US discount broker, were conducted on line in the first quarter of 1998, up from a third in 1997 (Kehoe, 1998).

- E*Trade increased the number of its active accounts by 243 per cent over the same period (Morgan Stanley Dean Witter, 1997).

- Auto-By-Tel's share of references resulting in a car sale, as a share of the total number of US domestic units sold, has increased from 0.33 per cent in the first quarter of 1996 to 1.88 per cent in the first quarter of 1997 (Meeker, 1997). Its revenue grew by 418 per cent over six quarters to mid-1997 (Morgan Stanley Dean Witter, 1997).

- In 1996, independent travel agents handled 80 per cent of US airline reservations; by 1998, their share had fallen to 52 per cent, with airlines dealing directly with customers via the Web or telephone (Kehoe, 1998). The American Society of Travel Agents estimates that 1 per cent of all US airline tickets were sold on line in 1997 (Margolis, 1998).

- In terms of merchandise sold on line, AOL has seen growth of 90 per cent from the beginning of 1996 to mid-1997. Subscribers' visits to the AOL Marketplace rose from an average of two in the first quarter of 1996 to 11 in the first quarter of 1997 (Morgan Stanley Dean Witter, 1997).

Table 1.1 gives a number of near-term (2000-02) estimates of the size of electronic commerce. The estimates vary widely, from a low of $10 billion to a high of $1.5 trillion, with a median of $154.5 billion. Compared to the median derived from the 1995-97 estimates, the annual average growth rate is approximately 200 per cent.

As illustrated above, the business-to-consumer segment of electronic commerce is very sector-specific. Box 1.4 presents some figures on the possible impact on selected sectors in the near term. The estimates represent a deepening of activity across the fairly narrow group of sectors that are currently aggressive users of electronic commerce. By 2001-02, larger sectors – banking, insurance, bill paying/ postal services – which are currently testing or developing e-commerce products will become more actively involved. Many of these services now use proprietary software or networks to provide services to a select group of customers. Over the next few years, these services will migrate to the Internet and will probably use a standard browser as the interface for their service. Coupled with more ubiquitous access devices, such as set-top boxes for TVs, it will be possible to offer the service to a much wider range of users and to begin to diffuse electronic commerce widely.

Box 1.4. **Predictions of near-term growth in selected e-commerce sectors**

In the expectation that 50 million people will soon pay an annual fee of $240 ($20/month) for Internet access, Internet access providers will generate $12 billion in revenues (Lesk, 1997).

E-commerce-specific software such as "turnkey" packages which allow merchants to set up a storefront on line should experience strong growth. Forrester Research estimates that this segment earned revenues of about $121 million in 1996 and should reach $3.8 billion by 2000.[21]

Forrester Research predicts that 50 per cent of all software distributed by Microsoft, Netscape, Oracle will be done over the Internet by 1999 (Erwin *et al.*, 1997).

Both JD Power, a marketing firm specialising in the automotive industry, and KPMG, an accounting/consultancy firm, estimate that by 2000, 20 per cent of new and used cars will be bought using the Internet (Griffiths, 1998). Chrysler predicts that by 2000 a quarter of its sales will take place on line (Anderson, 1997).

Jupiter Communications predicts that by 2002, 7.5 per cent of all music will be sold on line.[22]

Forrester Research expects 8 per cent of all travel tickets and 15 per cent of business travel (Forrester Research, 1997) to be sold over the Internet in 2001 and amount to $10 billion.

Piper Jaffrey estimates that by 2001 online trading of stocks will account for 60 per cent of discount commissions and 10 per cent of all retail stock brokerage commissions.

A Booz-Allen & Hamilton survey of European banks found that 154 had Internet sites, with sites increasing at a rate of 90 per cent per year. Over half had introduced or had plans to introduce online banking (*Financial Times*, 12 August 1996, p.1).

Electronic bill paying is estimated to increase to 18 per cent by 2000 (Institute for the Future, 1996).

Drivers/inhibitors for business-to-consumer electronic commerce

Factors influencing growth in business-to-consumer electronic commerce differ significantly from those that affect business-to-business electronic commerce. They are more likely to limit its growth and to hold it to 10-20 per cent of the overall total in the near term. While competition may force businesses to engage in business-to-business e-commerce, the business-to-consumer segment faces barriers such as concerns about security of payment, potentially fraudulent merchants, privacy of personal data, and difficulty and expense in accessing e-commerce merchants. In addition to these legal and psychological barriers, three economic factors will have a large impact on the growth of business-to-consumer electronic commerce: *ease and cost of access, convenience*, and the *appeal of mass customisation*.

Many observers feel that the cost and complexity of the PC, which is currently the primary access device, is a key factor shaping the demographics of the e-commerce consumer (IDC, 1997*b*). In addition, there is the cost of getting on line and finding the site with the products of interest. Even when the site is located, navigating it can be a challenge even to the experienced user. It may be that only when there is a very simple – what John Landry of Lotus calls a "brain-dead easy" – access device, something like a TV with very simple controls, will business-to-consumer e-commerce reach massive scale. While such devices are available now and are being refined (*e.g.* WebTV), it remains to be seen whether or not a broad spectrum of households will quickly adopt e-commerce. Even then, the economic impact may not be large, as the current demographic profile of e-commerce shoppers – high disposable income, young, well-educated – is what most retailers target and the profile attributed with generating most sales.[23] Nonetheless, a simplified access device should stimulate e-commerce shopping. The finding that the longer shoppers use the Internet, the more likely they are to buy on line and the less likely they are to shop in traditional stores supports this view (ActivMedia, 1998). The volume of commercial activity on France's Minitel, for example, did not peak for nearly a decade after it was first introduced (OECD, 1998*a*).

Once consumers have access, the main drivers of business-to-consumer electronic commerce appear to be convenience, choice, personalisation, amusement, and savings. Of these, the near-term importance of convenience is frequently singled out.[24] Given the current demographic profile and life-style of e-commerce shoppers, it is not surprising that they value services that offer convenience. Surveys indicating that such shoppers tend to shop at atypical hours bear this out: America Online reports that about 40 per cent of electronic shopping takes place between 22:00 and 10:00 (Margherio *et al.*, 1998), when most stores are closed. Likewise, Lands' End, the large US mail order clothing firm, reports a lunchtime spike in their online sales during the working week.[25] REI, a sporting goods and outdoors retailer, gets 35 per cent of its online orders between 22:00 and 7:00 ("Cyberspace Winners: How They Did It", *Business Week*, 22 June 1998). To some degree, the emphasis on convenience is due to long working hours, especially in the United States[26] and Japan, and limited opening hours for traditional retail establishments, especially in Europe. As long as this is the case, business-to-consumer e-commerce is likely to grow.

After convenience, a characteristic frequently cited as a spur to business-to-consumer e-commerce is the possibility of forming a one-to-one relationship between merchant and consumer which allows products to be customised. Current examples include the PC configuration, custom stock portfolios, personalised greeting cards, made-to-measure jeans, and custom-made CD compilations. Many e-merchants that do not offer customised products provide a huge variety of products with niches so small that they begin to approach custom-made products: bookstores offering millions of titles, general merchandise sites offering 90 per cent of all household needs, and car sites with links to every major manufacturer. This increased choice is a feature that consumers value, especially for locating speciality or hard-to-find items. Likewise, well-designed sites guide the user, remember consumer preferences, and in some cases reconfigure themselves to reflect past behaviour.

At the same time, the premium placed on convenience can work against strategies that emphasize choice as making decisions takes time. While e-commerce sites are helpful for finding the proverbial "needle in the haystack", too much choice can confuse and irritate customers. Ravi Dhar of Yale University found that as choice increased so did the possibility that consumers would not buy anything. John Gourville of the Harvard Business School suggests that if consumers are asked to make too many trade-offs they become anxious.[27] This research suggests, first, that choices must be real and not frivolous "versioning" (*e.g.* 35 versions of one brand of toothpaste); and, second, that selection must be easy (*e.g.* use of agents/pre-set preferences). The degree to which business-to-consumer e-merchants recognise this may have a significant impact on the near-term growth of electronic commerce.

The future (beyond 2002)

While many factors are likely to affect the future of e-commerce, including general economic conditions, the European monetary union, the millennium bug, and unforeseen technological advances, two of the dominant forces are certain to be the ageing of the "Nintendo" generation – those who grew up with video games and are comfortable with information technology – and the widespread diffusion of business-to-business electronic commerce in the near term. By engaging in business-to-business electronic commerce, firms open up and transform many of their operations (see Chapter 3 on industrial organisation), thereby positioning themselves so that the transition to direct sales to consumers should be natural and relatively easy. It is therefore likely that electronic commerce will be stimulated by both the demand and supply sides.

Figure 1.3 shows sectors identified in this chapter that may be affected by electronic commerce as it develops over time. Many of the sectors affected by business-to-business electronic commerce lack penetration estimates because in many cases the displacement effect is internal.

To judge the potential economic impact of business-to-consumer electronic commerce, the question is whether near-term growth will represent a "skimming of the cream" or whether it will represent the "tip of the iceberg", that is, whether a tipping point will be reached and electronic commerce will become a major mode of conducting business in the OECD area. History is littered with instances where the potential impact of new technologies was not foreseen (*e.g.* the mainframe computer, the photocopier) as well instances where the impact of a technology was vastly overestimated (*e.g.* the "paperless office", telephone/ mail order shopping). The impact of electronic commerce – whether large or small – will probably only be apparent at least five years from now and more likely 15 to 25 years from now (Myhrvold, 1997). It is likely to be first felt in the business-to-business segment, where growth and diffusion are expected to be significant while the growth of the business-to-consumer segment is likely to be more modest and sector-specific.

Figure 1.3. **Impact of e-commerce on a product basis, 2000-05**

Estimates of online shares in percentages

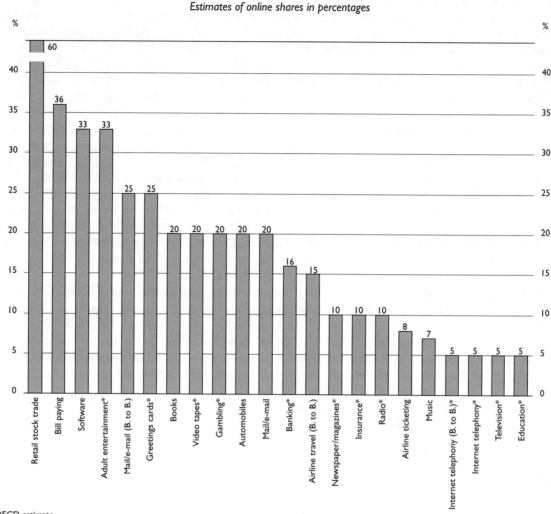

* OECD estimate.
Source: OECD, compiled from various sources.

On the basis of current experience and judging from the various e-commerce successes and failures to date, sectors likely to be significantly affected by electronic commerce in the future are those whose products have a high price-to-bulk ratio such as music CDs, commodities such as routine business flights, and intangibles such as software that can be delivered electronically. Products unlikely to be significantly affected include those with high tactile characteristics such as fur coats or high fashion clothing and expensive items such as furniture. But even these may be amenable to electronic commerce if trusted third parties provide accreditation or warranty as is now done for wine and used cars.

The future growth of electronic commerce is likely to follow "the reverse product cycle" of innovation in services: in the initial phase, incremental process innovations increase efficiency; in the second, more radical process innovations lead to substantial improvements in quality; and in the third, "... product rather than process innovations become dominant,... new industries emerge and the overall impact on output and employment is expansionary" (Barras, 1986). While all three phases will operate in the three time periods analysed here, the most significant new products can be expected to emerge in the more distant future.

The future of existing products

While the new modes of conducting business offered by electronic commerce will generate growth, products and methods that e-commerce renders obsolete will be displaced. Initially, electronic commerce may generate efficiency gains as new methods replace previous ones. In the process, businesses will fail and jobs will be lost. This is the natural evolution of economies, and there are many historical precedents to show that the economic efficiency that emanates from this "creative destruction" is beneficial to the economy and ultimately generates more growth and jobs (OECD, 1998b). Nevertheless, when assessing the growth prospects of electronic commerce, it is important to realise that some sectors may experience negative growth.

Aside from sectors already identified as likely participants in electronic commerce, the more distant future (beyond 2002) is likely to see other industries, whose primary function is the transmission of information, using e-commerce to provide that service. They include not only the so-called carriers or broadcasters, such as the communication, radio and TV industries, but also those whose main activity is to transmit information and knowledge, such as teachers, health practitioners, and many government services. This migration depends on the availability of sufficient bandwidth, since the information intensity of many of these activities (*e.g.* the need to transmit moving pictures) requires significantly more capacity than is typically available today. Achieving this added capacity is a function of continued technological development and diffusion and regulatory reform that supports competition and innovation.

The focus on products in this section is by and large restricted to the business-to-consumer segment. While business-to-business e-commerce is, and will probably continue to be, the dominant segment, it is more likely to change production *processes* rather than to generate new *products*. Likewise, the impact on the generic wholesale and retail sector will only be briefly touched on, as the bulk of e-commerce's impact on these sectors is associated with "disintermediation", whereby producers sell directly to consumers without the aid of intermediaries or where new electronic intermediaries compete directly with their "bricks-and-mortar" equivalent (*e.g.* online versus off-line bookstores). As in the case of business-to-business e-commerce, the bypassing of traditional distribution channels is mainly a change in process and is viewed as a change in the cost structure of doing business. These issues are analysed in some depth in Chapter 2.

Telephony, fax, video conferencing and the Internet

The Internet provides a standard technology for a wide variety of communications that previously used different systems (fixed-line, circuit telephone service, fax transmission and broadcasting). Internet bandwidth limitations cause the quality of some of these services to drop and make the service less reliable than current norms. Therefore, some observers estimate that the immediate impact will be larger on communication services that are not time-dependent (fax, voice mail, and pagers) and that only about 5 per cent of the voice market will shift to Internet in the near future, owing to sensitivity to losses in quality.[28] While this is a concern, some applications and consumers may be willing to trade off quality for a reduction of 50-90 per cent in the price of conventional telephone service (Atkins, 1997). Currently, it is estimated that networks adhering to the Internet protocol handle about 31 million minutes of traffic a year, a small fraction of the 530 billion minutes handled by public switched telephone networks (PSTN) in 1997 (Moozakis, 1998). With large carriers such as Deutsche Telekom engaging in pilot projects in the use of IP telephony and AT&T announcing that it intends to move its entire network infrastructure to an Internet protocol platform (Kujuba, 1998), this is likely to change in the future (OECD, 1997b). Analysys, a telecommunications strategy consultant, predicts that Internet telephony traffic will overtake traffic carried by the fixed network by 2000 (Reuters, 1998).

In addition, the use of telephony and fax services may change as electronic commerce is adopted. A factor that may temper this displacement is continuing consumers distrust of the Internet as a vehicle for payment, with the result that they continue to rely on the phone and fax to transmit the relevant information. Likewise, with the development of Internet telephony, most e-commerce sites in the near future will have a telephone link to a customer service representative who could maintain the role of the telephone in the sales process. Despite these mitigating factors, Forrester Research predicts that as a channel for selling, phone and fax will drop from 51 per cent in 1997 to 32 per cent in 2000 and that Internet commerce will increase from 15 per cent to 42 per cent (Erwin *et al.*, 1997). This will not have a demonstrable impact on the telephone system *per se*, but it could affect the size and number of call centres as fewer operators are needed as processing transactions becomes more efficient.

Entertainment

As TV and radio are "webcast", electronic commerce over the Internet may offer a new mode for the delivery of entertainment services. In addition, new products, such as multimedia content, which compete with TV and radio and other leisure activities, such as gambling, video rental and video game playing, are likely to be affected. WebCensus, a survey conducted by Hambrecht & Quist and LinkExchange, examined the time household Web users spent daily on various media. When asked what they sacrificed for the Web, 22 per cent watched less TV, 12 per cent read less print media, and 3 per cent listened to less radio (Hu, 1998). During peak evening viewing periods, the number of Americans logged onto America Online now regularly surpasses the number watching CNN or MTV (Jackson, 1997a). However, it is unlikely that the Internet will broadly displace TV or radio, although it may take over some key demographic slices of the population, thereby reducing the value of TV advertising time. It is more likely that TV and the Internet will begin to interact and encourage viewers to "click here" for more information about a programme or product. More generally, people have a limited amount of leisure time, and new activities will necessarily come at the expense of old (European Commission, 1997c).

Broadly, webcasting is the transmission of audio or video over the Internet (OECD, 1997c). Although it is in its infancy, 400 radio stations are already on the Internet (*e.g.* http://www.timecast.com). They range from large stations, such as ABC and CBS in the United States and CBC in Canada, to small live music stations in Brazil (http://www.convex.com.br/clube). Several TV stations are testing use of the Internet, and streaming video is already a common feature of many Web sites. Despite its relatively poor quality, video transmission over the Internet is used for conference calls, security, and surveillance. Even if quality never reaches the level of current TV broadcasts, this market is expected to become a significant segment of electronic commerce in the future with the sale of low-quality/low-cost applications for monitoring production processes, watching children, and security surveillance (ActivMedia, 1998).

Multimedia is a digitised interactive application involving more than one medium (video, text, graphics, sound). Its major uses range from entertainment to education (these are often combined to form "edutainment") to conveying information, to corporate applications. Corporate applications are the largest segment today, and are largely used to encourage online sales. Multimedia content facilitates electronic commerce whenever customer interaction is required, such as filling out forms. As a result, it aids in the collection of information and the development of detailed customer databases that include purchasing patterns, interests and preferences, and demographic information, enabling the mass customisation of products and services. At present, the growth potential of multimedia and its various applications is mainly limited by current bandwidth constraints.

Education

Although distance learning has existed for some time, the Internet makes possible a dramatic expansion in coverage and better delivery of instruction. Text can be combined with audio/video, and students can interact in real time via e-mail and discussion groups. Students in Korea can now attend US universities over the Internet and pay tuition fees by credit card (Chandersekaran, 1998). Such technical improvements coincide with a general demand for retraining and upskilling by those who, due to work and family demands, cannot attend traditional courses.

Distance learning via the Internet is likely to complement existing schools for children and university students, but it could have more of a substitution effect for vocational training and continuing education programmes. For some degree programmes, high-prestige institutions could use their reputation to attract students who would otherwise attend a local facility. Fears that information technologies may adversely affect education date back to the radio and surfaced again with the advent of television and video cassette recorders. Such fears were groundless, and the same is likely to be true for the Internet, especially since the Internet overcomes many of the deficiencies associated with the previous technologies. Instead, owing to the Internet's ease of access and convenience for distance learning, overall demand will probably expand, leading to growth in this segment of e-commerce but little displacement of existing programmes (Selingo, 1998). Nevertheless, competition should increase as geographical constraints subside. Once the domain of somewhat unconventional educational institutions, distance learning is now offered by a wide number of prestigious institutions.[29]

Health services

Provision of health services has two facets that are amenable to electronic commerce. One is use of the Internet to streamline the capturing, storing and processing of information such as patients' records, physicians' notes, test results, and insurance claims information. It is estimated that these processes account for about one-third of health-care costs in the United States and Denmark (Evans and Wurster, 1997; OECD, 1997c). The use of a standard electronic system would reduce these costs as well as errors (*e.g.* due to side-effects of drugs, wrongly prescribed drugs) and insurance fraud. The second use is for telemedicine. This can consist of at least three different services: teleradiology (transmission and diagnosis of X-rays, ultrasound images, or magnetic resonance images), telepathology (real-time transmission and diagnosis of information to a pathology lab during an operation), and virtual reality (the use of computer simulation techniques to train and instruct) (BIAC, 1997). While it is unlikely that surgery will be performed at a distance or that computer diagnosis will replace human diagnosis, a number of trials have shown that a wide variety of simple procedures, monitoring, and preventive medicine can be conducted by telemedicine.

The increased demand for health services as OECD populations age, budgetary pressures to contain health costs, and regulatory reform all should help to promote future e-commerce activity in health services. Militating against this trend will be policy concerns regarding privacy of patients' personal data and national licensing and health practice regulations that restrict the provision of certain services across borders.

Other professional services

Professionals whose occupations largely involve the exchange of ideas or advice (architects, engineers, accountants, lawyers, consultants) may gravitate to electronic commerce, especially to acquire and serve clients (Chittum, 1998). While clients are unlikely to engage such services without direct personal contact, e-commerce is likely to expand the market for them and increase the level of client interaction (*e.g.* review of draft legal agreements).

Publishing

Many magazines and newspapers have gone on line, and a few charge a subscription fee for access. To date, the success of this activity has been limited to a few niche areas; this limits the displacement that can be expected in the near future. This is especially true for magazines, which typically rely on subscriptions for 40-60 per cent of their revenue and which have found it difficult to gain online subscribers, as many users have become accustomed to receiving online content free of charge (Margherio *et al.*, 1998). Exceptions may include adult magazines, as the decline in circulation of some magazines is attributed to the Web, as well as scientific and academic journals and reference publications (*e.g.* legal opinions) (Hays, 1997).

Newspapers are far more dependent on advertisements, an e-commerce business model which has had some success.[30] In particular, the profitability of traditional newspapers could be threatened by the migration of classified ads – a source of about 37 per cent of revenues – to the Internet, where the possibility of making exact searches and fast comparisons gives e-commerce an advantage over the traditional paper (Margherio *et al.*, 1998). In addition, many e-commerce sites have adopted a business model whereby they provide a classified ad service without charge, try to generate significant traffic, and simply charge for advertising at that site (Evans and Wurster, 1997). If the model succeeds, it could undercut traditional newspapers. A 1996 Newspaper Association of America study concluded that newspapers could lose up to 50 per cent of classified ad revenues by 2001 if the trend continues, and "if that happens the average newspaper's operating margin will fall from 14 per cent to 3 per cent" (Margherio *et al.*, 1998). In that case, it is likely that many will go out of business.

Two other developments could pose threats to traditional newspapers. The first is the development of city-specific online guides. These could draw off a large portion of local advertising as well as classified ads. Such products would mainly affect local newspapers, entertainment guides (*e.g.* Pariscope), and local TV. The second is the ability to build one's own tailored online paper, which could challenge the "one size fits all" model of current newspapers. In general, newspaper readership is declining as a result of competitors (*e.g.* TV) and the changing behaviour of new generations. The advent of e-commerce is only likely to accelerate an existing trend. Nonetheless, many newspapers are adapting and using their established reputation and network of journalists to compete in the new environment (see, for example, http://www.nytoday.com).

Books, on the other hand, are enjoying a renaissance, possibly because of e-commerce bookstores and innovations in traditional bookstores. While publishers of popular books are unlikely to be adversely affected by e-commerce, publishers of reference material may be, because the ease of updating and searching online databases makes printed versions non-competitive. The demise of the *Encyclopaedia Britannica* as encyclopaedias on CD were bundled with the purchase of a PC in the United States shows how electronic commerce might more broadly affect paper reference publications (Evans and Wurster, 1997).

Finally, it is very probable that electronic commerce will lead to a decline in other printed products such as catalogues, telephone books, photocopies, etc.

Financial services

Financial services, including banking, stock trading, insurance, and provision of financial information, are likely to be significantly affected by e-commerce. As for other products, the displacement of existing activities will be offset by overall increases in the market for these services as prices decline and people make more frequent use of them. For example, there is more frequent stock trading now that commissions are low. Finnish banking, a leader in the use of electronic payment systems, offers a rough indication of what may happen to financial services in the OECD area. In moving banking out of branches and onto networks, Finland has seen a sharp 54 per cent annual growth in productivity (measured by transactions per employee, 1984-96) and a 3.5 per cent annual decline in employment, resulting in a cut of more than a third of the jobs between 1984 and 1996. James Culberson, President of the American Bankers Association, predicts a similar trend in the United States in the near future, with half of all transactions conducted electronically and one-third of all branches closing (Margherio *et al.*, 1998).

Letter delivery

E-mail is a very popular Internet application, and nearly 60 per cent of US households with online connections (about 20 per cent of households) (Margolis, 1998) and 85 per cent of US businesses (about 50 per cent of all businesses) (IDC, 1997c) use it daily. While much of this mail consists of small, spontaneous messages that complement existing letter mail, some substitution is inevitably occurring as well. The Universal Postal Union (UPU) estimates that because of e-mail, the share of physical mail in the overall communication market (mail, fax, phone, e-mail) in Western Europe and North America should drop from about 28 per cent in 1995 to less than 20 per cent as e-mail doubles from 12 per cent to 24 per cent (UPU, 1997). The biggest impact is expected in business-to-business mail, where e-mail is expected to displace about 12 per cent of the flow by 2005; in the business-to-consumer segment, e-mail is expected to displace 4-5 per cent. Compared to other sources, these estimates appear to be very conservative: US Postmaster General Marvin estimates that over the last five years business-to business first-class mail dropped by over a third because of e-mail.[31] Moreover, the rapid migration of bill paying to electronic commerce (over a third by 2005) (Institute for the Future, 1996) could seriously impact letter delivery, as bills represent a third of the US Postal Service's revenues and half of its volume (Childs, 1998). Morgan Stanley estimates that, by 1994, 44 per cent of "messages" were transmitted by e-mail, up from 29 per cent in 1991 (Meeker, 1997).

Although post offices are now responding by offering their own e-mail-based services (Strassel, 1997*b*), the probable overall impact is a shrinking of delivered mail as e-mail grows. This will affect postal services and their suppliers (*e.g.* trucks) as well as suppliers of postal equipment (*e.g.* postage meters) and the internal mail rooms of nearly every organisation. Offsetting this decline is an increase in the number of parcels delivered as a result of e-commerce. More generally, existing post offices may come to act as central warehousing and load consolidation points that provide delivery services across a standardised fixed route much like today's mail delivery (ActivMedia, 1998). This would avoid the problem of numerous delivery trucks coming to the same address but would put the post offices in direct competition with the parcel delivery firms that are already providing this service.

Stimulating product innovation

The greatest future economic impact due to electronic commerce is likely to come from the creation of new products or the radical transformation of existing ones (effectively making them new) and the consequent creation of new demand. Historically, these new, frequently unforeseen, products have been the engines of growth and the source of new employment (*e.g.* home electronics, the television/film industry, software). While extraordinarily difficult to identify or quantify with any precision, five characteristics of e-commerce are likely to be a springboard for the demand for new products.

Market extension/aggregation

Because a Web page is accessible to anyone with access to the Internet, electronic commerce greatly extends the market reach of firms, vastly expanding opportunities and revealing new demand that fuels economic growth. This phenomenon is already evident. W.W. Grainger, a leading North American distributor of maintenance and office supplies, reports that 30 per cent of its online customers are new or incremental customers. Dell reports that 80 per cent of consumers and half of the small and medium-sized enterprises (SMEs) that purchase over its Web site have never purchased from them before, and one out of four say that they would not have purchased if it was not for the Web site (Margherio *et al.*, 1998). Playboy reports that three-quarters of its e-commerce revenues were collected from customers who were buying from Playboy for the first time (Macavinta, 1998). The reach of e-commerce and the reduction in transaction costs associated with it also enable an aggregation of demand, creating a market which can sustain new niche products; in the past, the small market potential would have been economically unfeasible. Examples abound, from home-made salsa sauce from Texas to rare quilt patterns from France.

Online auctions, such as those used by airlines to sell unsold seats at the last minute, are another example of using e-commerce to aggregate demand, creating a new market that delivers value to the consumer (inexpensive flights) and revenue to the producer. American Airlines estimates, for example, that it has generated tens of millions of dollars in incremental revenue by selling seats that previously went unsold since it launched NetSAAver in 1996 (Margherio *et al.*, 1998). Another example is the creation of spot markets for products for which the market was too diverse and scattered but which electronic commerce makes feasible: Fastparts, Inc. sells to buyers at a discount, through a spot market, surplus inventory of electronic components from assemblers of electronic goods (*e.g.* computers), which is estimated to represent some 10 per cent of the total annual shipments of the electronic component industry. This allows sellers to recover about half of the value of the part, while buyers receive a price reduction of 30-50 per cent (Margherio *et al.*, 1998)

Radically redefining existing products

Old products are being radically transformed by the addition of intangible digital improvements that continue to erode the distinction between a good and a service. Examples abound, from networked Coke machines to satellite navigational systems in cars. The reduction in communication and information costs is a common element in much of this transformation. E-mail is an obvious example. It is seen as a substitute for physical mail, but it can be sent securely to many recipients across the globe, with verification, in a few hours. In addition to text, it can contain links to other documents and include audio and video clips and multiple attachments. With traditional mail, this would be either impossible or very difficult. This new functionality and interactivity is an aspect of electronic commerce that is likely to transform old products and thus generate new demand. Although hackneyed, the example of Amazon.com, the online bookstore, shows how the retail experience can differ from what it is in the traditional bookstore: millions of books to choose from, chats with authors, collaborative filtering to suggest books potentially of interest, reviews by critics and customers, games. It is questionable as to whether the same product is being sold. Redefining how products ranging from cars to wills are sold could create new demand.

Marketing "free" products

Electronic commerce's lower transaction costs, as well as its interactivity and ability to market on a one-to-one basis, make it possible to market items that previously could not economically be bought or sold and existed as non-market transactions. Two current examples are advertising and private information, but many "free" goods such as shareware (free software) and free content could follow this model. In the past, the only monetary benefit a consumer could have gained from reading an ad would be a coupon or rebate for a price reduction when buying the product or possibly an in-kind benefit such as frequent-flyer miles. With pay-per-view advertising, electronic commerce now enables advertisers to pay consumers to read an ad (Borland, 1997a). Similarly, in the past, private information about individuals collected by businesses for marketing purposes, such as name, address, and demographic and financial information, was often acquired from individuals without any direct compensation. With e-commerce, it is possible to establish a market for this information, and businesses can buy this "product" from owners just as they compensate workers for their labour. The creation of these new markets should be a significant source of new e-commerce-generated growth.

One-to-one marketing

As the number of e-commerce users rises, so does the capacity of businesses to gather, store and, most importantly, access transaction data that link consumers to products. These databases have become modern-day treasure troves and essential e-commerce tools. The importance of such data and analysis predates Internet e-commerce, but because of the interactive nature of the Internet some sites can prohibit users from viewing the site unless they accept a computer programme that provides information about "what has happened on your computer in the recent past" (a "cookie": see http://www7.netgrocer.com/cookie_explain.cfrr). According to Dataquest, the world-wide data warehousing industry grew by 34 per cent in 1997, with revenues reaching $1.47 billion. It is forecast to reach $1.88 billion in 1998. Businesses use the information gained in this way to use product suggestions and personalised interfaces as marketing tools. Amazon.com, for example, uses filtering tools to profile customers and determine their purchasing patterns. On the basis of information gleaned from this database, Amazon suggests other books that might interest customers, based on the purchasing patterns of those who have bought similar books (Wilson, 1998).

Database mining has become an attractive industry on its own. New companies, such as AIR MILES International Holdings N.V., specialise in tracking customer purchases at a wide variety of locations. In exchange for detailed purchasing information from retailers as diverse as gasoline stations, moving companies, department, grocery, liquor and hardware stores, AIR MILES offers a small incentive to customers in the form of points that can be converted into air miles with selected airlines or into other products and services such as movie tickets or free long-distance calls. From the user's point of view, swiping the AIR MILES card at the cash register when buying a dishwasher and a week's supply of groceries can provide enough points for two tickets to a major sports event. In Canada, one in every two households collects these air miles. The company also operates in the United Kingdom, the Netherlands, and Spain.

Thanks to consumers who willingly provide detailed purchasing information, AIR MILES and similar companies create extensive databases that can be used by participating merchants to plan sales campaigns and identify potential target markets. Marketing companies are now able to profile people's hobbies. Among Canadians who make purchases online, for example, 48 per cent are avid gardeners. As customer profiles become clearer, so do the marketing methods that take advantage of this information

(Wilson, 1998). However, significant concerns regarding privacy and ownership of such information must be addressed and may limit this activity.

POLICY IMPLICATIONS AND THE FUTURE RESEARCH AGENDA

E-commerce is growing very quickly, albeit from a small base. When compared to benchmarks such as catalogue shopping or credit card activity, it is clear that electronic commerce is in an embryonic stage and that technology and market dynamics are still casting its basic shape. This is especially true for the business-to-consumer segment, which is a small fraction of the business-to-business segment. Policies should therefore be crafted cautiously, and with due recognition of the evolving nature of electronic commerce. Although nearly all sources indicate that business-to-business e-commerce dominates the market, most existing analysis and available data focus on the business-to-consumer segment.

- *Future research in this area should rectify this imbalance and, given the importance of business-to-business e-commerce, some of the economic and social impacts stemming from it should be analysed.*

Current estimates suggest that the United States currently generates about four-fifths of total worldwide e-commerce activity. As countries seek to dismantle some of the barriers to global electronic commerce, this imbalance raises competitive concerns and some suspicions.

- *The causes of this imbalance, its likely duration, and any particular factors that might preserve or reduce it could be a valuable topic for study.*

Within the business-to-consumer segment, activity is very sector-specific and a number of factors may inhibit its future potential for growth. In order to set a policy agenda and a timetable, a more accurate sense of the growth and direction of business-to-consumer e-commerce would be useful.

- *Research directed towards identifying the key inhibitors and drivers of business-to-consumer e-commerce could guide policy and make it possible to better judge the importance of this activity.*

In both the business-to-business and business-to-consumer markets, digital products such as software, travel services, entertainment and finance are the leading e-commerce products. Their intangible nature forces a re-evaluation of existing rules and practices.

- *Better measurement of these e-commerce products is needed because of the potential policy implications. It is important to examine how their intangible nature affects policies concerning trade, competition policy, price movements, economic cycles, etc.*

Fundamental to all of these policy implications is a greater ability to measure electronic commerce accurately. Statistics that measure the level, growth, and composition of e-commerce are badly needed to focus the policy debate. Research in these areas should be directed towards defining activities that truly illuminate the e-commerce phenomenon so as to give policy makers a better idea of where it is important to implement e-commerce policies. In the current situation, the wide variety of disparate estimates does little to clarify the issues.

- *Work should be undertaken to develop a statistical methodology and apparatus for measuring electronic commerce.*

NOTES

1. The countries are: Canada (1997), Finland (1997), France (1996), Germany (1995), Japan (1994), the United Kingdom (1994), and the United States (1997).

2. Forrester Research (1998*a*) reports that in 2001, the EU will have revenues one-third those of the United States.

3. "Dell: Net to Make up Half of Sales", http://www.news.com, 28 April 1998.

4. "Net Biz Software to Top $3B", http://www.techweb.com, 13 May 1997.

5. Interview with J.L. Trétois, Development Manager, GEIS, 2 September 1997.

6. *Ibid.*

7. It is estimated, for example, that up to 70 per cent of EDI links are established primarily because a major corporate or government customer specifies doing so as a term of contract. See OECD/ISO (1996).

8. "Overview of the ANX Network Service", http://www.aiag.org/anx, 26 May 1998.

9. "FedEx Sees Surge in E-commerce", http://www.news.com, 22 May 1998.

10. Domestic final demand is the same as total final demand except that imports have not been included. See OECD (1995).

11. "CyberSex", *The Economist*, 4 January 1997.

12. Donna Hoffman of Vanderbilt University quoted by Sussman (1998).

13. "Top End Online Travel Market Closing as Bottom Tier Open to New Players: Online Travel Sites Must 'Differentiate or Die'", http://www.jup.com, 24 April 1997.

14. "Can Pay, Won't Pay", *The Economist*, 14 February 1998; and Reeve (1998).

15. "PC Week's Top 10 E-commerce Sites", http://www.pcweek.com, 14 January 1997.

16. "The US Post Office Girds for E-mail Competition", *Business Week*, 26 January 1998.

17. A current partial list of organisations experimenting with electronic bill paying includes: California utilities Edison (4.2 million customers) and Los Angeles Department of Water and Power (1.2 million residential customers); American Express (600 000 customers); Chase Manhattan Bank; AT&T (75 million customers will be offered the option); MCI; Bell South; Southern Bell Corp.; Shell Oil; JC Penny. See Rafter (1998).

18. "The Hottest Web IPO You Never Saw", *Business Week*, 14 April 1997.

19. Presentation by Ira C. Magaziner at the conference, "The Internet and Electronic Commerce", 28 January 1997, Prague, Czech Republic.

20. "Ticket Master Online Sales up 270%", http://www.news.com, 15 May 1998.

21. "Net Biz Software to Top $3B", http://www.techweb.com, 13 May 1997.

22. "Surf Music", *The Economist*, 16 August 1997.

23. Ody (1996) states that "75 per cent of retail sales volume comes from the top 30 per cent of shoppers". Evans and Wurster (1997) state that "10% of the population that now use personal-financial management software (*e.g.* Intuit) probably account for 75% of the profits of the banking system".

24. Meeker (1997) reports that 69 per cent of respondents who purchased products on the Web listed convenience as a major factor.

25. "Lands' End and E-commerce: A Perfect Fit", http://www.internetnews.com, 12 September 1997.

26. A recent Harris poll found that the median number of hours worked per week in the United States rose from 40.6 in 1973 to 50.6 in 1995, while leisure time fell from 26.2 to 19.2. See Meeker (1997).

27. *The Economist* (1998), "Market Makers", 14 March.

28. "Report: Net to Dial up $9 billion by 2002", http://www.internetnews.com, 17 April 1998.

29. For example, the Western Governors University – which is a co-operative project of 17 US state universities (Arizona, Colorado, Idaho, Nebraska, New Mexico, North Dakota, Oregon, Utah, Washington, Wyoming, Alaska, Hawaii, Montana, Nevada, Oklahoma, Texas, Indiana), that of the territory of Guam, the California Virtual University (which represents all the California state universities) and Penn State's "World campus" distance education programme – plans to offer 25 certificate programmes with an enrolment of 5 000 students by 2003. See Selingo (1998).

30. "Can Pay, Won't Pay", *The Economist*, 14 February 1998.

31. "The US Post Office Girds for E-mail Competition", *Business Week*, 26 January 1998.

Chapter 2

THE IMPACT OF ELECTRONIC COMMERCE
ON THE EFFICIENCY OF THE ECONOMY

Introduction: a friction-free economy?

Rapid technological progress in information and communication technologies (ICTs) along with their widespread diffusion have led to speculation about "frictionless" economies in which transaction costs are nearly zero, barriers to entry and contestability disappear, and markets clear instantly. Some think that electronic commerce, with producers selling directly to consumers over computer networks such as the Internet, will eliminate existing intermediaries ("disintermediation") and drastically reduce transaction costs.[1] These lower production costs will encourage the entry of new businesses and thus increase competition and pressure to pass lower costs on to consumers as lower prices. In addition, consumers will be able to search among thousands of merchants for the lowest prices, thereby increasing the downward pressure on prices and leading to a shift in market power from producer to consumer (Hagel and Armstrong, 1997). In general, it is thought that electronic commerce can significantly improve the efficiency of economies, enhance their competitiveness, improve the allocation of resources, and increase long-term growth.

Because electronic commerce is still at a very early stage in its development, much of this thinking is based on speculation or anecdotal evidence. This chapter begins to analyse these claims by looking first at price declines in key technologies that enable electronic commerce: information processing, communication, and data storage. The price declines in these supporting technologies allow firms to replace old inputs and processes by new, less expensive inputs, thereby changing the firm's production function and reducing its production costs. Because these are information and communication technologies, the main impact is on transaction costs. However, given the intangible nature of e-commerce, new transaction costs are generated, many of which are associated with creating trust and managing some of the risks perceived to exist on the Internet. The impact of e-commerce on transaction costs is analysed both for firm-specific transaction costs and for costs incurred between firms. Equally important is the redistribution of some of these costs among the various parties, including consumers. Finally, the potential impact of changes in firms' costs on prices is examined. Changes in these costs have a direct impact on business models and market structure; this is analysed in Chapter 3.

The falling cost of information and communication technologies

Electronic commerce is an Internet application. It runs on an infrastructure composed of computers, software and communication systems and uses the Internet's key infrastructure applications (e-mail, the World Wide Web, the browser). This constellation of technologies has supported the development of electronic commerce and in turn is the source of much of electronic commerce's value. As Figure 2.1 shows, advances in microelectronics have caused the price of memory chips (*e.g.* DRAM) and semiconductors (*e.g.* microprocessors) to decline steadily. While these price declines are among the most spectacular, many other elements of computing – disk drives for data storage, printers and other peripherals – have also seen significant price declines (Figure 2.2), so that the overall price of a mainframe has generally fallen by a factor of three between 1984 and 1994 and that of PCs has fallen by a factor of five (Figure 2.3). These falling prices allow firms to switch to new ICTs, which allow them to engage in

Figure 2.1. **World-wide memory chip and semiconductor price indices**
Index: 1992 = 100 (Log scale)

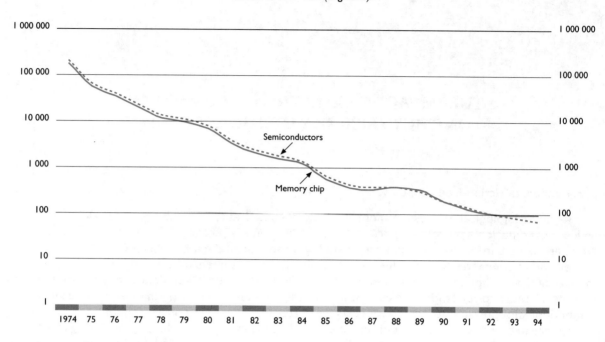

Source: Triplett, 1996.

Figure 2.2. **US disk drives, printers and other peripherals price indices**
Index: 1992 = 100

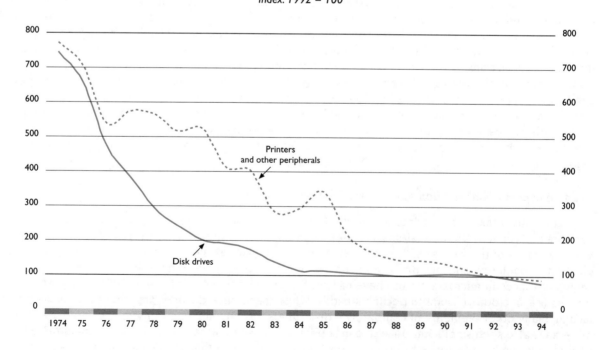

Source: Triplett, 1996.

Figure 2.3. **US mainframes and personal computers price indices**
Index: 1992 = 100

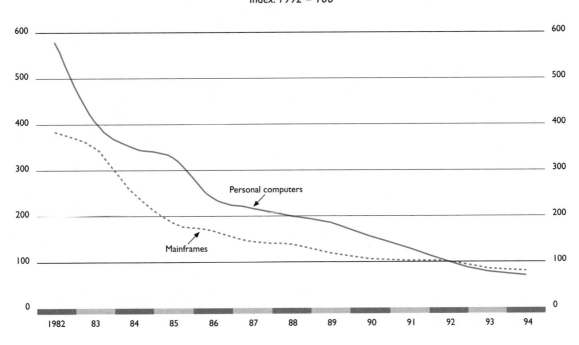

Source: Triplett, 1996.

electronic commerce. In fact, the cost of processing, analysing, storing and presenting data has fallen to such an extent that computing power is now widely diffused in seemingly frivolous applications like shoes, skis, and greeting cards.

Fibre optics technology, and radio and satellite transmission as well, have also fuelled large price declines in communications costs (Figure 2.4). However, because of the networked nature of the communications sector and its regulatory environment, the overall drop in phone call prices has been more modest (Table 2.1). Segments that are exposed to competition, such as the tariff basket for business communication charges in competitive markets and the price of leased lines (1.5/2 Mbits per second), have seen annual average declines of 4.1 per cent and 6.6 per cent, respectively, between 1990 and 1996 (OECD, 1997a). Likewise, the average price for Internet access charges in the OECD area, based on 20 hours of usage a month, fell by more than a factor of three, from $68 in 1995 to $20 in 1996, where it has since stabilised (OECD, 1997a).

New technologies such as digital subscriber lines (DSL), continued liberalisation of regulations, the arrival of new entrants, and the addition of significant new capacity (Table 2.2) have led some to suggest that communication prices may begin to follow a similar performance-to-price path as information technologies (Gilder, 1994; Forge, 1995).

The Internet and electronic commerce use a mixture of information and communication technologies (routers, ATM switches, the existing communications network) to connect PCs to servers. Many of these contain huge databases and maintain sophisticated software applications that ensure that the entire system operates smoothly. Thanks to the digital capability of this network and its packet switching protocol, data, voice, audio and video transmission can use the same system simultaneously, thereby vastly increasing the capacity and flexibility of the current communications system while undercutting the costs and prices of traditional modes of transmission. For example, the Internet can support a manufacturing EDI system at about one-quarter the cost associated with using a value-added network over a leased line (Meeker, 1997); the price of an Internet switched telephone call is approximately 20 per cent that of a traditional phone call (Atkins, 1997).

Figure 2.4. **Cable cost per voice path, 1974-97**
US$ thousand

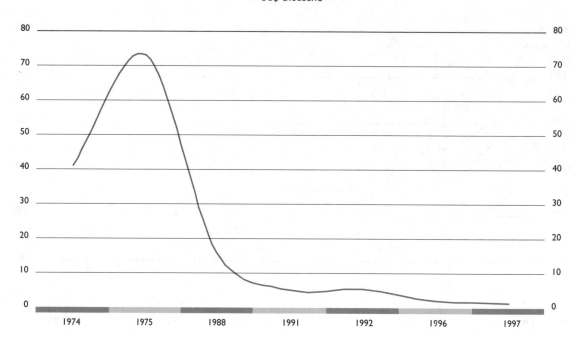

Source: Telegeography, 1997.

The impact on production costs

Assessing the collective impact of these technological developments and their associated price declines on production costs, productivity, and prices is very difficult. Indeed, the impact of computers alone on productivity has been extraordinarily difficult to ascertain and has led to a sub-field of economics that tries to explain the "productivity paradox": why the widespread introduction of computers has not resulted in increases in the official productivity statistics. As work on this question progresses, it is becoming clear that the paradox is unlikely to have a single solution, and the issue of whether or not computers significantly increase productivity has not been resolved. This is not surprising, since the broader impact of the telephone, which has been widely diffused for generations, on social interaction, location decisions, and business structure is still not well understood (Fisher, 1992).

A key element of this technological convergence is a shifting of the former trade-off between the richness of information (amount, customisation, interactivity) and its reach (exposure, coverage) (Evans and Wurster, 1997). Previously, a rich information flow was only obtained through the focused use of a few dedicated channels for a select audience (*e.g.* specialised publication, small meeting), while wide coverage meant sending a much more general message to a wide variety of recipients (*e.g.* TV, a company-wide memo). This trade-off dictated how interactions occurred, how businesses structured themselves, and how businesses interacted with each other and final customers (Coase, 1937; Williamson, 1975). While the combined effects of ICT on costs, productivity and prices for electronic commerce are likely to be difficult to determine, it may be that the sum of these technologies generates much greater utility than their individual parts, so that the productivity impact will be clearer. The Internet could represent that union, with electronic commerce as a key commercial application.

Changing firms' cost structure

The impact of electronic commerce on firms' internal production and transaction costs falls into three broad categories: the cost of executing the sale, costs associated with the procurement of production inputs, and costs associated with making and delivering the product. This list probably represents only a

Table 2.1. **OECD trends in collection charges**

Average of peak one minute to OECD countries expressed in US$[1]

	1991	1992	1993	1994	1995	1996	1991-96 Exchange rate	1991-96 Local currency
Australia (Telstra)	1.38	1.37	1.30	1.12	1.25	1.26	−8.42%	−7.26%
Austria	1.23	1.20	1.28	1.18	0.94	1.06	−13.76%	−23.58%
Belgium	1.13	1.10	1.12	0.76	0.77	0.88	−22.34%	−28.33%
Canada	1.37	1.29	1.22	1.00	0.94	0.96	−29.76%	−19.47%
Denmark (Tele Den.)	0.80	0.74	0.82	0.77	0.69	0.62	−21.84%	−24.48%
Finland (Telecom Fin.)	0.99	0.93	0.69	0.63	0.63	0.58	−41.72%	−9.34%
France	1.14	1.13	1.02	0.88	0.81	0.89	−21.54%	−26.12%
Germany	1.00	0.97	0.97	0.91	0.93	0.65	−34.88%	−32.19%
Greece	1.36	1.18	0.97	0.81	0.78	0.81	−40.15%	−10.12%
Iceland	1.54	1.52	1.35	1.09	1.25	1.11	−28.14%	−19.45%
Ireland	1.43	1.30	1.37	0.79	0.81	0.84	−41.30%	−41.76%
Italy	1.44	1.36	1.37	0.87	0.77	0.69	−52.27%	−34.21%
Japan (KDD)	2.19	2.36	2.51	2.85	2.77	2.16	−1.59%	−38.83%
Luxembourg	1.26	1.04	0.97	0.96	0.81	0.80	−36.68%	−33.81%
Mexico	n.a.	n.a.	n.a.	2.96	2.78	2.03	−31.21%[2]	−32.91%
Netherlands	1.01	0.99	0.97	0.92	0.89	0.78	−23.34%	−18.46%
New Zealand (TCNZ)	1.66	1.54	1.36	1.38	1.48	1.64	−0.93%	−9.79%
Norway	0.93	0.72	0.71	0.58	0.55	0.49	−47.07%	−36.94%
Portugal	1.39	1.37	1.56	1.25	1.14	0.97	−30.22%	−19.71%
Spain	1.77	1.73	1.57	1.25	1.03	1.08	−39.05%	−27.16%
Sweden (Telia)	1.06	1.04	1.08	0.80	0.70	0.66	−38.26%	−20.33%
Switzerland	1.17	1.14	1.00	0.90	0.94	0.79	−32.55%	−38.85%
Turkey	2.74	2.11	2.35	1.78	1.28	0.83	−69.60%	
United Kingdom (BT)	0.89	0.79	0.78	0.66	0.59	0.61	−31.13%	−19.48%
United States (AT&T)	1.34	1.33	1.33	1.40	1.42	1.57	−16.84%	−10.74%
OECD average[3]	**1.34**	**1.26**	**1.24**	**1.06**	**1.01**	**0.95**	**−29.46%**	**−23.00%**

1. The average of a one minute tariff based on one initial minute plus three additional minutes, divided by 4. OECD average is a straight average. All calculations are in exchange rates 1990-95, except for the last column. The average in last column is the average of the reduction rate of each country.
2. Mexico is excluded from the OECD average or as a destination country. Mexican data are for 1994-96.
3. All averages in local currency exclude Turkey.
Source: OECD, 1997a.

subset of the cost impacts associated with electronic commerce as firms implement the technology, since by and large they only represent savings over existing processes and thus do not factor in quality improvements. Similarly, beyond mere substitution, it is likely that electronic commerce techniques may foster completely new ways of conducting business. While these are hard to envision, they may lead to more significant cost savings. For example, when electricity first replaced water power, it typically used the same site near the water and the machines were vertically aligned to take advantage of the belts connected to the water wheel. While this represented an improvement over water power, large productivity gains were only obtained when new, horizontal buildings were constructed to fit the technology, allowing for the formation of assembly lines (David, 1990). A similar pattern may occur for electronic commerce.

The cost of executing a sale

The key areas of cost reduction when carrying out a sale via electronic commerce rather than in a traditional "bricks-and-mortar" store involve physical establishment, order placement/execution, customer support and after-sales service, and staffing.

Physical establishment. Estimates of the costs of setting up and maintaining an e-commerce Web site range from e-commerce in a box at $349 (Jackson, 1998), to about $8 000 for start-up and $10 000 for yearly maintenance for a service (Joachim, 1998), to hundreds of millions of dollars for a state-of-the-art site.[2] However, it is less expensive to maintain such a storefront than a physical one because it is always "open", can be accessed by millions around the globe, and has few variable costs, so that it can scale up to meet demand. By maintaining one "store" instead of thousands, duplicate inventory costs are eliminated.

Table 2.2. **Deployment of fibre optic cable in the OECD area**

	1993	1994	1995	Compound annual growth rate 1993-95 (%)	Measure
Austria	45 298	64 558	92 320	43	Fibre/km
Czech Republic	1 408	39 187	90 336	701	Fibre/km
Denmark	9 300	10 300	n.a.	n.a.	Km
Finland	164 024	327 416	425 955	61	Fibre/km
Germany	68 400	81 100	86 000	12	..
Greece	2 745	4 615	7 025	60	Cable/km
Iceland	156	180	315	42	Km
Ireland	8 600	9 600	11 200	14	Fibre/km
Italy	1 333 000	1 719 000	1 964 000	21	Fibre/km
Japan	168 300	212 629	248 731	22	Km
Mexico	8 701	16 796	21 610	58	..
Norway	11 400	12 700	13 800	10	Cable/km
Portugal	15 280	99 600	134 128	196	Km
Spain	24 857	29 339	36 041	20	..
Turkey	20 700	24 850	28 300	17	Km
United Kingdom	2 300 000	2 600 000	2 800 000	10	Km
United States	7 545 539	9 055 120	10 714 811	19	..

Source: OECD, 1997a.

Order placement/execution. By placing the necessary information on line in an accessible format, electronic commerce merchants generally transfer transaction costs (*e.g.* obtaining product information, selecting the product) to the customer. As a result, even when customers execute the transaction in a traditional way (off-line), for example by buying a PC over the phone or coming to an auto dealer's showroom to test drive a car, they come "pre-qualified". They know more precisely what they do and do not want and are more likely to buy. This greatly increases the efficiency of the sales process. Micron Computers reports a productivity gain of a factor of ten: their Web sales people spend on average two minutes on the phone with a customer who has looked at their Web site but 20 minutes with traditional customers (Kehoe, 1998). Auto dealers report similar gains: they spend about $25 to deal with an e-commerce-generated bid but several hundred dollars for a face-to-face transaction.[3]

In addition, e-commerce is very effective at reducing the costs of attracting new customers. While far from "friction-free", advertising is typically cheaper than for other media and more targeted. For example, while Carpoint (an e-commerce auto referral site) typically charges dealers about $200 in advertising and fees per car sold, car dealers typically spend $450 per car sold through traditional media (Kehoe, 1998). In addition, many merchants can send e-mail to prospective customers, and the WWW, with its hyperlinks, makes it relatively easy to sell a variety of products ("cross-sell") to existing customers. Cross-selling to a customer is roughly seven times cheaper than attracting new customers.[4]

Finally, the electronic interface allows e-commerce merchants to check that an order is internally consistent and that the order, receipt, and invoice match. While this simple process may seem trivial, both General Electric (GE) and Cisco report that one-quarter of their orders (1.25 million in the case of GE) had to be reworked because of errors. At Cisco, the use of electronic commerce for ordering instead of phone, fax or e-mail has automated the consistency check and has reduced the error rate to 2 per cent. To address the problem, GE has developed its Trading Post Network (TPN), which allows requisitions to be posted electronically for outside bid by any supplier and has significantly reduced the error rate in orders. It has also generated other benefits, such as a 5 to 20 per cent drop in materials costs due to increased supplier competition and a 50 per cent reduction in the procurement cycle (Margherio *et al.*, 1998).

Customer support/after-sales services. In what are increasingly knowledge-based economies dominated by sophisticated products, customer service and after-sales service are a major cost for many firms. Traditionally, this meant placing service personnel in the field to visit clients, staffing call centres, publishing extensive documentation, or issuing software. For many firms, these costs are substantial, accounting for more

Table 2.3. **Cisco's e-commerce customer support cost savings**

US$ million

Product manual printing costs	270
Software distribution	130
Telephone technical support	125
Total	**525**

Source: Meeker, 1997.

than 10 per cent of operating costs. Through electronic commerce, firms are able to move much of this support on line so that customers can access databases or "smart" manuals directly; this significantly cuts costs while generally improving the quality of service. A classic example is the Federal Express Internet site which allows customers to order package pick-up, generates a bar-coded label for the package, permits customers to pay for the service and allows them to track the delivery. With over 1 million "tracks" a month, half of which would have meant phone calls to FedEx's call centre, the system has saved FedEx millions in labour costs (Margherio *et al.*, 1998). Forrester Research estimates that it generally costs $500 to $700 to send a service representative into the field, $15 to $20 to handle a customer question over the phone, and about $7 to set up and maintain an Internet-based customer service system (LaTour Kadison *et al.*, 1998).

Cisco, the largest supplier of routers for Internet traffic, provides insight into how aggressive use of e-commerce to provide customer support can significantly reduce costs. As of 1997, Cisco had moved 70 per cent of its customer support on line, including everything from manuals to software to employee recruitment (Meeker, 1997). This has eliminated an estimated quarter-million phone calls a month, saving over $500 million, which represents about 9 per cent of total revenue or 17 per cent of total operating costs (Margherio *et al.*, 1998) (Table 2.3).

Staffing. Changes in the nature of what constitutes a store and the productivity of sales and customer services staff have a direct impact on the number and nature of staff hired. By and large, e-commerce shops require far fewer, but high-skilled, employees. Amazon.com, the e-commerce books merchant, has only 614 employees[5] (for sales of $148 million), while Barnes & Noble, the largest physical US bookstore, has 27 200 (for sales of $2.8 billion).[6] While these numbers are not strictly comparable, they give a rough sense of the difference in employment levels and sales per employee ($267 000 per Amazon employee versus $103 000 for Barnes and Nobel). A comparison of NECX, a catalogue turned e-commerce seller of PCs, and CompUSA, the largest retailer of PCs in the United States, provides some idea of the impact on skill requirements. In 1996, CompUSA had 106 stores, each of which generated on average $38.4 million in revenues and employed 103 persons, the majority of whom were cashiers, salespersons, and stockers/warehouse workers.[7] NECX generated $50 million from its Web site in 1997, but employed only 38 people, half of whom provided skilled, technical support (webmaster, Unix administrator, junior-level support person, four EDI support people, and 12 programmers) to the site (Goff, 1998).

Federal Express reports that their online customer service system has represented a savings of 20 000 new hires (about 14 per cent of their total labour force). Cisco reports that, thanks to its e-commerce Web site, they did not have to hire 1 000 new staff for their sales/support group (out of a total of 4 500 sales and marketing employees and 11 000 total staff).[8] GE reports that their TPN has resulted in the transfer of 60 per cent of their staff involved with requisition and that labour costs associated with procurement have declined by 30 per cent (Margherio *et al.*, 1998). These cases suggest that personnel savings are significant and represent a major cost savings associated with electronic commerce. But as Chapter 4 shows, the nature of employment is also changing: employment that supports an e-commerce Web site is relatively highly skilled. It is more akin to a fixed asset (*e.g.* a building) than traditional retail employment, which is relatively low-skilled and has a variable cost. This will limit to some degree the cost savings obtainable.

Purchase orders/procurement

Just as electronic commerce can significantly reduce selling costs, it can also lower the costs associated with buying. While the actual transaction takes place outside the firm, the costs associated with procurement constitute significant internal costs. Even for low-value requisitions for office supplies or travel, the typical purchase order costs between $80 and $125 to process, a sum that in many cases exceeds the value of the material being bought (Margherio *et al.*, 1998), owing to the error-prone and time-consuming process generally required to control purchasing costs and the fact that a typical purchase must go through several departments. Attempts to circumvent these processes usually result in even higher costs because negotiated discounts are not obtained or incompatible material is ordered. Internet-based e-commerce procedures now make it possible to apply EDI-type systems to relatively small purchases, thereby drastically reducing errors, ensuring compliance with organisational norms, and speeding the process. Estimates of the savings gained range from 10 to 50 per cent (Girishankar, 1997*b*), although in many cases the largest savings are not monetary: MCI reports that using e-commerce to buy PCs reduces its computer purchase cycle from four to six weeks to 24 hours (Margherio *et al.*, 1998), Bell South has cut the time needed to approve an expense report from three weeks to two days (Davis, 1998), and by replacing its EDI system with an Internet-based system, the US General Services Administration (GSA) has more than halved the time needed to complete a purchase (Girishankar, 1997*b*).

Inventories

Directly related to savings in time associated with procurement are savings in inventory carrying costs: the faster an input can be ordered and delivered, the less the need for a large inventory. In aggregate, in the United States, the average value of non-farm inventories represents some 2.3 per cent of yearly final sales and 4.2 per cent of sales of final goods. Since services are typically not inventoried, this may be a more appropriate indicator (http://www.bea.doc.gov/bea/dn/nipatbls/nip5-12.htm). This is about the same as the sales of all motor vehicle equipment in the United States. Approximately 37 per cent of all inventories are "carried" by manufacturers, while 25 and 27 per cent of total non-farm inventories are held by wholesale and retail trade, respectively. Each stage of the value-added chain therefore holds considerable inventories. It is estimated that for retailers, the cost of carrying an inventory for a year is equivalent to at least 25 per cent of what they receive in payment for the product (Taylor, 1997). Therefore, a two-week reduction in inventory represents a cost savings of 1 per cent of sales. As most retailers operate on margins of 3 to 4 per cent, this is significant.

The impact on costs associated with decreased inventories is most pronounced in industries where the product has a limited shelf life (*e.g.* bananas), is subject to fast technological obsolescence or price declines (*e.g.* computers), or where there is a rapid flow of new products (*e.g.* books, music). With computers as one of the main products sold via electronic commerce both to consumers and businesses, and the fact that computer components lose about 1 per cent of their value each week, this industry has been an innovator in reducing inventory costs. While the experience of one firm is not generally applicable, it does give insight into some of the potential inventory savings that electronic commerce could provide (Box 2.1).

Box 2.1.   **Dell, e-commerce and inventories**

Typically, a computer (PC) is made by a manufacturer, sits in a warehouse, and is shipped to a retailer, where it sits on a shelf until it is bought, a process that on average takes two months from production to sale. Since 80 per cent of the cost of a PC represents components and since their average price drops by 30 per cent a year, every day that can be shaved off inventory means that the manufacturer can use cheaper (and in most cases more powerful) components, and can maintain the same profit margin while selling a better product at a lower price. Dell has done this very successfully through electronic commerce and claims that parts only sit in inventory for eight days before being shipped out directly to the customer (Court, 1998). In this way, Dell reportedly enjoys a 100 per cent advantage in inventory turnover compared to traditional competitors, resulting in a 10 to 15 per cent price advantage (Margherio *et al.*, 1998). Competitors are being forced to adopt similar methods, as Dell's cost advantages are reflected in its profits: compared to Compaq, the largest US PC manufacturer, which earned $16 million in profits on $5.7 billion in sales in the first quarter of 1998, Dell's profits of $305 million on $3.9 billion suggest that this is a very profitable strategy (Court, 1998).

The general tightening of supply chains as business-to-business e-commerce becomes more pervasive is likely to have a significant effect on inventories and their associated costs. Ford's deployment of an intranet which connects 120 000 workstations at offices and factories around the world is attributed with contributing to reducing the time needed to get new models into full production from 36 to 24 months. Ford hopes to extend this system so as to manufacture on demand; the goal is to manufacture and deliver the car two weeks after the order, thereby saving billions of dollars in inventory and fixed costs (Cronin, 1998).

Recent tests by the US Automotive Industry Automation Group (AIAG) Manufacturing Assembly Pilot (MAP) programme, which piloted an EDI system across the Internet to a wide spectrum of suppliers and original equipment manufacturers (OEM), suggest that these benefits could be widespread. The pilot generated a 58 per cent reduction in lead times, a 24 per cent improvement in inventory levels, and a 75 per cent reduction in error rates. When deployed more widely in 2000, it is expected to save the US automotive industry an estimated $1 billion a year (http://www.aiag.org/about/accomplish.html).

A key factor in reducing the costs of inventories is improving the ability to forecast demand more accurately. Electronic commerce merchants who allow consumers to customise their order or select from a wide variety of choices obtain valuable information on consumer preferences. This should improve their ability to forecast demand. In a traditional store, a consumer might buy a computer with unwanted features or lacking certain features because that model was available. In such a situation, the merchant is ignorant of the consumer's true preferences. The electronic commerce merchant who offers a "built-to-order" computer, instead, knows exactly what consumers prefer and can adjust the product line accordingly. In addition, the links that electronic commerce provides along the supply-chain make it possible to pass this information on to partners, thereby lowering their costs and probably the overall price. This practice, known as collaborative planning forecasting replenishment (CPFR), is estimated to lead to a reduction in overall inventories of $250 to $350 billion, or about a 20 to 25 per cent reduction in current US inventory levels (Ernst & Young, cited in Margherio *et al.*, 1998). While this estimate seems optimistic, pilot studies on the US auto market obtained a 20 per cent savings (Frook, 1998a). Even a 5 per cent reduction would have a significant economic impact. Gains can also be achieved from having the correct type of stock on hand so that customers can buy what they want, when they want it. Japanese supermarkets like Sotetsu Rosen have used this technique and have basically eliminated (0.04 per cent) out-of-stock items (Ministry of International Trade and Industry, 1998).

Distribution

Although shipping costs can increase the cost of many products purchased via electronic commerce and add substantially to the final price (see next section), distribution costs are significantly reduced

Table 2.4 **E-commerce impact on various distribution costs**

US$ per transaction

	Airline tickets[1]	Banking[2]	Bill payment[3]	Term life insurance policy[4]	Software distribution[5]
Traditional system	8.0	1.08	2.22 to 3.32	400 to 700	15.00
Telephone-based		0.54			5.00
Internet-based	1.00	0.13	0.65 to 1.10	200 to 350	0.20 to 0.50
Savings (%)	**87**	**89**	**71 to 67**	**50**	**97 to 99**

1. Traditional refers to a travel agent booking the ticket using a computer reservation system. Internet-based refers to a customer booking an "electronic ticket" directly with the airline.
2. Cost per transaction at a branch bank estimated by Booz-Allen & Hamilton, quoted in Margherio *et al.*, 1998. Cost per transaction by telephone estimated by Booz-Allen & Hamilton, quoted in Margherio *et al.*, 1998. Cost per transaction by Internet estimated by Booz-Allen & Hamilton, quoted in Margherio *et al.*, 1998.
3. IBM preliminary estimates, quoted in Margherio *et al.*, 1998.
4. InsureMarket estimates for agent fees based on term life insurance policy of $400 000 with $700 annual premium quoted in Margherio *et al.*, 1998.
5. Bollier, 1996.
Source: See notes.

(by 50 to 90 per cent) for digital products such as financial services, software, and travel, which are important e-commerce segments. For these products, the cost reduction associated with electronic commerce could have large economic impacts and further fuel the migration of these sectors to electronic commerce (Table 2.4). In the case of airlines, electronic tickets now account for about half of all tickets for some major carriers; this has resulted in substantial savings and is forcing competitors to follow suit.[9] For sectors such as music, where songs can be downloaded directly from the producer, or news, where the journalist e-mails the reader directly, huge savings are reaped over traditional forms of distribution. This reduction in distribution costs is especially important for international trade, as the ability to "download" some products without incurring shipping costs is thought to be a strong stimulus to trade, particularly for small and medium-sized enterprises (SMEs). Even for tangible goods, e-commerce methods can reduce the administrative costs associated with trade and customs clearance by over 25 per cent (WTO, 1998).

Changing the cost structure of the value-added chain

Just as electronic commerce reduces the internal costs of many transactions, it also changes the cost structure that dictates a firm's relationships with other businesses. This set of relationships is called the value-added chain, the network of upstream and downstream businesses, from raw materials to final sale, through which a product travels. At every stage of processing, an intermediary often performs a service which facilitates this flow – adding value but also adding cost. In many cases, this service is information-intensive – matching a buyer to a seller, certifying parties in a transaction, providing support for the transaction (*e.g.* financial or legal services) – and often involves some type of risk sharing. Electronic commerce, especially in intangible products, may reduce the involvement of intermediaries in the value-added chain and thus lower costs.

The previous section showed that, in some cases, this is true for services that were formerly provided internally by a company but which can now be performed by the consumer thanks to the information and communication technology bundled with electronic commerce. While the cost of inventories has been considered an internal cost to the firm, it is in fact a reflection of a firm's interactions with others in the value-added chain. This section will analyse the impact of e-commerce on costs incurred by firms to sell their product, principally the use of services provided by third-party agents or brokers. It will also examine how electronic commerce is creating new intermediary functions as well as relying on traditional suppliers.

Disintermediation

Intermediaries who help producers sell to consumers are of two types: distributors such as wholesalers and retailers, collectively referred to as margins, which are located between the producer of tangible goods and the consumer; and services which act as intermediaries for other services (*e.g.* travel agents selling seats on airlines). To begin to understand the potential economic impact of the disintermediation associated with electronic commerce, the two are analysed separately because the demand for, and provision of, goods versus services by e-commerce differs significantly.

Margins. In the chain of activity between the final producer and the final consumer, intermediaries perform three services – transportation, wholesaling, and retailing – known as margins. In most OECD countries, margins typically add about 33 per cent to the final price of goods (Table 2.5). In the Unite States, for all personal consumer expenditures (PCE) (goods and services), margins add about 15.6 per cent to the final price, of which 0.6 per cent represents transportation, 3.8 per cent wholesale costs, and 11.2 per cent retail costs (Table 2.6). In terms of economic impact, the largest effect would be the elimination of the services provided by wholesale and retail trade.

To explore this, Table 2.6 presents a sensitivity test of the impact of electronic commerce on distribution margins (wholesale and retail trade), which breaks down all US consumer expenditures into three broad categories: sectors that have been, or are expected to be, significantly affected by business-to-consumer electronic commerce; products whose margins account for 50 per cent or more of the final sales price; and broad categories of products unlikely to be affected by e-commerce. In the first sensitivity test, it is assumed that all products currently involved in some e-commerce migrate completely to an e-commerce model, with producers selling directly to consumers, thereby completely eliminating all

Table 2.5. **Distribution margins for goods, selected OECD countries**

	Margin on personal consumption of goods	Margin on food products	Margin on clothing	Margin on leather and shoes	Margin on drugs and medicines	Margin on motor vehicles	Margin on electrical appliances
United States, 1987	38.0	32.8	45.9	50.1	40.8	18.9	38.7
Japan, 1985	34.5	27.8	52.4	33.9	n.a.	28.1	41.5
France, 1987	29.8	29.5	40.9	42.7	41.3	24.6	38.1
Australia, 1986-87	37.4	34.5	46.1	49.0	71.9	30.8	34.8
Austria, 1988	26.8	21.4	38.4	37.6	34.7	16.0	29.8
Netherlands, 1990	36.6	31.8	43.6	38.8	52.9	18.3	36.1
Sweden, 1985	n.a.	21.7	39.3	35.4	44.8	14.4	17.6

Note: The distribution margin is the difference between final consumption expenditure at purchaser prices and final consumption expenditure at producer prices. Margins exclude net indirect taxes.

Sources: Based on input-output tables as follows: United States from 1987 benchmark input-output table in BEA (1994); Japan from 1985 input-output table in Management and Coordination Agency (1990); France from INSEE (1996); Australia from ABS (1990); Netherlands from CBS (1992); Sweden based on SCB (1989). Austria from EC (1994).

intermediaries. In all, these products represent 27 per cent of 1992 US personal consumer expenditures or over $1 trillion worth of sales, vastly in excess of most current estimates of e-commerce and above most future estimates when inflation is taken into account. Nevertheless, the impact of disintermediation is relatively modest: a 6 per cent decrease in wholesale trade margins and a 9.6 per cent decline in retail trade margins. If motor vehicle sales are eliminated, the impact is only a 3 per cent decline for both wholesale and retail trade.

A second sensitivity test assumes that, in addition to products already identified as likely candidates for electronic commerce, half of the products for which the cost of wholesale and retail intermediary services represents a significant portion of the final cost (50 per cent or more) will also be traded directly by e-commerce. The assumption that half of these products would be sold through electronic commerce adds an additional $150 billion in e-commerce sales, raising the total amount of consumer expenditures conducted by electronic commerce to 31 per cent. For 1992, this test results in an additional displacement of 8 per cent for US wholesale activity and 15 per cent for retail.

Adding the two sensitivity tests together results in the disintermediation of 14 per cent of US wholesale services and 25 per cent of US retail services (inclusive of motor vehicles, which account for 6.5 per cent of total PCE margins) for 1992. While non-trivial, the total amount of consumer expenditures assumed to be carried out via e-commerce without the benefit of any intermediaries, even under these extreme assumptions, is roughly the same as current US direct marketing sales of $1.9 trillion. Given that direct marketing sales take place without the aid of traditional intermediaries, the future impact of e-commerce disintermediation is unlikely to be any more pronounced than what has already occurred through direct mail, telephone, newspapers, TV and radio (Direct Marketing Association, 1998).

The relatively small amount of disintermediation associated with margins is due to the fact that many of consumers' major product expenditures are for products which are already sold directly to consumers (*e.g.* electricity) or for products that are themselves an intermediary service (*e.g.* stock trading) which does not require any additional intermediary (margins). In fact, many of the sectors identified in Chapter 1 as information sectors where digitisation might easily occur (banking, education, health) use relatively few intermediaries. In the case of tangible goods like books or CDs, the new e-commerce merchants are not disintermediating, they are simply competing with existing intermediaries for the retail role. Moreover, many firms will sell products in both distribution channels in the near term as they experiment with electronic commerce; this is another factor that may limit the amount of disintermediation. In some cases, this experimentation will reveal the complementary of the traditional store to electronic commerce, insofar as the former allows customers to physically examine and immediately take ownership of tangible products and may provide consumers with a sense of trust that they may lack in a purely cyber-transaction. Thus, "disintermediation" due to the elimination of the wholesale and retail sectors as an intermediary is likely to be important for some sectors, but relatively small overall.

Table 2.6. **Input-output commodity composition of personal consumption expenditures (PCE) in producers' and purchasers' prices, 1992**

US$ million

	Producer value	Wholesale margin	Retail margin	Purchaser value	W&R margins as share of purchaser value
Electronic commerce products					
Telephone and telegraph	70 669	0	0	70 669	0.0
Computing equipment and software	7 441	1 054	3 518	12 076	37.9
Household insurance	244	0	0	244	0.0
Physicians	166 429	0	0	166 429	0.0
Dentists	37 636	0	0	37 636	0.0
Other professional medical services	85 216	0	0	85 216	0.0
Veterinarians	5 108	0	0	5 108	0.0
Health insurance	43 224	0	0	43 224	0.0
Brokerage charges and investment counseling	28 719	0	0	28 719	0.0
Bank service charges, trust services	30 934	0	0	30 934	0.0
Services furnished without payment by financial intermediaries	137 479	0	0	137 479	0.0
Money orders	576	0	0	576	0.0
Tax return preparation services	2 888	0	0	2 888	0.0
Postage	6 701	0	0	6 701	0.0
Expense of handling life insurance	69 380	0	0	69 380	0.0
Legal services	44 864	0	0	44 864	0.0
Employment agency fees	1 721	0	0	1 721	0.0
Classified ads	676	0	0	676	0.0
New domestic autos	41 222	1 508	5 727	49 567	14.6
New foreign autos	23 656	866	3 289	28 449	14.6
Net purchases of used autos	17 223	739	13 215	31 177	44.8
New and used trucks	42 637	1 825	8 511	54 069	19.1
Motor vehicle insurance	25 728	0	0	25 728	0.0
Books and maps	9 795	1 809	5 181	17 148	40.8
Magazines and sheet music	7 012	1 128	2 892	11 590	34.7
Newspapers	7 743	397	2 015	10 369	23.3
Video cassette rental	6 290	0	0	6 290	0.0
Cable TV	19 883	0	0	19 883	0.0
Film development	5 099	0	400	5 499	7.3
Motion picture theaters	4 939	0	0	4 939	0.0
Spectator sports	5 131	0	0	5 131	0.0
Commercial amusements, n.e.c.	19 489	25	467	19 981	2.5
Lotteries	9 783	0	0	9 783	0.0
Casino gambling	13 931	0	0	13 931	0.0
Parimutuel net receipts	3 366	0	0	3 366	0.0
Private higher education	28 804	0	0	28 804	0.0
Commercial and vocational schools	13 105	0	0	13 105	0.0
Government higher education	23 624	0	0	23 624	0.0
Total electronic commerce products	**1 067 877**	**9 351**	**45 215**	**1 126 485**	**4.8**

Displacement of intermediary products. A potentially larger impact involves the displacement of products whose basic function is to convey information that is asymmetrically possessed (by travel agents, insurance agents, stockbrokers, real estate agents, etc.). Even in such cases, however, many sellers will value the buffering and risk-sharing service offered by these intermediaries and will retain them (Hawkins, 1998). The intermediaries most vulnerable to disintermediation are those that act as "human modems" and simply pass on information without adding much value (*e.g.* times and prices on a standard flight). In nearly all cases, e-commerce accelerates an existing trend. For example, the use of discount brokers in the case of stock trading or the many travel services directly available from the provider.

The bulk of the available evidence concerns the compression of commissions for traditional travel agents and discount stockbrokers, *i.e.* in those cases where electronic commerce has allowed producers to sell directly to consumers or where the electronic nature of the transaction means that commissions based on volume (*e.g.* dollar value of the stock trade) have been displaced by flat fees. In both these cases, the impact has been large and has resulted in an average annual decline in commissions

Table 2.6. **Input-output commodity composition of personal consumption expenditures (PCE) in producers' and purchasers' prices, 1992** *(cont.)*

US$ million

	Producer value	Wholesale margin	Retail margin	Purchaser value	W&R margins as share of purchaser value
Broad categories of products					
Food, tobacco and alcohol	542 504	53 156	109 661	715 356	22.8
Clothing and leather products	36 161	4 893	27 281	68 652	46.9
Personal articles and services	68 803	2 593	12 701	84 710	18.1
Housing	642 574	0	0	642 574	0.0
Furniture, household supplies and utilities	247 368	11 151	51 969	313 506	20.1
Health equipment and supplies	98 568	7 380	19 802	126 060	21.6
Hospitals	270 322	0	0	270 322	0.0
Personal business services n.e.c.	21 386	72	872	22 354	4.2
Motor vehicle maintenance and fuel	153 668	37 195	32 179	228 535	30.4
Public transportation	36 437	0	0	36 437	0.0
Recreational and sporting products	23 650	2 427	10 731	37 031	35.5
Audiovisual products and services	38 397	5 054	15 944	59 744	35.1
Leisure and entertainment	32 942	13	549	33 573	1.7
Education	23 495	0	0	23 495	0.0
Religious, welfare and non-profit activities	126 235	0	0	126 235	0.0
Travel (net)	–16 358	0	0	–16 358	0.0
Total	**2 346 152**	**123 934**	**281 689**	**2 772 226**	**14.6**
Wholesale and retail high margin products					
Shoes and other footwear	14 926	3 382	14 474	32 903	54.3
Women's clothing without luggage	55 724	7 185	57 510	120 938	53.5
Jewelry and watches	13 153	2 541	15 893	31 645	58.3
China, glassware, tableware and utensils	8 156	1 231	9 963	19 577	57.2
Durable house furnishings n.e.c.	8 850	1 433	8 815	19 407	52.8
Hand tools	2 575	748	2 401	5 754	54.7
Writing equipment	1 010	356	934	2 311	55.8
Lighting supplies	2 122	601	1 956	4 778	53.5
Ophthalmic products and orthopedic appliances	4 633	1 143	7 201	13 001	64.2
Stationery and school supplies	2 298	594	2 671	5 721	57.1
Toys and sport supplies	16 183	4 976	11 367	32 882	49.7
Greeting cards	3 745	562	4 571	9 129	56.2
Flowers, seeds, and potted plants	4 541	408	6 475	11 961	57.5
Total	**137 916**	**25 160**	**144 231**	**310 007**	**54.6**
Total electronic commerce products	**1 067 877**	**9 351**	**45 215**	**1 126 485**	**4.8**
Total broad categories of products	**2 346 152**	**123 934**	**281 689**	**2 772 226**	**14.6**
Total wholesale and retail high margin products	**137 916**	**25 160**	**144 231**	**310 007**	**54.6**
Total	**3 551 945**	**158 445**	**471 135**	**4 208 718**	**15.0**

Source: US Department of Commerce, 1998.

of 57 per cent for the dominant online stock trader and 43 per cent for the commissions paid by one large US airline.

Air travel. Travel agents' commissions, marketing and advertising, labour and other expenses for central reservation systems are the airline industry's second largest operating expense, with travel agents alone accounting for about 9 per cent of total operating costs (*Financial Times*, 8 July 1996). Currently, about 80 per cent of all airline tickets are purchased through a travel agent, with the airlines selling directly most of the remainder (Margherio et al., 1998). However, the arrival of electronic commerce has coincided with a steady erosion of agents' commissions and aggressive attempts by the airlines to provide the service directly (Table 2.7).

Stock trading. A similar fate is befalling discount stockbrokers who typically simply execute orders from clients without adding value such as investment advice (and for those who do, the trade-off of lower prices is decreasing demand for their services). Discount brokers' commissions now represent about 14 per cent of the 1997 total of all retail stock trading in the United States; and e-commerce brokers currently

Table 2.7. **Impact of e-commerce on commissions**

US$ per transaction

	Trade of 1 000 shares of IBM stock[1]	Flight from New York to Los Angeles[2]
1993	285	60
1994	285	60
1995	285	50
1996	228	50
1997	228	25
1998	30	10
Annual average decline (%)	**57**	**43**

1. IBM stock price as of 29 May 1998; 1993-95 discount broker; 1996-97 Internet discount of 20 per cent; 1998 full Internet trade.
2. Flight based on a $600 price as of 23 July 1998 (http://www.travelocity.com) with rates of $10 applied as cited in Margherio *et al.*, 1998 and news accounts.

Sources: OECD interview with Charles Schwab (col. 1); Margherio *et al.*, 1998 (col. 2).

account for 4 per cent of that total. While this is small, the arrival of e-commerce brokers has led to significant price competition, with the average commission for the top ten online trading firms dropping from $34.65 in 1996 to $15.95 in 1997 (Newsedge, 1998). Indeed, several firms offer trades of 5 000 shares or fewer for less than $10. While the services provided by these firms are not strictly comparable, they have forced the commissions for standard services of large firms such as Charles Schwab to decline as well, reducing overall profits (Table 2.7) (Wise, 1998).

Re-intermediation

As electronic commerce causes the disintermediation of some intermediaries, it creates both greater dependency on others and also some entirely new intermediary functions. The principal service provided by many of these new intermediaries is establishment of trust, a very important factor for electronic commerce businesses, as buyer and seller may never meet and the openness and expanse of the Internet make fraud easier than in traditional commerce. Box 2.2 provides an example of new intermediary activities for which demand is increasing due to electronic commerce.

To give a sense of how these intermediaries could add costs to e-commerce transactions, three of the potentially largest intermediary services are examined: advertising, secure online payment, and delivery.

Advertising/branding. The relative ease of becoming an e-commerce merchant and setting up "stores" (Web sites) results in such a huge number of offerings that consumers can easily be overwhelmed. This increases the importance of using advertising to establish a brand name and thus generate consumer familiarity and trust. For new e-commerce start-ups, the process can be expensive and represents a significant transaction cost, one which is also present in the traditional world of commerce but on a narrower geographical scale. One of the disadvantages to the "born global" character of electronic commerce is the fact that competitors are also global, necessitating advertising which is global in reach. This can be expensive, especially for SMEs and start-ups. To some degree, this dynamic may favour merchants with an established brand image ("mind share") and carry that image into the world of electronic commerce. If so, this would tend to increase the costs of gaining brand recognition for new, purely e-commerce merchants.

Brands are typically created by advertising, which is currently a significant cost of conducting electronic commerce. This is evident in recent deals struck between leading e-commerce merchants and Internet "real estate" with significant consumer traffic. These sites, frequently called Internet "portals", are search engines like Yahoo!, browsers like Netscape Communicator, and large Internet access providers like America Online (AOL). As Table 2.8 shows, AOL's advertising revenue has been significant.

Associated with this has been the development of a system of affiliates, whereby e-commerce merchants pay for referrals, direct links from portals, or techniques that drive traffic towards their site. In many cases, commissions paid to affiliates can be large: e-Toys pays 25 per cent of the sale price to the referring affiliate, Amazon.com has 30 000 affiliates and shares from 5 to 15 per cent of the sale (Karpinski, 1998).

Box 2.2. Network-based intermediaries

Directories. Directory service intermediaries provide searching facilities. There are **general directories** (*e.g.* Yahoo and EINet Galaxy), **commercial directories** (*e.g.* The All-Internet Shopping Directory) which are the equivalent of paper-based industry guides, and **specialised directories** (*e.g.* Jeff Frohwein's ISDN Technical Page) which are topic-oriented and may provide consumers with technical and evaluative information about a good or a particular producer, in addition to simple search support. A directory's only source of income is advertising.

Search services. Search sites (*e.g.* Lycos and Infoseek) provide users with the capability to conduct key-word searches of extensive databases of Web sites/pages. Typically, search sites do not allow browsing of the database directly and are rarely topic-specific.

Malls. A site that has more than two commercial sites linked to it. It is an intermediary, that, like traditional physical malls, provides infrastructure for the producer/retailer in return for a fee (perhaps rent or percentage of sales). Often these malls have a geographic focus (*e.g.* The Aloha Mall or The Alaskan Mall). They may target a particular type of producer/retailer (*e.g.* The Asian American Mall) or they may be composed of a variety of "stores" that sell a variety of products (*e.g.* The Pinnacle Mall or Cybersuperstores).

Publishers. "Traffic generators" that offer content of interest to consumers (*e.g.* Information Week or Wired Magazine). They may appear more or less to be online newspapers or magazines. They may charge flat fees for advertising or may also extract a transaction fee for sales.

Virtual resellers. Malls provide cyber-infrastructure, but they do not own inventory or sell products directly, unlike virtual resellers, who do.

Web site evaluators. Sites that offer some form of evaluation and help to reduce some of the risk to consumers [*e.g.* Point Communications (top 5 per cent of the Web) and GNN]. They may extract value by charging a fee to producers to be evaluated, or they may charge consumers for their service.

Financial intermediaries. Payment systems will take many forms, including credit authorisation by major credit card companies such as Visa or Mastercard, electronic equivalents to writing cheques (Check-free), cash payments (Digicash), and sending secure electronic mail authorising a payment (First Virtual). In an electronic commerce environment, these financial intermediaries may extract per transaction fees in order to absorb some of the risk associated with money flows.

Spot market makers and barter networks. A new set of intermediaries, similar to auction houses, flea market owners, and commodities exchanges may arise. One thriving example of the use of the network to help create a spot market are the news groups that act as markets for various products. There are often local market groups or local Freenets on college campuses. There are also specialised groups (computer equipment, trading cards, etc.) and those that deal in used goods. In addition to the newsgroup-based facilities, there are also many Web-based services, including Barter Net and netTrader.

Intelligent agents. Software programmes that begin with some preliminary search criteria from users, but that also learn from past user behaviour to help optimise searches.

Table 2.8. **America Online's deals, 1997-98**

Date	Company	Terms
February 1997	Tel-save	$100 million plus % profits
June 1997	CUC	$50 million over 3 years
June 1997	Auto-By-Tel	$18 million over 3 years
July 1997	Amazon.com	$19 million over 3 years
December 1997	N2K (music)	$12 million
January 1998	Barnes & Nobel	$40 million over 4 years
February 1998	Intuit	$30 million
April 1998	Realtor.com	$14 million over 40 months

Source: Goldman Sachs, 1997.

The cost of establishing and defending a brand through advertising and affiliate deals represents an important e-commerce transaction cost and is a main reason why many business-to-consumer e-commerce merchants have yet to report a profit. The "bookstore war" between Barnes & Noble and Amazon.com provides an illustrative example. While Barnes & Noble enjoys a brand image from their traditional book shops, it is not turning a profit from its online operation, despite predicted sales of $100 million in 1998, because it is spending $30-40 million on marketing and paying $20 million to AOL.[10] Amazon is not faring much better. With sales of $148 million in 1997, it generated a loss of $29.2 million owing to "....heavily [investing] in marketing and promotion, product development and technology, and operating infrastructure development"(US Security and Exchange Commission, 1998). Of these three investments, marketing and promotion account for over two-thirds.

The development of intelligent agent systems that allow consumers to scour the Internet for a particular product reduces the importance of brands and portals. These very new systems have not yet been widely diffused. While they are a potentially attractive option for some products, the nature of the Internet makes creating trust in an unknown merchant located by an intelligent agent difficult. In the near term, therefore, it is unlikely that this development will displace the costs associated with advertising.

Secure online payment. The openness, global reach, and lack of physical clues that are inherent characteristics of e-commerce also make it vulnerable to fraud and thus increase certain costs for e-commerce merchants as compared to traditional stores. While a variety of payment systems are being tested, the credit card is the dominant online payment method so far, and e-commerce merchants are exposed to potentially higher levels of fraud resulting from stolen cards or illegally obtained card numbers. Cybersource, a firm that specialises in detecting e-payment fraud, estimates, on the basis of a client survey in October 1997, that 39 per cent of all e-commerce orders (based on numbers of orders) are fraudulent (Cybersource, 1998). The system-wide average fraud rate for credit cards is less than 0.5 per cent (based on value) (de Aenelle, 1997). Other sources report similar e-commerce credit card fraud rates (Krochmal, 1998). Anecdotal evidence suggests that the credit card fraud rate is especially high for digitally delivered products, which tend to be the most popular e-commerce consumer purchases.[11] Because of the rule on distance retail (if the credit card is not physically present, the merchant is liable for all the costs associated with the fraud even if the bank has authorised the transaction), e-commerce merchants could face added costs because of their exposure to fraud.

New techniques are being developed to protect the use of credit cards in e-commerce transactions, but the need for greater security and user verification leads to increased costs. The leading standard for these transactions is the SET (Secure Electronic Trading) system developed by MasterCard and Visa. Unlike normal credit card transactions, this system uses digital certificates to verify the user, making the system about three times slower (20 to 30 seconds) than traditional transaction processing (Nelson, 1998). These additional precautions will also increase costs, depending on the volume and the merchant, by 1 to 6 per cent of the value of the transaction (Institute for Technology Assessment, 1997).

Delivery/logistics. A key feature of electronic commerce is the convenience of having purchases delivered directly. In the case of tangibles, such as books, this incurs delivery costs. Given that the good cannot be physically examined or carried home as in traditional commerce, the delivery agent plays an important role in assuring customers that purchases will arrive, and this explains why package tracking services have become so popular. Although advances in delivery now make it possible to ship groceries by plane to any destination in the United States from a warehouse in Texas, delivery costs cause prices to rise in most cases, thereby negating many of the savings associated with electronic commerce and substantially adding to transaction costs (Jackson, 1997b). Goldman Sachs conducted a survey of prices for a market basket of 30 products sold by Wal-Mart both online and off-line; while the prices for the two market baskets did not differ by much, the final price of products purchased online was higher by 9 per cent owing to shipping costs (Goldman Sachs, 1997). While these comparisons are not exact, since the consumer pays indirectly for delivery when shopping at a traditional store, in terms of gasoline, car depreciation and especially time, delivery costs are a large enough factor for some e-commerce merchants that they are relocating to reduce them (Rawsthorn, 1997a). For e-commerce between businesses, the expense of enhanced distribution services may also represent an additional cost, but in many cases the increased cost of delivery is offset by reduced inventory carrying costs. Also the use of advanced forecasting systems and third-party, as opposed to internal, transportation services means that trucks run fully loaded, do not incur empty "back-haul" journeys and more accurately deliver what is needed. In the case of one Japanese supermarket, this has resulted in a 20 per cent reduction in the number of deliveries (Ministry of International Trade and Industry, 1998).

The fact that many of the intermediary services required by e-commerce merchants seek to create more trust in transactions suggests that known incumbent intermediaries already trusted by consumers may have an advantage over new ones. This would affect the overall impact of disintermediation and re-intermediation (Hawkins *et al.*, 1998).

Shifting of costs to consumers. Some portion of the reduction in firms' costs can be attributed to the shifting of costs formerly borne by the firm to the customer in the form of self-service. For example, customers are now expected to learn about the product, answer their own customer-support questions, and pay for shipment of the product. It is difficult to ascertain what portion of the firms' lower costs is due to shifting and what portion to actual reduction. As some consumers will prefer not to pay these costs or to accept the lower quality of service, this potentially limits the reduction (Travel & Tourism Intelligence, 1998). At the same time, it is likely that e-commerce firms are now reducing, as a competitive feature, costs that used to be routinely accepted as customer costs. For example, in the online sale of software, sellers now perform many of the support tasks that used to fall to users: installation, keeping track of licences, ensuring that users have the right version, and ensuring that upgrades are made on schedule. Gartner, a consultancy group, estimates that this cuts firms' internal technical supports costs by 55 per cent (Moad, 1997).

Bailey and Bakos (1997) explore thirteen case studies of firms participating in electronic commerce and find that, for the majority, new roles arise for electronic intermediaries that seem to outweigh any trends towards disintermediation. They identify four functions of market intermediaries: *aggregation* of buyer and seller (to achieve economies of scale/scope and reduce bargaining asymmetry); *agent of trust*; *facilitation* (to reduce operating costs); *matching* buyers and sellers. Although the sample is too small for formal empirical analysis, it indicates that there is a general perceived increase in the role of intermediation services (Table 2.9).

In sum, the evidence is mixed. It appears that more intermediation may be as plausible an outcome as less. In any event, it is clear that the nature of e-commerce and the change in relative costs it generates will cause a restructuring of the intermediation function, with some services gaining while others lose. In many cases, these new intermediary services will address the issues of trust and risk sharing that plague e-commerce. New entrants may often provide the solutions, but, because of need to engender confidence, established intermediaries able to adapt to the new environment may be well positioned. The demand for e-commerce intermediaries will vary considerably by sector, but, in nearly all cases, they will be information-intensive and will exploit the information infrastructure to deliver the service.

Table 2.9. **Does the move to electronic markets increase the importance of these intermediation services?**

	Sample	Aggregation Provision of one-stop shopping	Trust Provision of authentication and secure communications	Facilitation Exchange of messages between customers and suppliers	Matching Provision of marketing information to suppliers
Retail Business to business	2	Yes	Yes	Yes	Yes
Retail Business to consumer	3	Maybe	Yes	Yes	Yes
Automotive Business to business	2	Yes	Yes	Yes	No
Automotive Business to consumer	3	No	Yes	Yes	No
Information goods Business to consumer	3	No	Yes	Yes	Yes

Source: Bailey and Bakos, 1997.

Market entry

Changes in firms' relative cost structure affect the competitiveness of existing firms and firms' incentives to enter new markets. Anecdotal evidence suggests that barriers to entering various product markets and international markets have declined and that some characteristics of e-commerce may favour small businesses over large. In terms of stimulating competition, one of the most important impacts of e-commerce has been the emergence of new entrants in product markets where Internet e-commerce has dramatically changed the sector's competitive dynamics. While many observers point to the Internet booksellers' success in forcing their "bricks-and-mortar" competition to come on line and match their price discounts, the largest competitive challenge has probably come from new entrants that provide digital services at a much lower cost than traditional suppliers.

The early stage of electronic commerce makes predictions based on the current situation difficult, but, for some segments of the e-commerce market, small start-ups unencumbered by existing relationships with traditional retail outlets or a large sales force may be at an advantage. In these cases, entrants can adopt a business model that forces larger, established competitors to "cannibalise" their existing relationships or be seen as non-competitive. Examples of this phenomenon include Sony's decision to bypass its traditional retailers and sell music directly[12] or GM's GMBuyPower.com Web site, which "... reduces dealers to little more that test drive centres and distribution points" (Noer, 1998).

While it is typical for smaller firms to lag behind larger firms in their adoption of ICT, a recent Industry Canada/Statistics Canada survey found that expense was the most important factor delaying the implementation of e-commerce by small firms, and that lack of skills and the complexity of e-commerce were ranked as much less important (Industry Canada, 1997). However, as the cost of implementing e-commerce falls and as the benefits become more widely known, small firms' entry should be more pronounced. This is already the case in the United States where "... companies less intimidated to jump in are the smaller ones because they have less to lose, a lot of Gen Xers with some smart ideas" (Scannell, 1998).

Firms' relative cost structure, and the degree of domestic and foreign markets contestability, also contribute to determining firms' business strategies and competitive behaviour. The role of these and other factors in shaping the structure of markets affected by electronic commerce is discussed in Chapter 3.

Economy-wide efficiency gains

While electronic commerce is a far from frictionless mode of exchange devoid of transaction costs, it offers significant cost savings both within and between firms, especially for the processing and delivery of digital products. Even for tangible goods, e-commerce can provide closer and faster links with suppliers and customers, thereby reducing costs, especially those associated with carrying inventories. Such qualities are fuelling the growth of electronic commerce (Cohen, 1998) and are especially important to wholesalers and retailers for whom the impact of even small savings on typical profit margins of 2 to 3 per cent can be large. Forrester Research estimates that e-commerce can double these margins from 2.2 to 5.6 per cent on average because of payroll reductions due to reductions in sales staff (2.4 points) and catalogue printing and shipping costs (1 point) (La Tour Kadison *et al.*, 1998).

While the profits of some wholesalers and retailers may increase, in some cases, as discussed above, their activity will be reduced or eliminated. To obtain a rough estimate of the potential impact of cost reductions attributable to e-commerce on the economy as a whole, the methodology developed for the OECD's regulatory reform work (OECD, 1997*g*) was used. Based on an input-output model, electronic commerce was assumed to reduce total wholesale and retail trade activity for consumer expenditures by 25 per cent (similar to the estimates in Table 2.5). It was assumed that this reduction would lead to a decline in the use (cost) of buildings and related services (construction, real estate and utilities) by 50 per cent, or a 12.5 per cent decline in total for retail and wholesale trade. The smaller size of the wholesale and retail sector would lead to less use of labour and capital by these sectors, both of which were assumed to decline by 30 per cent for these services, or 7.5 per cent for the total retail and wholesale sectors. The partial equilibrium resulting from these changes in costs leads to a reduction in aggregate distribution costs of about 5 per cent (United States: −5.2; Japan: −5.3; Germany: −5.9; France: −4.2; United Kingdom: −4.5) and in total economy-wide costs by about one-half to two-thirds of a percentage point (United States: –0.7; Japan: –0.7; Germany: –0.6; France: –0.5; United Kingdom: –0.6). While small, this is still a considerable gain, since a reduction in these costs is a rough proxy for productivity gains (total factor productivity – TFP) which has only averaged an annual increase of 0.8 per cent across the G7 economies in the recent past (1979-97) (OECD, 1998c).

Given that the cost savings due to business-to-business e-commerce are significant and that the business-to-business segment represents a much larger portion of the overall total, these estimates based on a business-to-consumer scenario are conservative. The economy-wide savings from the substitution of e-payment systems for paper cheques in the United States are estimated at $30 billion, and the extension of similar efficiencies to the greater economy are assumed to be "...orders of magnitude higher" (Litan and Niskanen, 1997).

The impact of electronic commerce on prices

The translation of lower costs into lower prices is not automatic. It depends on the presence of sufficient competition. While the potential for this exists, the phenomenon is not, at the moment, broadly evident (see Chapter 3). Many observers predict that electronic commerce will result in very efficient competition that will cause prices to drop and the balance of market power to shift from producers to consumers. As described above, this has only occurred for a few select products, such as commissions for online stock trading or deep discounts on overstocked items. For sectors such as air travel, the reduction in travel agents' commissions has not been accompanied by a price decline in air fares (Stohr, 1997). However, online trading seems to have had a negative effect on the price of seats on major US stock exchanges (with a seat on the New York Stock Exchange falling by one-third in four months) (Barboza, 1998). Of the four known surveys that measure the impact of e-commerce on prices, each of which has methodological flaws, only one unequivocally finds evidence of price declines (Table 2.10). Morgan Stanley cites the lack

Table 2.10. **A survey of studies analysing the impact of e-commerce on prices**

Survey	Survey date	Coverage	Caveats	Key findings
Ernst & Young[1]	January 1998	Comparison of 3 on-line and off-line vendors for 32 consumer products (n = 96).	Shipping costs and taxes not included Off-line stores all located in Cleveland, Ohio.	Online prices were lower for 88% of products, same for 6%. In total, on-line was 10% less expensive.
Forrester Research[2]	July 1997	150 companies in 12 major industrial categories engaging in business-to-business e-commerce.		Lower costs mean higher margins, most of which are currently being retained.
Goldman Sachs[3]	August 1997	Comparison of a 30-item market basket sold by Wal-Mart.	One store, arbitrary selection of products.	Online prices were 1 per cent higher, 9 per cent with shipping costs included.
OECD[4]	February/March 1997	Comparison of 24 000 prices for three products: books, CDs and software.	Shipping costs and taxes not included. Off-line stores are not strictly off-line but are "hybrids" with both an on-line and an off-line presence. Prices for off-line stores are those posted on their Web sites.	On-line prices are slightly higher than those of "hybrid" stores and change more frequently.

1. http://www.ey.com/wired/pricing survey.
2. http://www.forrester.com.
3. Goldman Sachs, 1997.
4. http://www.oecd.org/dsti/sti/it/ec/.

of price benefits as a potentially limiting factor for the overall growth of business-to-consumer electronic commerce (Meeker, 1997). A recent survey of the 100 largest firms on the Web found that about half did not display any price information, less than 5 per cent listed prices of competing products, and less than 1 per cent offered any form of dynamic price negotiation or customisation (Information Strategy, 1998).

Among the many reasons for the lack of significant price discounts due to electronic commerce is the rather embryonic state of business-to-consumer electronic commerce. So far, customers have tended to be affluent, young, well-educated males who are experimenting with electronic commerce and cite convenience as a primary reason for using it. Thus, online prices may be higher than off-line because the consumers' affluence allows merchants to extract a higher price. However, the demographics of e-commerce are changing and as they better reflect the population at large and as additional e-commerce merchants increase competitive pressures the situation may change.

On the other hand, online merchants add value in the form of convenience and other characteristics that can be costly, and consumers (especially busy, affluent ones) may be willing to pay for this. The "convenience factor" may mean, therefore, that it is inappropriate to compare prices for products sold on line and off line. Moreover, online shopping may more readily encourage "impulse" purchases, again allowing the merchant to sell at a higher price. Lastly, as merchants experiment with e-commerce, they are unwilling to undercut their traditional distribution and retailing channels and frequently charge the same price even though their online costs are lower.

Different pricing schemes

The interactive online environment and the intangible nature of many of the products sold on line are likely to mean that e-commerce merchants will employ a variety of pricing schemes. The most common is likely to be the widespread adoption of differential pricing. For the business-to-consumer segment, merchants can compile information about consumers' buying habits via devices such as "cookies", which allow for a finer segmentation of the market and make it possible for merchants to charge different prices to different consumers for the same product, or, in economic terms, to reduce the consumer surplus. The low cost of buyer-seller interaction inherent in e-commerce also makes auctions and reverse auctions, where the buyer sets a price, a viable pricing mechanism for a wide variety of products. Forrester Research estimates that online auctions will increase from $2.9 billion today to $52.6 billion by 2002 (Frook, 1998b).

For the business-to-business segment, businesses with a large product line used to be locked into set prices because of the high costs and the time required to diffuse new price data to distributors, retailers and salespeople (Cortese, 1998). E-commerce lowers these barriers, making more frequent price changes more likely. New pricing strategies are likely to emerge such as IBM's recent announcement to drop the price of one of its products by 60 per cent in exchange for 20 per cent of the revenue it predicts that the product will generate (Denton, 1997). Just as in the business-to-consumer segment, business-to-business e-commerce transactions can provide in-depth information about clients, allowing firms to adjust prices. Federal Express, for example, uses its transaction data to identify unprofitable customers who are either dropped or charged a higher price (Grant, 1997).

More fundamentally, many of the products currently traded by e-commerce are digital products with high initial development costs (fixed) but low reproduction costs (variable). In addition, many are so-called "non-rival" goods (that is, one person's use of the product does not diminish the value of simultaneous use of the product by others). In a competitive market, the price for such goods would be pushed to the marginal cost which is close to zero. In fact, many digital e-commerce products are priced at zero and given away, thereby contributing to what is known as the "free economy" of the Internet. For some products, trying to establish a brand or a market niche or simply to attract attention (Goldhaber, 1997), this pricing scheme is sensible. Others, however, will follow a pricing strategy that tries to create monopolistic competition by differentiating products so that different prices can be charged to different consumers on the basis of their willingness to pay (Varian, 1996; 1998). This could lead to a wide variety of pricing practices, such as the bundling of various information products, time sensitivity (e.g. real time versus delayed), subscriptions, rentals, site licensing, reliance on after-sales fees and flat fees. For example, if software can be downloaded nearly instantly, why should people buy copies? Why would they not rent what they want when they want, as for videos?

Figure 2.5. **Impact of US industry on inflation**
Implicit gross domestic income price index

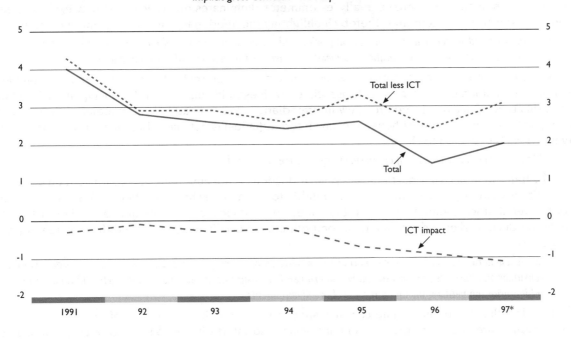

* Estimated.
Source: Margherio *et al.*, 1998.

In general, it is thought that the lower transaction costs associated with the use of the Internet will allow a wide continuum of content aggregation schemes ranging from individual products (separate articles) to small bundles (*e.g.* a software "suite") to large collections (*e.g.* the complete work of the Beatles). It is expected that these different strategies will reduce the number of consumers who would not buy a product because the price was too high (the "deadweight loss") as well as the number of consumers who would be willing to pay more than the price being asked (the "consumer surplus") (Bakos and Brynjolfsson, forthcoming). In sum, while e-commerce may not change current price levels, it may well change the price-setting structure and, in the case of content, make it more efficient.

Ultimately, the impact of e-commerce on prices will depend on competition. As the ability to search thousands of e-commerce stores in a few minutes or through an intelligent software agent improves, and as the expected growth of e-commerce generates more entrants, competition should be sufficient to transfer the cost savings associated with e-commerce into price savings. The overall impact of these price changes on prices is impossible to gauge at this time, although the impact of the underlying ICT technologies on prices in the United States has been significant (Figure 2.5).

POLICY IMPLICATIONS AND FUTURE RESEARCH AGENDA

A key reason why electronic commerce, especially the business-to-business segment, is growing so quickly is its significant impact on costs associated with inventories, sale execution, procurement, intangibles like banking, and distribution costs. If these reductions become pervasive, e-commerce has the potential to be the application that ushers in the large productivity gains that prove the worth of ICTs. Achieving these gains is therefore contingent on a number of factors, including access to e-commerce systems and the needed skills. However, what is unique about e-commerce over the Internet and the efficiency gains it promises is the premium placed on openness. To reap the potential cost savings fully, firms must be willing to open up their internal systems to suppliers and customers. This raises policy issues concerning security and potential anti-competitive effects as firms integrate their operations more closely. Another source of efficiency associated with e-commerce is the opportunity for "boundary crossing" as new entrants, business models, and changes in technology erode barriers that used to separate one industry from another. More generally, e-commerce illuminates differences that may exist between products, industries and countries, thereby highlighting the need to reform inconsistent regulations.

- *Work is needed to better assess the economy-wide and sector-specific impact of e-commerce on productivity and to explore the notion that this application may lead to a sustained higher level of economic efficiency.*

While e-commerce can dramatically reduce some production costs, it does not offer a "friction free" environment. Rather, owing to new costs associated with establishing trust and reducing the risks inherent in this type of activity, it requires new intermediaries. Widespread "disintermediation" (producers selling directly to consumers without aid of any intermediaries) is not likely, but the nature of intermediary functions is expected to change.

- *Monitoring of the restructuring of intermediary functions is needed.*

The translation of cost reductions into price reductions is not automatic. It is contingent on sufficient competition. Currently, price reductions attributable to e-commerce have only been evident in a few sectors (*e.g.* retail stock trading). However, the lower costs associated with e-commerce should lead to greater product, market and international competition, especially in services, and thus to greater price competition.

- *While a general assessment of the impact of e-commerce on prices may be premature, sectoral studies on a variety of consumer and business products should be undertaken to measure its impact and identify factors that encourage and inhibit price competition, including the use of intelligent agents.*

It is clear that electronic commerce will change the structure, if not the level, of pricing as more and more products are subject to the differential pricing associated with customised products, fine market segmentation and auctions, and as the ease of changing prices increases. While these changes will generally improve economic efficiency, they may raise some consumer concerns. While consumers are accustomed to paying different prices for products such as cars, they may be less comfortable with differentiated pricing for smaller, common purchases. In addition, the more widespread use of variable pricing, the advent of greater price competition, and the ability to change prices quickly may affect expectations about prices and therefore have some bearing on monetary policy. In any case, changes in the structure of price setting will affect the ability to measure changes in prices and inflation accurately.

- *Work needs to be carried out to understand how these new methods may affect the structure of price setting and the resulting impact on the frequency of price changes, on markets and on measurement.*

NOTES

1. Michael Vlahos, Senior Fellow, Progress & Freedom Foundation, http://www.gip.org/GIP2B.HTM.

2. E*Trade's site is estimated to have cost $485 million, according to Judy Balint, Senior Vice President, Global Marketing & Strategic Business Development, E*Trade, speaking at IDC E-commerce Forum, 10-12 May 1998, Monaco.

3. "Who will Deal in Dealerships?", *The Economist*, 14 February 1998.

4. J.G. Sandom, Senior Partner, Director of OgilvyOne Interactive, OgilvyOne Worldwide, speaking at IDC E-commerce Forum, 10-12 May 1998, Monaco.

5. 31 December 1997, US Securities and Exchange Commission, Form 10-K405, filed on 30 March 1998, http://www.sec.gov/Archives/edgar/data/1018724/0000891020-98-000448.txt.

6. 31 January 1998, US Securities and Exchange Commission, Form 10-K filed on 1 May 1998, http://www.sec.gov/Archives/edgar/data/890491/0000889812-98-001106.txt.

7. Form 10-K, US Securities and Exchange Commission, http://www.sec.gov/archives/edgar, 22 April 1998.

8. Meeker, 1997; US SEC, http://www.sec.gov/Archives/edgar/data/858877/0000891618-97-004205.txt.

9. United Airlines reports that 52 per cent of their tickets are e-tickets while Continental Airlines reports it issues 40 per cent in electronic form. See Caruso (1998).

10. "Barnes and Noble Sees $100M in Online Sales", http://www.techweb.com, 19 January 1998.

11. Software.net, a leading e-commerce merchant for electronically delivered software, had a fraud rate of 60 per cent of orders although these had gone through the standard bank authorisation procedure. See Cybersource (1998).

12. "Surf Music", *The Economist*, 16 August 1997.

Chapter 3

THE IMPACT OF ELECTRONIC COMMERCE ON FIRMS' BUSINESS MODELS, SECTORAL ORGANISATION AND MARKET STRUCTURE

Electronic commerce is transforming the marketplace by changing firms' business models, by shaping relations among market actors, and by contributing to changes in market structure. Given the dynamic nature of these processes and their firm-, sector-, and time-specificity, it is difficult to single out the impact of electronic commerce. Nevertheless, it is possible to see some emerging patterns, and some conclusions can be drawn from business case studies. This chapter addresses three themes associated with electronic commerce and the organisational changes it entails: changes in firms' business models, changes in market structure, and opportunities for economic growth created by organisational change.

Electronic commerce creates the possibility of new models for organising production and transacting business, by offering intermodality and complementarity – not only substitution – in business models. This chapter begins by looking at the core characteristics of firms entering electronic markets and offers some evidence on the extent to which business models are changing in various sectors. The catalytic role which early adopters can play *vis-à-vis* incumbents in established markets is a key driver of business reorganisation on electronic markets, and the flexibility and adaptability of the work force is a key enabler of this process.

Next, the market structure likely to emerge as a result of organisational changes associated with electronic commerce is examined. The Internet opens up certain proprietary relationships, extends relations between sectors, makes the electronic market accessible to smaller businesses and allows them to address international markets. The nature of competition and firms' strategies and competitive advantages in domestic and international markets also change. Work can be performed from a variety of locations, and firms are exposed to global competition. Several key factors that contribute to the degree of openness on electronic markets – leaving aside the question of disintermediation, which is discussed in Chapter 2 – are analysed. One is the type of Web-based competition that will emerge in each electronic market. Increasingly, new entrants compete to set standards and provide the interface, and Web-based alliances play a strategic role in determining the emerging standard. Online firms also compete to capture customer information, and virtual communities could play a role in striking the balance of market power between consumers and suppliers. Other factors that could counterbalance the pro-competitive effects of electronic markets (see Chapter 2) are: first-mover advantages related to the presence of positive network externalities; national differences in the regulatory environment; and the degree to which the choice of the transaction structure (open or closed) is path-dependent (see Box 3.3 below) and sector-specific.

The final section considers the ways in which organisational changes at the firm level associated with electronic commerce can translate into improved performance and growth at the economy-wide level and suggests a few areas for future research. Because there is evidence that small innovative firms are an engine of growth, it would be valuable to know whether electronic commerce offers small innovative firms any special advantages for entering new or existing markets. Another issue is the nature of the innovation associated with electronic commerce. This point is not often stressed in the literature, but it is extremely important, given the direct and indirect impact of innovation processes on productivity and growth through technology diffusion. Two novel aspects of organisational change and electronic commerce are worth exploring: the role of inter-firm collaboration and networking for successful innovation and the role of customer-supplier relations as a source of technology transfer. An additional interesting line of research concerns whether the combination of new business processes and work organisation associated with electronic commerce favours high-performance work. There is evidence, in fact, that streamlined business processes, flat organisational hierarchies, and continuous learning and skills acquisition contribute to a favourable environment for innovation and improve performance.

Electronic commerce: a new business paradigm?

Advanced information and communication technologies, together with new networking capabilities, allow firms, from the very large to the very small, to communicate, transact and collaborate at lower cost and with greater ease and flexibility than ever before. This may stimulate noteworthy changes in models of organisational behaviour and lead to the creation of "cyber-traders" and/or virtual enterprises. It is more likely, however, that incremental changes will be made as firms adopt and adapt new technologies to fit their way of doing business. After looking at the core characteristics of firms operating on electronic markets, this section discusses key drivers and enablers of business reorganisation. Annex 3.1 presents evidence on the extent to which business models in various sectors are changing.

New entrants and the evolving business environment

The so-called "cyber-traders" (see Box 3.1) have garnered a great deal of the attention associated with electronic commerce and the Internet. It is becoming increasingly evident, however, that the attention paid to these companies substantially surpasses their economic significance. Most cyber-traders are consumer retail firms and, while many have achieved remarkable success and high growth rates, their contribution to total retail trade is not quantitatively significant. They have emerged because the electronic marketplace is a good place to experiment with new technologies and new ways of doing business. Whether this is a temporary or long-term phenomenon, however, remains to be seen. Large firms may use the same technologies and techniques and eventually displace cyber-traders, as they will be able to integrate these strategies into their traditional operations and target several niches simultaneously.

While most analysts would agree that cyber-traders are on the fringes of mainstream electronic commerce, many point to what has been termed the "internetworked" enterprise (Tapscott, 1996) as an emerging model in the new information economy. Such an enterprise is characterised by a "virtual" organisational structure, defined as commercial collaboration among firms and individuals carried out in an electronic environment, where entry to and exit from the structure is flexible and determined as needed (Hawkins, 1998). This organisational structure, which often leverages Web-based alliances, can theoretically "harness the power of market forces to develop, manufacture, market, distribute and support their offerings in ways that fully integrated companies cannot duplicate" (Chesbrough and Teece, 1996).

Virtual organisational structures leverage the capabilities and resources of many players to pursue a strategy of risk sharing. There are, however, risks associated with a virtual business structure. Integrated centralised companies, the polar opposite of the virtual firm, do not usually reward risk takers but do have established processes for conflict resolution and co-ordinating all the activities needed for innovation.

Box 3.1. Cyber-traders

Cyber-traders are businesses without a significant physical presence which operate almost exclusively in cyberspace. Using the new technologies, they typically specialise in niche markets and are highly adaptable to consumer wants and needs. These start-up companies own or control very little of the supply chain or physical production, but they provide convenient service. Many are small operations set up virtually overnight and known only by their Web address. Others, like Amazon.com and CDnow are much larger operations and have become almost household names. CDnow, for example, operates as an intermediary between customers and music distributors, providing fast delivery of compact discs, often within 24 hours. Other firms have emerged that sell new products and services, often centred around Internet or related technologies or the capabilities they offer, including computer products, such as new software programmes and computer-mediated services, and thereby spur the growth of intermediaries.

As a result, firms, and their managers, must often find a balance between incentives and control. Finding the appropriate balance depends on the business activity, the degree of risk that collaborating firms can absorb, and the level of control over information and communication that is needed for the enterprise as a whole to function. Risk increases as firms adopt more "virtual" characteristics and co-ordination through the marketplace becomes increasingly difficult. Control is likely to be more effective under the classical, hierarchical firm structure (Hawkins, 1998).

Accompanying the need for some degree of control within the firm's organisation is the value that firms place on a stable supplier community. Firms value historical experience when selecting partners and, through commercial exchange or collaborative efforts, often develop commercially sensitive information pools with them (Garcia, 1995). These features of the evolving commercial environment (greater risk of co-ordination failures, more difficult governance, sensitive information pools) need to be addressed by policies that focus specifically on commercial governance.

The role of early adopters in new business models

It is important to ask whether "internetworked" enterprises are truly sources of opportunity within the virtual marketplace and whether Internet commerce should be linked to revolutionary changes in the organisation of business processes and structures (Hawkins, 1998). Some 80 per cent of Australian business leaders believe that e-commerce will drive revolutionary changes in their business by the year 2003 (Andersen Consulting, 1998). Companies convinced of the revolutionary impact of e-commerce tend to be foreign-owned. They operate in various industries, but are not very likely to produce consumer products. A similar survey of European attitudes to e-commerce reveals that European business leaders are more cautious than their Australian counterparts (Andersen Consulting, 1998). Only 43 per cent of European respondents felt that e-commerce offers a real competitive advantage to their company today, as compared to 64 per cent in Australia.

Annex 3.1 offers some evidence of business substitution and indicates the degree to which this implies organisational changes at the sectoral level. In some cases, Internet commerce constitutes the logical extension of firms' business models and simply accentuates some of their characteristics. In others, Internet commerce can mean the adoption of new business models that replace or complement existing ones. In all cases, electronic commerce creates new opportunities and challenges for market participants and offers the possibility of new models for organising production and transacting business. E-commerce thus offers intermodality in conducting commercial transactions and complementarity in business models; it provides an evolving paradigm which can be adapted to the needs of different firms in different contexts.

Even if virtual enterprises do not bring about radical, economy-wide organisational change, it can be argued that leaders who are active in electronic commerce and early adopters of certain forms of business structure can force competitors to adopt a certain type of supplier-customer relationship. In particular, cyber-traders, even if they do not yet seem to represent a new commercial paradigm, are often at the cutting edge of new technologies and innovative market experimentation. Thus, they may play an important testing role for other, more traditional companies.

An example of potential business model "enforcement" concerns Dell and Compaq as suppliers of computer equipment to General Electric (GE) (Ghosh, 1998). GE is setting up a system of Internet bidding and expects to purchase almost entirely over a Web-based bidding system in five years. At present, Dell sells computers directly to customers and expects to handle half of its business over the Internet by the year 2000; Compaq, instead, sells through distributors. It appears likely that Dell's strategy is forcing competitors in the computer industry to develop Internet channels of their own (see Box 3.2).

Early adopters are beginning to emerge in other industries, such as auto retailing (General Motors and Auto-By-Tel) and trade publishing (Cahners and VerticalNet). New intermediaries in personal financial services are likely to require the unbundling of retail banking's integrated business system. Some intermediaries will specialise in creating and managing customer relationships, others in developing new products, and still others in providing back-office processing services and support (McKinsey, 1997). Companies such as Compaq will have to weigh the importance of protecting existing relationships, which account for most of their current revenue, against the advantages of establishing future strategic positions and revenue streams.

Box 3.2.   **Pirating the value chain: the case of the personal computer industry**

Currently, computer manufacturers like Apple, Compaq and IBM purchase computer components from suppliers like Intel (microprocessors) and Seagate Technology (hard disk drives). Manufacturers supply machines to distributors such as Ingram Micro and MicroAge, which in turn supply retailers such as CompUSA. This is the physical value chain for much of the industry (excluding manufacturers such as Dell and Gateway 2000, which sell directly to customers). Internet commerce is blurring the boundaries in that chain. Ingram Micro and MicroAge are setting up Internet-based services that would allow anyone to become an online retailer of computers. At the same time, retailers like CompUSA are establishing their own brands of computers, which they intend to sell both in stores and over the Internet. They will order parts electronically from component suppliers. Finally, Apple and other computer makers have also made the choice to sell computers over the Internet.

Competition is even coming from outside the value chain. United Parcel Service has announced that it is setting up a service for virtual merchants. Using Internet software, a merchant can create a product catalogue and a storefront on the Web. UPS will then manage the operations. The merchant or its customers will be able to schedule deliveries, track packages and co-ordinate complex schedules over the Web. Conceivably, an online PC vendor could let consumers create customised machines, made up of components drawn from several different manufacturers. UPS would then gather the parts overnight, deliver them to an assembly facility, pick up the assembled product, and deliver it to the customer.

Online providers of information about computers, such as CNET, are already becoming resellers of software and hardware products. The Internet search service Yahoo! also sells hardware and software through its site by linking seamlessly to partners' sites. Even ancillary players in the industry value chain – including banks like Barclays and First Union, and telecommunications providers such as AT&T – have established shopping services on their sites and could sell computers (or anything else) to their customers.

Source: Adapted from Ghosh, 1998.

Although early adopters may be in a position to define new business models, in which case the impact on business-to-business relations could be large, the process is not so simple. It would be fatal for firms to try to adjust business models to technologies unless there is a clearly defined strategic rationale for doing so. Companies that stand to lose margin to others currently provide real value to customers in the form of merchandising skills (which Ingram Micro does not have but CompUSA does), logistics expertise (which CompUSA does not have but UPS does), and information management (which CNET can do better than Apple) (Ghosh, 1998). One interesting case concerns IBM, which in 1996 launched Informat, an electronic-content delivery initiative, and World Avenue, a cyberspace mall (Ghosh, 1998). IBM thought it could use its computer network to deliver content and challenge the physical distribution chain, but it soon realised that it lacked the editorial and circulation skills of publishers and the merchandising and advertising skills of retailers. As a result, both initiatives were abandoned in the following year.

In the case of business-to-consumer electronic commerce, which has not yet reached critical mass, it may be very risky for a company to bypass distributors and to have to weigh the gain of a few Internet customers against the loss of a large number of traditional ones. The degree to which producers are able to impose their desired channels depends in fact on various factors – *e.g.* institutional, social, subjective – and a variety of path dependencies.

It would be interesting to know in which sectors early adopters are most likely to enforce their business models and where conflicts involving transaction channels are most likely to occur. It is possible that enforcement of new business models might be more frequent in industries where switching costs are low or where costs are lowered by adoption of information and communication technologies (ICTs). When Federal Express (FedEx) launched its Web site (November 1994), which allowed customers to track packages on the Web, UPS (United Parcel Service) accelerated its development efforts, and launched a similar service six months later. Today, both services are functionally very close. The third major competitor (DHL) made a similar service available in 1996 (Bloch *et al.*, 1996).

Key enablers of business re-engineering: workers and innovation

Becoming virtual implies substantial organisational adjustment. The virtual enterprise is a "real-time" enterprise that must adjust immediately to changing business conditions. A key enabling factor in business re-engineering is the flexibility and adaptability of staff. Much organisational learning and adjustment will be required from workers in the electronic commerce environment and new skills will have to be developed (see Chapter 4).

The virtual enterprise will be characterised by flatter hierarchies and a team-based work organisation so as to respond more quickly to changes in the business environment and customer demands. Because electronic markets have the power and capacity to open channels of human communication and collaboration dramatically within an office, across space, and across time, collaborative work increasingly takes place in teams on high-capacity networks (Tapscott, 1996). Horizontal collaboration in independent team-based structures is replacing traditional vertical hierarchies. In the new model, teams are both clients and servers for other teams that are both internal and external to the organisation.

The value added created by these teams is not linked in linear fashion but generated through an ever-changing open network. The model is designed to encourage flexibility, innovation, entrepreneurship and responsiveness. As an example, the Boeing 777 is the first aircraft to be designed without physical models and blueprints. It was designed by teams and involved customers and suppliers in a workgroup design system and was engineered concurrently, thereby reducing development time dramatically. It was also tested in various performance situations and weather conditions several times prior to production (Tapscott, 1996). To the extent that electronic market players pioneer or are forced to adopt these flexible forms of work organisation and combine them with new and streamlined business processes, electronic commerce will favour high-performance work (see below).

In this evolving business environment, market actors need to innovate continuously and perhaps differently than in traditional markets. As a trading environment, electronic commerce is unique in providing unparalleled opportunities to capture, manipulate and manage all the information generated in a transaction. This helps improve business planning, efficiency in production and distribution, and vendor and customer support. This is "efficiency" innovation and it diffuses very rapidly.

The Internet has also provided an extremely challenging environment for flexible product development, one that allows designers to continue to refine and shape products even once they are on the market (Iansiti and MacCormack, 1997). Designers can sense customer needs (either by broad consumer testing, internal testing or testing by lead users), test alternative technical solutions, and integrate the acquired knowledge into a coherent product design.

From proprietary to open networks: the impact on sectoral organisation and market structure

As a standardised system accessible to all at minimum cost, the Internet takes over at the point where proprietary systems reach the limits of their possibilities.[1] The Internet extends the benefits of EDI to all of a firm's suppliers, opens up certain proprietary relationships, extends relations between sectors, makes the electronic market accessible to smaller businesses and allows them to address international markets. The shift to standardised networks also contributes to the shortening of the product cycle, improves procurement procedures, and affects transaction costs between producers, intermediaries and consumers differently (see Chapter 2). This in turn lowers entry barriers and creates greater incentives to enter the market, thereby generating competitive effects. The result is an expanding market, more transactions and more providers. Thus, as there is a shift in the use of the electronic link, there may also be a change in an industry's market structure.

Electronic commerce is changing the way firms compete and market players interact, as well as changing the size and nature of the marketplace. The following discussion starts by examining changes in the competitive behaviour of firms involved in electronic commerce on domestic and international markets. It then turns to changes in the size of the market and the open and global nature of electronic commerce. It considers the emergence of virtual communities as a factor that can affect the relative strength of market players. Finally, it presents factors that might counterbalance the competitive effects stressed in Chapter 2, such as: first mover advantages related to the presence of positive network externalities;

international differences in the regulatory environment; and the degree to which the choice of the transaction structure (open or closed) is path-dependent and sector-specific.

Internet commerce and the changing nature of competition

Key factors for competing in online markets include the ability to create strong brand recognition, to build user communities and attract advertising, to provide ease of use, variety of value-added services, functionality and features and quality of support, to establish strategic alliances and to expand on international markets. Key features of competition in electronic markets are the entrance of non-industry competitors and the spread of Web-based strategies focused on setting dominant standards and making strategic alliances.

The emergence of non-industry competitors

Apart from incumbent firms in established sectors and new start-ups, new competitors in online markets are often companies or new intermediaries coming from other sectors, *e.g.* software companies. Microsoft, for example, is positioning itself to become a trusted intermediary in retail banking. Its platform includes leading players in each product segment of retail banking, *e.g.* Schwab and Fidelity for mutual funds, E*Trade for online trading, CheckFree for electronic payments, and over 50 major banks for credit and transaction products (McKinsey, 1997). In another example, Amazon.com purchased (4 August 1998) two Internet start-up companies, one providing a Web-based virtual database technology shopping service and one providing a Web-based address book. Through these acquisitions, Amazon hopes to evolve from an online bookseller to become an Internet commerce hub, like Yahoo! and other Web portals. In so doing, Amazon could come into conflict with sites such as Yahoo!, which it now pays to send it traffic (Robert D. Hof, San Mateo, California).

The ability of non-industry competitors to take over a significant part of the business of incumbent firms should not be underestimated. Killen & Associates (1996) estimate that in the banking industry 25 per cent of the global electronic payment market will be taken by non-banks and high-technology companies (Bloch *et al.*, 1996). In the pharmaceutical industry, the emergence of HMOs (health management organisations) and other intermediaries between customers and suppliers has reduced the share of customer value going to manufacturers from 67 per cent to 60 per cent (Bloch *et al.*, 1996). Charles Schwab, by offering convenience (24-hour access, a single statement), extensive information and advice (SelectFunds list, software), range of choice (1 200 mutual funds) and low price (half of the funds are no-load, no-fee), has already captured 50 per cent of US online trading in mutual funds (McKinsey, 1997).

Competing on standards and the first mover advantage

At this stage, everything that constitutes a market – products, industrial structures, trade and competition rules, regulations and laws – is in the process of being defined on the Internet. The first aim of players entering the new market is to influence these elements in their favour, by proposing and helping to select innovative products that fit their technological options, by segmenting the market to suit themselves, by helping to define the ground rules (recommendations, proposed organisation, standardisation, etc.).

Web-based competition is often driven by three types of strategy. One involves setting the dominant technology standard. In the computer and multimedia industries, for example, Novell has become a standard for local area networks, while Netscape is trying to build a platform for electronic commerce. Second, firms increasingly compete on acquiring customer information. In customer Web sites, the platform is shaped around detailed customer information (*e.g.* Microsoft and Intuit in financial services). Such information is used to find new customers more efficiently, improve products and services or tailor them to individual needs, and build loyalty. Companies that use customer information to provide value added to the customer are positioned to gain access to more customers (Hagel and Rayport, 1997).

A third strategy involves segmenting the market and exploiting a niche. Market Web sites are organised around a narrow product category, with Web shapers developing a market for transactions and aggregating a critical mass of players (*e.g.* Schwab's OneSource and InsWeb) (McKinsey, 1997). The development of niche markets in intangible products with high information content may contribute to the development of dominant long-term positions on electronic markets. The greater the information content of a product, the easier it is to buy and sell via a network. Financial services, for example, are pure information products (*i.e.* they are based on the gathering and analysis of information), and even transaction services may be reduced to a set of entirely electronic accounting entries. This is why financial services are becoming the biggest market for electronic commerce, both business-to-business and business-to-consumer. Moreover, as the Internet is not yet a mass market, the "high-tech" profile of Internet users has a strong influence on business-to-consumer offerings. These factors are important, since they show areas in which growth niche markets in electronic commerce can be found.

It is often important to be first movers and fast adapters in the online environment, especially in relation to establishing a brand reputation, to defining standards and to exploiting new markets. Electronic markets are characterised by the presence of positive network externalities. Positive network externalities are features of all products, but in particular of network information technologies (Katz and Shapiro, 1985). The first player to enter an electronic network benefits from positive network externalities on a global scale and can very rapidly acquire an edge in terms not only of information (global reputation of certain brands) but also of economies of scale and stature (price advantage). The lack of transaction security owing to technical or legal problems amplifies the effects of reputation and communication.

Although the Internet is a naturally open environment, the nature of Web-based competition may, in certain cases, favour the emergence of dominant positions on electronic markets. The aim of public authorities in this context is both dual and ambiguous. On the one hand, they need to take advantage of such dominance to spur the market, and on the other, they need to reduce the risk of abuse of this power by helping to ensure that the market is open to as many players as possible.

The role played by strategic alliances

Web-based strategies follow the assumption that the best way to handle risk is to share it by leveraging the capabilities and resources of many players. While strategic alliances are nothing new in the business landscape, Web-based strategies pursue alliances that are different from conventional ones in at least three respects: they involve a much larger and more varied group of companies; they rely on much more informal business relationships and co-ordination mechanisms than the usual detailed legal arrangements; and they require leadership by one or two companies to define standards for all Web members and create incentives that attract more companies to it (McKinsey, 1997). A wide resource base and risk spreading often make these players pursue more aggressive strategies than traditional actors.

International strategic alliances, typically joint ventures, as well as direct acquisitions and licensing agreements, are a common way for online firms to expand on international markets (see the example of

Table 3.1. **E-commerce firms' presence on international markets**

Company	Percentage share of on-line revenues (1997)	International alliances and acquisitions	Markets
E-Trade	63%	Nova Pacific Capital (Australia), VERSUS Technologies Inc. (Canada)	Australia, New Zealand, Canada
Schwab Charles Corp.	37%	Charles Schwab Europe, 1995 (UK)	Europe
CDnow		Lycos Bertelsmann GMBH & Co AG, 1998	Some European countries
		Rolling Stone Network	World
		Wholly-owned subsidiary in Japan Shinseido Inc. (Japan)	Japan
Music Boulevard (NK2)	100%	MSI (Netherlands)	Europe
		MTV Networks	Europe, Brazil, Japan, Asia
Amazon	100%	None	

Source: OECD, based on data from the US Securities and Exchange Commission.

online brokering in Annex 3.2). Table 3.1 provides some recent examples of ways in which US e-commerce firms expand on foreign markets.

"Virtual" communities and the shifting balance among market actors

Electronic commerce is expected to affect relations among actors in the marketplace. Changes in the value chain and the entry of new actors work in this direction. Electronic commerce as a mechanism for delivering information also affects market players, as information can determine their relative bargaining power. With the growth of information-intensive electronic transactions, firms start competing on "information content or quality" instead of prices or quantities, and problems of asymmetric information and asymmetric access to the electronic link become more relevant.

However, these drivers of change are not different from those associated with the spread of information technologies. The novelty of electronic commerce lies in the emergence of virtual communities that can play a role in reshaping market structure. Such communities might eventually set in motion an unprecedented shift in power from suppliers to consumers, as they can provide new sources of customer information (a crucial element of Web-based competition, see above). As communities bring together customers with shared interests and characteristics, the profiles they create will yield rich data sets about both individuals and customer segments (Hagel and Armstrong, 1997).

Companies are increasingly adopting electronic commerce solutions in the hope of developing new markets. The key to exploiting new markets involves combining content and communication, and virtual communities can play a powerful part by acting as catalysts and creating the "critical mass" needed for business-to-consumer electronic commerce to grow. For example, they could help expand the reach of very small and localised producers by helping them to market their products at a very low price, or they could create new demand by stimulating interest in new products and by diffusing information.

Changing the size of the market: competing globally

With the Internet, electronic commerce is rapidly expanding into a fast-moving, open global market with an ever-increasing number of participants (Beltz, 1998). The open, and potentially global, nature of electronic commerce is likely to increase market size and change market structure, both in terms of the number and size of players and the way in which players compete on international markets. Digitised products can cross the border in real time, consumers can shop 24 hours a day, seven days a week, and firms are increasingly faced with international online competition. But how large and global is the market?

How large is the market?

The Internet is helping to enlarge existing markets by cutting through many of the distribution and marketing barriers that can prevent firms from gaining access to foreign markets. Many small and medium-sized firms (SMEs) are using the Internet as a "business-to-business" tool to open and/or maintain a presence in foreign markets. Internet-based e-commerce's potential to facilitate SME access to global markets is illustrated by several case studies in the report, *Putting Australia on the New Silk Road* (Australian Department of Foreign Affairs and Trade, 1997). Electronic commerce lowers information and transaction costs for operating on overseas markets and provides a cheap and efficient way to strengthen customer-supplier relations, through electronic e-mail, remote online databases and video links. It also encourages companies to develop innovative ways of advertising, delivering and supporting their product and services.

Internet-based electronic commerce is also creating new opportunities for trade by radically changing delivery models for digitised products and services. The best example is that of electronic software distribution (ESD), *i.e.* transmission of software over the Internet. Even if ESD is still limited, its potential in the rapidly growing area of international trade in software may be significant. Among the major distributors of software over the Internet, those with international customers seem to export more than one-third of their product (OECD, 1998d). Other services, from financial services to education to medical services to others yet to be devised, all have the potential to become more globally traded.

While electronic commerce on the Internet offers the potential for global markets, certain factors, such as language, transport costs, local reputation, as well as differences in the cost and ease of access to networks, attenuate this potential to a greater or lesser extent. For example, because automobiles are manufactured, expensive, non-standard products requiring after-sales service, they are not traded electronically world-wide. The case of financial services is diametrically opposed. Trading (order, payment, delivery) is carried out entirely over networks. The case of information products, such as software, films, research, etc., might be the same. At present, books and recorded music lie somewhere between the two, as the products are inexpensive, can be delivered by mail at low cost, and require no after-sales service. It may therefore be cheaper to buy a book at Amazon.com than from a bookstore or from the virtual site of a national firm. Annex 3.2 presents estimates and evidence on the extent to which certain goods and services have an online international market.

How global is the competition?

On traditional markets, firms seeking to compete with a firm with a global presence will first lay the groundwork on a smaller geographical market where they will test their products and build brand recognition and reputation. The existence of geographical and time barriers shields the local development of multiple players. In addition, these barriers limit players' ability to exploit economies of scale. On the contrary, as markets on the Internet have no geographical boundaries, a new entrant cannot, in principle, take advantage of a geographical niche or use a neighbouring market as a springboard. The only neighbouring markets that can serve as a springboard are product markets (*e.g.* a firm might add music publishing to book publishing). This is why the current trend is for existing network players to extend their market and globalise their offer. The characteristics of information networks and the related technologies enable these firms to occupy the ground, geographically and quantitatively, to an extent not before possible.

However, the Internet is far from being a truly global market at this stage, as the United States accounts for about 80 per cent of world-wide electronic transactions (see Chapter 1). Being a first mover on foreign markets can be especially crucial for completely new entrants (as opposed to companies that already conduct off-line activities in the sector), and cyber-traders may be using foreign markets as springboards. Table 3.2 shows the trend in international revenue share of three new entrants. For all three, international revenue shares have been declining over time and Amazon.com and CDnow expect shares on international markets to decrease because of increased domestic marketing and advertising expenditure. It is possible, then, for international markets to function at the moment as niche markets for start-ups that otherwise face greater competition at home. Once these have established a certain brand reputation and expertise, they may then reinforce their position on domestic markets (especially if the domestic market is larger).

Changes in the source of international competitive advantage

As electronic commerce develops internationally, changes in delivery channels are likely to affect firms' relative competitive advantage on international markets. The ultimate impact on trade flows will depend on relative prices, inclusive of transaction and transport costs and duties (relative cost structure); on consumer access to and willingness to use online markets (critical consumer mass); on brand recognition and "closeness" to the local market. The ability of online retailers to track individual customer purchases and demo-

Table 3.2. **On-line revenues: percentage share of international markets**

Company	1998	1997	1996
CDnow	21	35	
Music Boulevard	26	33	
Amazon	21	26	35

Source: OECD, based on data from the US Securities and Exchange Commission (CDnow: March 1997 and 1998; Music Boulevard: September 1997 and April 1998; Amazon: September 1996 and 1997, March 1998).

graphic data for use in direct marketing and in developing one-to-one relationships with consumers is likely to reduce the competitive advantage of firms present on local markets. An important part of online firms' strategy is to address foreign markets. N2K, for example, offers registration and ordering instructions on Music Boulevard in English, Japanese, German, French and Spanish and has also launched a complete Japanese version of Music Boulevard (Edgar database, US Securities and Exchange Commission).

Insofar as e-commerce reduces production and transaction costs (see Chapter 2), transport costs will have greater weight in firms' relative cost structure and location decisions. Hence, firms which enjoy a greater competitive advantage in online markets (typically US firms) might still tend to establish a physical presence on foreign markets through foreign direct investment (FDI). Transport costs might instead completely lose relevance in the case of digitised products (such as software or music) which can be delivered electronically over the Internet. In this case, various stages might be envisaged. First, the development of online markets in Europe might shift European consumer demand towards those markets (because of convenience, choice, etc., as transport costs are modest within Europe). This would change relative market shares within Europe (European firms and non-European companies based in Europe that are first on the online market are likely to acquire a first-mover competitive advantage). Second, as electronic delivery will become the predominant channel for delivery, transport costs will be eliminated. At that point, companies are most likely to fully exploit their competitive advantage in online markets regardless of their location.

How open is the market structure?

Even if the growth in transactions over the Internet is leading to greater competition, it is not clear that there is a direct relation between the adoption of open links and open market structures. Statistics on the growth of intranets show that the commercial development of the Internet may be as much about creating essentially "closed" spaces in an open environment as it is about creating a universally open trading space (Hawkins, 1998). On the one hand, as discussed above, the use of electronic networks as a marketplace might help to create dominant positions in the long term. On the other hand, there may be path-dependent, sector-specific strategies that favour closed rather than open structures.

Firm and sectoral strategists face a wide diversity of existing and/or potential transaction structures when planning electronic commerce applications. Different transaction structures reflect the diversity of industry and market structures, product characteristics, and buyer and seller expectations (Hawkins, 1998). Much of this diversity is determined by the various evolutionary path dependencies (see Box 3.3) established in different business areas over time. Production dependencies (the choice of an electronic network depends on the specific nature of the transaction), market and strategic dependencies (the use of a specific network might increase the cost of switching to a different one and might favour market power), and environmental and institutional dependencies all influence the choice of the network, and this in turn might have an impact on industry's organisation structure.

Box 3.3.   Path dependencies

A firm is a set of competencies embedded in its staff, its organisation and its techniques, most of which are inherited from the past. The term competencies refers to all of an organisation's capacities, including its managerial capacities and its functional skills (financial, commercial, technical and productive) (Ansoff, 1988). It therefore covers not only expertise and knowledge but also equipment, know-how, collective and institutional learning, patents and protected technologies, access to raw materials and components, relations with customers and suppliers, modes of production and information management, modes of organisation and corporate culture. These competencies, specific to each firm, may be explicit or tacit. They represent both a potential for and a restriction on growth (Nelson and Winter, 1982) and are what Arthur *et al.* (1987) call path dependencies.

The literature shows that there is a whole range of outcomes in computer-mediated business relationships. For instance, financial information services, previously disseminated via proprietary systems, such as Reuters, Dow Jones Market (Telerate), Knight Ridder or Fininfo, are now – to some extent at least – available on the Internet. The shift from proprietary systems to standardised networks has opened up the electronic network market to new actors such as newspapers, brokers, and individuals. The transaction structure is more of a hybrid, with new players (*e.g.* Briefing, Quote.com) and traditional vendors offering new services that compete with traditional ones. Most financial markets still sell their information to specialised intermediaries via proprietary connections, and, in most cases, the Internet sites are merely showcases. Some financial services are still available exclusively through proprietary systems. They are either innovative services requiring dedicated systems, or services requiring the high security and confidentiality that proprietary systems offer.[2]

For firms in supply and production chains, instead, the logical endpoint could well be smaller, less open structures rather than expansive open ones. In the upstream production-oriented part of the automobile industry, for example, electronic communications have a productive function as well as a commercial one. The former is particularly important for the definition of electronic links. It presupposes first, that some traded inputs are specific and the information relating to them is dedicated and secret and, second, that the components' flow is integrated into the production cycle. Since in this industry such flows are just-in-time, relevant information flows must be reliable and fast. This is why some data exchange systems will remain proprietary. Correlatively, transactions that are remote from the productive function and from just-in-time flows can be executed on open networks. The advantages of doing so are all the greater in that manufacturers can benefit from the competition among a maximum number of suppliers.

Electronic commerce and organisational change: channels for performance and growth

This section discusses the ways in which organisational changes at the firm level that are associated with electronic commerce can translate into improved performance and growth at the economy-wide level. The role played by electronic commerce in this respect offers important areas of research which are not yet covered in the literature. Because there is evidence that small innovative firms are an engine of growth, it would be interesting to examine whether electronic commerce gives small innovative firms any special advantages for entering new or existing markets. Another issue is the nature of innovation associated with electronic commerce, a point that is usually not stressed in the literature on the latter but is extremely important, given the impact that innovation processes have on productivity and growth, both directly and indirectly, through technology diffusion. There is also the question of whether the combination of new business processes and work organisation associated with electronic commerce favours high-performance work.

Does electronic commerce give smaller innovative firms special advantages for entering new or existing markets?

Basically, two types of firms enter electronic markets: start-up firms directly conceived to operate in this environment and established firms that migrate to electronic commerce. The economic significance of start-up firms is very small but is growing fast. Established firms adopt electronic commerce solutions at various rates and along industry-specific paths (see above). It is the "scalability" of the Internet that offers small niche players many of the same advantages enjoyed by large diversified firms in terms of expanding the range of e-commerce customers and transactions (Hawkins, 1998). This may be particularly important for small innovative firms trying to enter the market.

The problem of asymmetries in firms' abilities to control the terms of entry into and exit from the electronic marketplace is another SME-related issue that could be worth exploring. As large firms embrace e-commerce, more small firms are being compelled to follow to be able to do business with larger firms. These and many other factors can make opportunity costs relatively greater for SMEs than for large firms.

The role of electronic commerce in innovation processes and technology diffusion

Firms adopting electronic commerce often invest in research and development (R&D) for information and communication technologies. Reuters, a $5 billion global financial news and information company, has substituted a "high-value-added, real-time online business information services" business model for much of its traditional "news agency" model. In the process, it has become a major investor in R&D for ICT products and services (Hawkins, 1998). For example, it is investing in pay-per-view technology and a smart card that will allow Reuters subscribers to access services from anywhere in the world via the Internet (Margherio *et al.*, 1998). In 1997, the firm had the ninth largest overall R&D spending in the United Kingdom, more than that of British Aerospace or British Petroleum (Hawkins, 1998). Table 3.3 shows the amount of operating and development expenditure (inclusive of R&D expenditure) for three well-known cyber-traders.

By adopting information technologies, the mechanism of innovation changes. R&D breakthroughs seem to become the outcome of a series of many small innovations, rather than a single big one. Wal-Mart's and Bennetton's successful inventory strategies seem to have been built in this way. The future of R&D in business might be to move away from the hard sciences and technologies towards understanding consumers' demand patterns, self-organising structures, supply chains, markets, organisations and their behaviour (Forge, 1995).

Focused innovation is not only conducted at the R&D stage but carries over to implementation and marketing. The success of the Sabre reservation system lies not only in the technology but also in its marketing, as it is presented as a separate company to attract other airlines (Forge, 1995).

Innovation and technology diffusion lie at the heart of economies' growth processes. Recent OECD work (OECD, 1998*b*) points to the role of ICTs and organisational change in innovation and technology diffusion (see Box 3.4). The extent to which electronic commerce plays an independent and sizeable role in overall changes in the innovation process is still extremely limited. Nevertheless, the increasing role played by networks (Internet and intranets) in the innovation process constitutes a channel through which electronic commerce can stimulate successful innovation. Manufacturers of Internet equipment are heavy investors in R&D. As Table 3.4 shows, R&D expenditures in US companies have been increasing at an average rate of 55 per cent a year.

What is unique about these technologies is the system-wide gains in efficiency they achieve as they link different actors in a wide cross-section of industries. Fostering such system-wide improvements requires rethinking technology and innovation policies, such as technology diffusion programmes, which tend to focus on a single industry, such as manufacturing, whereas services such as wholesale trade, transportation and retail trade make the largest contributions to system-wide gains. This suggests the need to broaden the notion of "innovation" to include consumer goods and services (OECD, 1997*c*).

Electronic commerce may also play a role as a source of technology transfer via customer-supplier relations. These, together with the purchase of equipment and the hiring of skilled personnel, are by far the most important source of technology transfer in many countries (OECD, 1998*b*). In many of the cases examined above, direct links established between customers and suppliers can create a valuable technology/innovation channel.

Table 3.3. **Net revenues/sales and operating and development expenditures for e-commerce firms**

US$ thousand

Company	Country	Net revenues/sales[1]				Operating and development expenditure[2]				Operating and development expenditure as a percentage of net revenue/sales		
		1996	1997	1998	CAGR %	1996	1997	1998	CAGR %	1996	1997	1998
Amazon	United States		16.01	87.73	448.1		1.58	6.73	327.2		9.84	7.67
CDnow	United States		2 600	10 000	284.6		322	1 100	241.6		12.38	11.00
N2K	United States	1 656	11 263		57.0	7 955	14 852		86.7	480.4	571.2	
E*Trade	United States	51.60	142.74		176.6	2.79	10.76		285.4	5.41	7.54	

1. Amazon and CDnow: percentage of net sales (March); E*Trade: percentage of net revenue (September).
2. Expenses for store management, design, development and network operations personnel, systems and telecommunications.
CAGR = Compound average growth rate.
Source: OECD, based on data from the US Securities and Exchange Commission.

Table 3.4. **Revenues and R&D for manufacturers of Internet equipment**

US$ million

Company	Country	Revenues				R&D expenditure				R&D as a percentage of revenue		
		1995	1996	1997	CAGR %	1995	1996	1997	CAGR %	1995	1996	1997
3Com	US	1 404	2 057	2 093	22.1	145	214	270	36.3	10.4	10.4	12.9
Bay Networks	US	2 233	4 096	6 440	69.8	211	399	698	82.0	9.4	9.7	10.8
Cabletron Systems	US	833	1 100	1 407	29.9	89	127	162	34.7	10.7	11.6	11.5
Cisco Systems	US	1 593	2 327	3 147	40.5	166	233	335	42.0	10.4	10.0	10.7
Total		6 063	9 580	13 087	46.9	612	973	1 465	54.8	10.1	10.2	11.2

CAGR = Compound average growth rate.
Source: OECD (1999, forthcoming).

Box 3.4. **Changes in innovation and technology diffusion processes: the role of ICTs and organisational change**

The process of innovation and technology diffusion is undergoing substantial change

The main driving forces are increasing market pressures (stemming from globalisation, deregulation, and changing patterns of demand and new societal needs), as well as the increased use of ICT technologies (which can increase multi-disciplinary production of new knowledge and diminish the cost of information access and processing).

In this new mode, technology diffusion involves much more than the mere purchase of advanced equipment. Genuine innovative efforts, such as organisational and managerial changes, are often required to exploit fully the potential of new technologies.

Innovation has become a complex activity, involving many different types of knowledge and actors

Smooth interplay among actors is essential for successful innovation. Inter-firm collaboration, networking and the formation of clusters of industries are examples of such interaction. To reinforce their innovation competence, many firms are investing heavily in new ICTs and increasingly in "intangibles" (*e.g.* skills and qualifications, purchase of technologies and know-how, and organisational restructuring in order to realise the potential of the new ICTs).

As regards external links, the number of actors involved in the process of innovation is increasing (*e.g.* enterprises large and small, universities, public and co-operative research labs, hospitals). There is also a widening variety of types of interactions (user-producer interactions, outsourcing of R&D, formation of R&D alliances and research joint ventures to pool resources, formal and informal links to the scientific community, etc.). Firms are more likely to innovate successfully if they are able to access and implement acquired knowledge rapidly. This accounts for a positive relationship between internal innovation capabilities and the use firms can make of external linkages. Firms with higher internal innovative efforts also have a greater ability to co-operate with other actors and to adopt knowledge produced outside the firm.

"Networks of innovation" have become the rule

The development of intranets and the Internet favours networking of the economy and may change the relative importance of sources of information for innovation by firms. Intranets favour the diffusion of information within the firm and the Internet will certainly increase links with research institutions and universities.

Networking has also become an effective innovation technique in its own right. Indeed, some authors argue that networking must now be considered as powerful as hierarchy and the market as a co-ordination mechanism. Empirical studies have confirmed that collaborating firms are more innovative than non-collaborating ones. Even non-collaborating firms do not work in isolation, but are involved in a number of interactions: they purchase embedded technologies, consultancy, and intellectual property and scan for ideas from a variety of sources.

Source: OECD, 1998*b*.

The high-performance workplace and its impact on productivity

There is evidence that firms and establishments adopting new organisational structures have stronger and more productive external linkages with their customers and their suppliers of inputs and services (OECD, 1996*b*). Moreover, the combination of streamlined business processes, flat organisational hierarchies, and continuous training and skill acquisition constitutes a favourable environment for innovation and improved performance. Firms' strategies based on these elements are often termed "high-performance work practices". At least some, if not all, of the features of the new work organisation (OECD, 1998*b*) have much in common with the features of enterprises in electronic markets:

– more horizontal inter-firm links for subcontracting or outsourcing;

– the new work organisation is an essential complement to effective use of technology;

– latter hierarchies;

– better use of better trained and more responsive employees;

– more multi-skilling and job rotation, blurring differences among traditional work activities;

– more small self-managing or autonomous work groups which take more responsibility.

A series of recent surveys (OECD, 1998*b*) shows that organisational flexibility associated with high-performance workplaces has a positive impact on firm and establishment performance. In particular, high-performance workplaces are associated with: *i*) higher labour productivity, better wage performance and satisfactory unit cost performance; *ii*) higher sales owing to increased market shares, customer satisfaction due to better product quality and improved customer relations; and *iii*) positive employment performance (particularly in association with technology adoption) and lower staff turnover due to better working conditions and higher wages. Future work along these lines could specifically address firms operating in electronic markets, in order to assess the impact of electronic commerce on productivity growth and performance.

CONCLUSIONS AND FUTURE RESEARCH AGENDA

Electronic commerce is transforming the marketplace by changing firms' business models, by shaping relations among market actors, and by contributing to changes in market structure. Given the dynamic nature of these processes, the impact of electronic commerce will be firm-, sector-, and time-specific. Conclusions offered at this stage can therefore only be preliminary.

- *There is need for a continuous monitoring of the electronic marketplace. Case studies should address the sectoral and market specificity of organisational impacts. Research on the evolving nature of the commercial environment will help policy makers on issues of commercial governance, which are critical to the development of electronic commerce.*

Even if cyber-traders do not present a new commercial paradigm today, they play a catalytic role for other, more traditional companies that are entering electronic markets. Key market actors can thus contribute to the evolution and diffusion of e-commerce by forcing e-commerce solutions in sectoral and national contexts and, particularly, on suppliers.

- *Future research should analyse the role of e-commerce players in different national contexts, as well as the scope for governments to lead and encourage e-commerce solutions.*

Electronic commerce does not always lead to greater market competition, but it changes firms' competitive advantages, the nature of firms' competition, as well as the market on which firms compete.

- *Ongoing assessment of potential new barriers to market entry is needed. Future research could use firm-level data to analyse the competitive behaviour of e-commerce adopters on the domestic and international markets, while sectoral studies could address the dynamics of market structure, especially in the business-to-business segment. The existence of asymmetries in firms' ability to control access to the electronic marketplace should also be investigated. This research will assist policy makers to address competition issues, as well as to formulate policies targeted to SMEs.*

The open, and potentially global, nature of electronic commerce is likely to increase market size and change market structure, in terms of the number and size of players and the way in which players compete on international markets.

- *Research should look at the extent to which electronic commerce is really "global" or still mostly confined to national markets, and whether it is affecting countries' relative competitive advantage.*

The extent to which firms can reorganise in the new electronic environment will crucially depend on the flexibility and adaptability of the work force.

- *Future research should investigate the role played by workers in business re-engineering, study emerging forms of work organisation on electronic markets, and address the need for "upskilling" of workers and redefining their functions in electronic environments.*

The impact of e-commerce on the marketplace will also depend on the existence of a critical mass of consumers.

- *Issues of trust and confidence, privacy and consumer protection in the electronic marketplace should be addressed from an economic perspective.*

A novel aspect of e-commerce is the emergence of virtual communities in online networks.

- *The role of virtual communities in shaping new relations and shifting market power among suppliers and consumers should be investigated.*

E-commerce favours the combination of streamlined business processes, flat organisational hierarchies, continuous training and skills acquisition, inter-firm collaboration, and networking. All these elements contribute to a favourable environment for innovation and improve performance.

- *Empirical research is needed to quantify the contribution of electronic commerce to the size and quality of product and process innovation.*

Annex 3.1

ELECTRONIC COMMERCE AND NEW OPPORTUNITIES FOR BUSINESS SUBSTITUTION: SOME EVIDENCE

In some cases, Internet commerce constitutes the logical extension to firms' business models and simply accentuates some of their characteristics without implying revolutionary changes. For instance, in the computer industry, there are some early adopters of business solutions which minimise inventory risk, which is quite high, given the frequent and sizeable drops in the cost of material and rapid obsolescence.

The best example is that of Dell. At the heart of the Dell strategy there is a model of "virtual integration" (Magretta, 1998). This model encompasses two very different business models: a vertically integrated model, which offers a tightly co-ordinated supply chain, and a virtual corporation model, which is based on focus and specialisation and can reach very fine market segmentation. In 1994, Dell pioneered what became known as the "direct business model" within the computer industry. The distribution chain was eliminated and close relations with customers and suppliers were established by the use of customised intranet sites. The key element in Dell's strategy is to speed up every element of its business. Internet commerce is growing fast at Dell – from $2 million a day in the first year, to $3 million a day, with peaks of $6 million at Christmas, now – but it does not seem to have radically changed the company's business model. Rather, "Internet commerce is a logical extension of Dell's direct model".

In other cases, Internet commerce can entail the adoption of new business models which can replace or complement existing ones. Some examples of business substitution by established firms migrating to electronic are found in Annex Table 3.3.4. Obviously, these few examples do not allow generalisation, and as business substitution follows a sectoral dynamics, sectoral differences will also reflect different positions along the substitution path. However, Annex Table 3.3.4 suggests the existence of interesting differences that could be object of further research.

Music retail

The availability of multimedia features on the Internet, including audio, video and graphics, make it an ideal medium for promoting, marketing and selling music. Purchasers of music recordings can preview their purchases by listening to high-quality sound samples, viewing text and video clips, and searching an extensive catalogue of available titles. The Internet also allows users to download music digitally in a compressed format to a personal computer (PC) and store it on a CD using a read/write CD-ROM drive.

Internet-based retailers have certain advantages over traditional retail channels. Traditional retail stores limit the amount of inventory they carry and tend to focus on carrying a greater percentage of hit releases. Traditional retail stores stock an average of 10 000 stock keeping units (SKUs) and megastores stock an average of approximately 39 000 SKUs out of a total of more than 200 000 SKUs generally available in the United States and offered by online companies such as N2K (US Securities Exchange Database, N2K financial statement).

Annex Table 3.1. **Shifting from physical to electronic markets: changes in the business model**

Sector	Degree of business substitution
Music	Radical
Publishing	Radical
Transport	Partial
Information services	Mixed evidence
Retail banking	Radical
Marketing and advertising	None

Source: OECD.

For the moment, established online music retailers such as CDnow and N2K have relied on strategic alliances with Internet service providers such as America Online or aggregators such as Excite and Yahoo! to market and distribute their music. Other models are trying to emerge. NetRadio has established a CDPoint online store and plans to use "radio retail" to "buy-what-you-hear". Both DJ.com and Imagine Radio have partnered with CDnow to send their listeners to the online store and provide direct links from their downloadable "tuners".

Digital delivery of music thus has the potential to revolutionise the music distribution model. Digital recordings, once captured, can make an infinite number of perfect copies. Record companies will have to pool together, get permission from each of their artists, and choose a standard from among many technologies being offered, thereby giving up a significant degree of control over the distribution process. "This is the first time the music industry is realising its products into a channel in which they have little or arguably no control. A study found that nearly 80 000 illegal music files were already available on the Internet." (Lipton, 1998).

Publishing

The case of the *Encyclopaedia Britannica*, completely devastated by the advent of the CD-ROM encyclopaedia, is a dramatic one (Annex Box 3.4). Now the company, under new management, is trying to rebuild its business around the Internet.

Annex Box 3.1. *Encyclopaedia Britannica* and the advent of CD-ROMs

Since 1990, sales of the Encyclopaedia Britannica multi-volume sets have decreased by more than 50 per cent. The reason is simple: it costs in the range of $1 500-$2 200 to buy the paper version, while an encyclopaedia on CD-ROM, such as Microsoft Encarta, sells for about $50 and customers often get it free because it is bundled with their personal computers as CD-ROMs. Interestingly, the largest part of Britannica's cost structure was not the editorial content, which constituted only about 5 per cent of costs, but the direct sales force.

	Sales price ($)	Cost of production ($)	% of cost attributable to content
Encyclopaedia Britanica	1 500 to 2 200	200 to 300	5
CD- ROM encyclopaedia	50	1.5	

When Britannica realised the threat from CD-ROM encyclopaedias it created a CD-ROM version, but to avoid undercutting its sales force, the company included it free with the printed version and charged anyone buying the CD-ROM alone $1 000. Revenues continued to decline, the best salespeople left, and Britannica's owner, a trust controlled by the University of Chicago, finally sold out. Under new management, the company is now trying to rebuild the business around the Internet.

Source: Evans and Wurster, 1997.

Transport

In other cases, new business models have only partially replaced traditional ones. Federal Express (FedEx), for example, has substituted a sophisticated "logistics information" business model for parts of its original model (*i.e.* a "mover of boxes"). Starting in 1982, three successive programmes were introduced (see Annex Box 3.4), the last of which, InterNetShip, extended online capabilities to the Internet; this programme is used by nearly 8 per cent of the customers who interact electronically. At the same time, FedEx continues to operate and own a physical forwarding and delivery infrastructure; its proprietary network, FedEx COSMOS, handles 54 million transactions a day.

Travel

SABRE is an example of a company that is repositioning itself. It used to leverage a huge data network and computer operations in travel agencies around the world, providing them with information and reservation services (see Annex Box). The advent of the Internet makes it much more feasible for them and for airlines to go directly to consumers. Therefore, SABRE is outsourcing its computer and network operations and focusing more on the value added of their information database (content versus infrastructure) (Bloch *et al.*, 1996).

Annex Box 3.2.   Organisational change at FedEx: from courier company to logistics and networking provider

FedEx changed from courier company to a logistics and network provider. There were five key elements in the change.

Personal multimedia: In 1995, a new interactive training system was launched to teach basic interaction skills such as customer-contact methods and features of service categories to its 35 000 couriers and customer-service agents. Interactive multimedia training can occur at the beginning or at the end of a shift or whenever the individual can best fit in what are very personalised instructions.

The high-performance team: A customer calls for a pickup and speaks to an agent in a call centre. The request is transmitted to the COSMOS (customer, operations, management and services) database and then relayed to the dispatch centre in the local market, which, in turn, passes the request to a small computer located aboard a FedEx van (called DADS). Once the order is received, everything is taken care of by the network. Teams interoperate through electronic mail. The company has one of the largest single e-mail networks in the world – some 70 000 employees.

Enterprise infostructure: FedEx developed the service quality index (SQI) which measures failure rates. The index is based on ten events that frustrate or disappoint the customer, events that are weighted on a ten-point scale. Every time the parcel changes status, information is recorded through sensors and entered into the COSMOS database which contains all the basic customer information – name, account number, address, package pickup location data – and communicates with a number of other systems and devices to maintain a complete record of each shipment handled. The courier picks up the package and uses the Supertracker, a small, portable, battery-operated, menu-driven computer with a bar code scanner, to scan the package's bar code. The courier then places the Supertracker into a port located on the DADS computer. The package information is automatically transmitted to the dispatch centre and the COSMOS database. As the package moves through the system and is scanned, this information is continuously updated. Before a night is over, FedEx will have scanned 2.4 million shipments, up to nine times each, as they move through the network.

Interenterprise computing: The FedEx PowerShip network automates shipping by printing the mailing labels, calculates the cost to its customers, and provides tracking and shipping. PowerShip is just one of the network-based products that FedEx provides to its customers, so that their PC can be integrated with FedEx's client/server application. FedEx either supplies a PC and the software to the customer, or integrates the customer's system with the FedEx system, or supplies the software, which can run on any PC equipped with a modem and a laser printer.

The Internetworked business: The latest step was to extend online capabilities to the Internet with InterNetShip.

FedEx connects its customers electronically

Service	Date	Customers using service
FedEx PowerShip	1982	Largest customers
FedEx Ship	1995	Mid-size/less frequent customers
InterNetShip	July 96	Any customer

Source: Margherio *et al.*, 1998.

_____

Source: Tapscott, 1996.

Information services

In the case of "information services", the business substitution is more subtle but just as real. Case studies of content providers (Margherio *et al.*, 1998) offer a diversified picture. The online business model of the *New York Times* differs from the off-line model. In the latter, the New Journal controls the entire chain (content, advertising, manufacturing, distribution), in the online world all the production-related activities disappear. On the other hand, Dun & Bradstreet, one of the leading providers of business-to-business credit, marketing purchasing, and decision-support services world-wide, seems to be organising itself on the Internet much as it does in traditional markets.

Banking

"Banks will not become obsolete, but their current business definition will, specifically in terms of the concept of a bank as an integrated business where multiple products are originated, packaged, sold, and cross-sold through proprietary distribution channels" (Evans and Wurster, 1997). That has happened before in banking. Some 15 years ago, US corporate banking was doing business on spreads; today, corporate banking consists of small businesses that compete product by product. While credit flows directly from lender to borrower, banks now make money by providing services such as risk rating, advice, market making.

The institutional market (business-to-business banking) has already contributed to disassembling the value chain and cutting out specialist and market makers over the past 20 years. For institutional traders, electronic trading systems such as Instinet, Posit, and AZX have accounted for nearly 20 per cent of the daily volume on the major US stock markets over the last decade. Until recently, however, it was inconceivable that a similar mechanism could provide similar benefits to individual investors (see Annex Box).

Evidence of business substitution in the retail banking sector is still mixed. On the one hand, traditional retail banks seem to be slow to react to business opportunities in online markets. On the other, non-bank entrants enter the market with completely new business models. The new entrants, whose business models focus on a specific customer segment or on a specific transaction category, could constitute a real threat to traditional incumbents (McKinsey, 1997).

Marketing and advertising

Marketing and advertising is the sector that is probably most affected by the use of the Web. Most people surfing the Web are looking for information. For suppliers, Web advertising offers the ability to target and deliver directed messages to an audience with specific demographics and interests; and the ability to collect, track, analyse, and leverage consumer behaviour/buying patterns facilitates the growth of online marketing. A global study evaluating 1 800 Web sites, with representative samples from different industries and countries for 1996, reveals that the business purpose of a commercial Web site is primarily promotional; but the value added to the customer is primarily logistic in nature (rates and fares are quoted and there are facilities locators), while Web sites rarely create "custom value", defined as value that responds to a customer's preferences (*e.g.* searching a database of real estate listings based on preferred price range, location, size and style of home) (Ho, 1997). According to the same study, the marketing approach taken is not very different from the traditional one: product news, catalogues and portfolios, previews and samples, special offers and discounts, contests.

Annex Box 3.3. SABRE

The SABRE (Semi-Automated Business Research Environment) computerised reservation system began in 1959 as an internal organisational database for American Airlines. In the mid-1970s, the scheduling system was adapted for use outside American Airlines and released to travel agencies over a proprietary network in order to provide flight information through a central repository. The SABRE system proved very successful and provided the model for all future computerised reservation systems, not only for airlines but also for other segments of the travel and tourism industry. Currently, one traveller in three world-wide is routed through the SABRE system.

The emergence of online services like CompuServe presented the SABRE Group with an opportunity to expand. In 1986, EasySABRE was introduced as CompuServe's online travel agent, and CompuServe subscribers no longer needed to use a travel agent as an intermediary. The information traditionally accessed by travel agents was now directly available online.

Two years ago, the SABRE group further expanded their business model to include the World Wide Web. First, the command-based EasySABRE system was made publicly accessible through the Web. Second, SABRE created Travelocity, a Web site offering all of SABRE's features with an attractive graphical interface. The site provides schedules for over 700 airlines and can make reservations for more than 400. The Travelocity site also posts last-minute bargains and consolidator fares and provides an e-mail fare-tracking system which can send news on bargain flights to subscribers instantly. For major routes, passengers can even be informed via pager if their flight will be delayed. Other travel arrangements are also available, including car rental information for over 60 rental companies, and a hotel reservation system which integrates photographs, location maps, and reviews for over 35 000 hotels world-wide.

SABRE makes the transborder nature of electronic commerce clear. Since information is easily transmitted across national boundaries, international operations are facilitated, and expansion at a fast pace and low cost becomes possible. American Airlines did not need to establish a separate database in each city in which it operates around the world. Instead, it has been able to market access to its network anywhere, while maintaining its "production" facilities in the United States.

The development of Travelocity also underscores the importance of the Internet's open protocol system. It is now easier than ever before to extend a network directly to end users, as the infrastructure is already in place at the user's end. SABRE no longer needs to supply hardware or networking functionality to many of its end users. A simple IP address suffices. It is important to note, however, that SABRE is not switching to the open standard and eliminating its ties to traditional travel agent networks. The TCP/IP protocol is integrated into an existing business model in order to expand to reach new customers rather than to displace its old client networks.

The SABRE example does not bear out the view that the disintermediation brought on by electronic commerce will displace "middlemen" like travel agencies. While online travel sites have become popular (Travelocity is ranked in the top 25 per cent of Web sites in terms of "hits" and is ranked even higher in terms of number of visitors), 80 per cent of all tickets are still issued through travel agencies. The 20 per cent of passengers who have chosen the Internet are largely those who traditionally bought airline tickets by phone.

This should not be taken to mean that online services pose no threat to traditional agents. Travel agents face a clear challenge from this competition and may lose business as the technology improves and users become more comfortable as online consumers. As a result, travel agencies are working vigorously to improve service off line and to offer online services of their own. Moreover, as new distribution channels have become available to airlines, airlines have capped and reduced commissions paid to travel agents. Since travel agencies remain popular with travellers, airlines hesitate to cut their ties with them. Travellers complain that the SABRE system cannot provide the customised itineraries that are best created through person-to-person contact. In addition, consumers often feel that if something goes wrong, no one is accountable. It is likely, at least in the near future, that online services will simply be another channel of distribution. The most apparent result of the introduction of SABRE will likely be a higher level of service to consumers both on line and at the travel agency.

Annex Box 3.4.   **From Spring Street Brewing Company to Wit Capital**

Spring Street Brewing, a beer company, launched in 1995 the world's first Internet public stock offering in order to raise capital. After ten months, more than 860 000 shares had been sold to 3 500 new stockholders. The capital totalled $1.6 million, the amount needed for a viable marketing and sales initiative. Spring Street's initial public offering shows that the Internet was the perfect medium for a small, early-stage enterprise to find and reach potential investors and raise capital.

The second step was to use the Internet to create a trading mechanism, Wit Trade, which would act as clearing agent for stocks transactions. Wit Trade showed that the Internet can be used to provide moderate liquidity. More than a thousand would-be buyers and at least that many would-be sellers met over the Internet to buy, sell, and swap Spring Street stock without needing to go through brokers, deal with dealers, or have a seat on the stock exchange. They saved fees and commissions, and, by executing trades directly with other investors, they avoided the spreads charged by the market makers and specialists who are the middlemen of every traditional stock market trade.

The next idea was to create an investment bank and brokerage firm, Wit Capital, that would arrange stock offerings and facilitate stock trading on the Web. The company would develop a digital stock market in which sellers and buyers would interact directly. The idea was to deliver through the Internet to individual investors an open-architecture, low-cost public medium that is perfect for small-scale transactions, a model comparable to the one used by institutional investors. Since brokers had not the slightest interest in routing their orders to this new trading system and losing part of their commission, a new brokerage firm had to be created and a new and direct relationship had to be created with each and every individual investor. In 1998, Wit Capital will open a digital stock market and begin to offer no-spread direct trading.

Price comparison
US$

	Wit Capital	Schwab (voice order)	Merrill Lynch (voice order)
1 000 shares @ $25 market order	$14.95	$155.00	$428.00
1 000 shares @ $25 limit order	$19.95	$155.00	$428.00

Survey July 1997. Services may vary and other discounts may apply.
Source: Wit Capital (WWW/WitCapital.com).

———————
Source: Klein, 1998.

Annex 3.2

THE INTERNATIONALISATION OF BUSINESS: HOW GLOBAL IS E-COMMERCE?

To what extent is electronic commerce really global today? Annex Table 3.3.4 presents some estimates of international revenues by companies selling on line. For companies selling exclusively on line, international revenues attain one-third of total revenues.

Annex Table 3.2. **International trade of selected e-commerce firms, 1997**

Company	Segment	Online revenues as % of total	International revenues as % of total
CDnow	Music	100	35
Music Boulevard	Music	100	33
Amazon	Books	100	26
Barnes & Nobel	Books	0.50	30
FastParts	Electronic components	100	30
Virtual Dreams	Pornography	100	25
Dell	Computers	almost 50	20
1-800-Flowers	Flowers	10	15-20
Sabre	Travel	67.30	17.50
E*Trade	Consumer brokerage	63	2.80

Sources: CDnow, Music Boulevard, Amazon, Sabre, E*Trade (US Securities and Exchange Commission); Barnes & Noble (Cowles/Simba Information, "Electronic Advertising and MarketPlace Report", 4 March 1997); FastParts (Erwin *et al.*, 1997); Virtual Dreams ("CyberSex", *The Economist*, 4 January, 1997); Dell ("Dell: Net to Make Up Half of Sales", http://www.news.com, 28 April 1998); 1-800-Flowers (www.1800flowers.com).

Banking

One of the strategic challenges in corporate banking is how to address the issue of internationalisation. The Internet is a potential gateway to low-cost international expansion (offering domestic services to corporations abroad) through a virtual presence (almost two-thirds of the top 100 banks expect to use the Internet as a platform for global expansion). At the same time, however, the Internet might hinder this development due to the general increase in global access and competition (customers using local banks in foreign countries) and the emergence of virtual alliances between small local banks that jointly offer global services (Booz-Allen & Hamilton, 1997*b*).

Information services

Information services for businesses are above all a necessary complement to transactions involving physical goods and services. Therefore, for businesses, electronic services follow the distribution of cross-border physical products, and "regional proximity" partly determines the distribution of exports of physical products, since transport costs increase with physical distance.

Regional proximity may, however, be a much smaller factor in the case of electronic services for private households. For this target group, electronic services are an end-product for which transport costs (*e.g.* for telecommunication transfer) play a negligible role. Therefore, in the consumer sector, a world mass market, especially for entertainment services, is a very real possibility, as the film and music industries have already shown. Clear market dominance may be attained by the suppliers of consumer services from one country, as has been the case for the

United States. However, the rising importance of regional and local information for consumers, which is stressed in many market research studies, may partly counterbalance this situation (European Commission, 1996).

To prevent the erosion of their margins, leading financial information firms are seeking to increase exports of their services and to use the competitive edge gained at home to dominate regional markets. This increases concentration at the regional (*e.g.* European) level. These strategies are enabling market leaders to maintain high, albeit falling, growth rates and to increase their market share (see Annex Box 3.5).

Annex Box 3.5.   **Financial information services**

A 1997 study by Compagnie Bancaire indicates that 80 per cent of Internet financial services are provided by US companies and the remainder largely by UK firms (Tommasi, 1997). This confirms the findings of a European Commission study (1996) that UK firms account for 81 per cent of the European market for financial services.[3] Many explanations are offered. One is the predominance of English in this environment. Another is the reputation of UK and US firms, with historically strong institutions and healthy financial markets.[4] They may also have benefited from the availability and use of Audiotex services in the United Kingdom and their move to the Internet (Confederation of Information Communication Industries, 1995). Finally, there is the relative weakness of other markets, where bank lending dominated stock markets as a source of company finance.

The United States and the United Kingdom were first to open up their financial markets to the rest of the world over the Internet. This should make Wall Street and the City even more dynamic and enable them to attract most of the world's savings. Less dynamic markets can expect to fall even further behind unless ways are found to increase their attractiveness. In France, for example, the market is very institutionalised. While this has created a kind of public service that makes financial information accessible to all at very low cost, it is also the source of its weakness. To take off, the financial information market will have to offer services with high value added, in particular financial analysis.

The growing dispersal of investment and savings could aid the development of more specialised financial service groups. The Compagnie Bancaire report forecasts that, as investors become more independent, they will move away from instruments like unit trusts/mutual funds towards more individual forms of investment. However, the new-found freedom among private investors is expected to increase the risk of markets crashing or overheating as a result of speculation, rumours and false information. Because it is hard to control information placed on the network, the door is left open to abuse, fraud, or misinformation (*Wall Street Journal*, 8 June 1995).[5] Liberalisation will therefore need to go hand in hand with regulatory reforms that create a safe environment for the growth of Internet-based financial services.

Brokering

American Internet brokers have started moving into the United Kingdom and are increasingly setting their sights on the continent as well. Their arrival poses a challenge for European online trading firms, whose ambitions are, for the moment, limited to national markets. Analysts expect the arrival of the Americans to accelerate the vast changes in the securities business that are already under way as Europe becomes a single market. In April, Charles Schwab started an online trading service, and in June the E*Trade group, based in California, announced a joint venture with a British partner and a licensing agreement in Germany.

Under competitive pressures at home that are driving down profit margins, American brokers are being drawn to Europe. To build a European business, they are applying various formulae. Though most American online brokers accept European customers for trades on United States exchanges, they refrain from actively advertising so as to avoid irritating European regulators. Schwab, for example, only offers European customers the chance to trade on individual European exchanges, while E*Trade is signing up with local customers and licensing its systems. European banks and brokers are fighting back. Barclays PLC, one of the largest British banks, with 2 500 branches in the United Kingdom, will launch its own online brokerage service in September (*International Herald Tribune*, July 1998).

Music

International revenues represented about 21 per cent of revenues in the first quarter of 1998 for CDnow, and 25 per cent of 1997 online revenues for Music Boulevard (the online shop of NK2). However, there is little incentive for customers in countries with a fairly developed market to buy products already available at home. The UK music market, for example, is the most developed in Europe and is dominated by five large multinationals with nearly a 77 per cent share (Janson and Mansell, 1998). Even if US record companies export to the United Kingdom or have established a strong base there (*e.g.* Tower Records), online ordering is still coupled with physical transportation, which is time-consuming and expensive.

Annex Table 3.3 presents some estimates and comparisons of the time and cost of delivering CDs ordered online from the United States and the United Kingdom (Tower Records and Internet Music Shop) to continental Europe. Shipping a CD from CDnow costs $13 on average and can take three weeks as compared to $3 and 7-10 days from the UK-based Internet music shop. Tower Records, which can ship records both from the United States and from Europe (as well as Asia), is a clear example of a company establishing presence abroad in order to conquer market shares by avoiding transport costs. Interestingly, the UK-based Tower Records does not yet ensure secure online ordering (although it is preparing to do so) and orders are still done by mail. This may reflect the fact that online shopping in the European market is still a relatively modest phenomenon. High transport costs are forcing CDnow and Music Boulevard (both owned by N2K) to locate their operations outside North America. N2K has now established a wholly-owned subsidiary in Japan, the world's second largest market for recorded music sales. These subsidiaries can tailor the market better and offer faster and cheaper delivery (Rawsthorn, 1997*b*).

Annex Table 3.3. **Shipping time and charges from US- and UK-based CD stores to continental Europe**

CDs in stock

	Shipping rates (US$)	Quantity (No. of CDs)	Shipping time	Carrier
cdUSA	19.95 24.95 29.95	1-5 6-10 11-29	2-3 days	DHL Worldwide Express
CDnow	11.89-16.49 1.69-2.69 1.20-2.20	up to 3 next 3 each additional item	3-4 weeks	
Music Boulevard	6.99 + 2.25 additional item 20.99 + 2.25 additional item	1 1-3	7-14 days 2-5 days	Air Mail DHL Worldwide Express
CD UNIVERSE	5.99 + 1.5 additional item 9.95 + 2.25 additional item 24 + 2.5 additional item		5-10 days 2-5 days overnight	Air Mail Global Priority Express Mail
Tower Records from the US	20 25 30 35 40 45	1-3 4-6 7-9 10-12 13-15 16-18 (maximum)	2-3 days/not guaranteed	Federal Express
Tower Records from the UK	2.3 4.4 5.9 7.5 9 10	1 2 3 4 5 6	5-7 days	UK Royal Mail
Internet Music Shop	3 2	1 each additional item	7-10 days	1st class mail

Source: www.cdusa.com; www.cdnow.com; www.cduniverse.com; www.towerrecords.com.

NOTES

1. Proprietary systems tie the choice of a particular service to specific hardware. Each network in a proprietary system delivers services that are limited in nature, identity and number. With proprietary systems, often the only way to obtain a variety of data is to install several different terminals. Standardised networks can provide a range of different services via the same infrastructure, and hence the same terminal; with standardisation, only one terminal is needed.

2. At least for the time being, as the trend is for all networks to switch to the ICP/IP standard, which uses cryptography and access codes to make the system secure

3. Estimate based on user group turnover. In 1994, total EU revenues from demand by firms in the financial sector amounted to ECU 1 834.3 million. That year, UK revenue from the same source was ECU 1 497.1 million. UK network service providers therefore account for 81 per cent of the revenue from demand for financial services.

4. For instance, the UK market is currently benefiting from the consolidation and increased representation of UK securities on the market, and from a change in the composition of the stock market (see "UK to Become Counting-house of the World", *Financial Times*, 7 April 1997). The market is also reported to have a time zone advantage over other markets (see "Measuring the City's Fund Strengths", *Financial Times*, 15 January 1997).

5. "Exchange Warns of Internet Risk", *Wall Street Journal*, 8 June 1995.

Chapter 4

ELECTRONIC COMMERCE, JOBS AND SKILLS

Introduction

This chapter focuses on the potential impact of electronic commerce on jobs and skills. Given the current relative size of electronic commerce with respect to other factors that may contribute to overall labour market turbulence (*e.g.* technology, trade, policies), it is necessarily speculative in nature. At this stage, the impact of electronic commerce on employment can only be very small, but, in the longer term, its effect may be felt more strongly. It may worsen or improve countries' trade balances or the skill matching between employment and the labour force; and it may allow economies to reap the benefits of increased productivity at the micro and sectoral level.

The overall effect of electronic commerce on employment will be the balance of direct new jobs, indirect jobs created by increased demand and productivity, and job losses (due to workers, *e.g.* retailers or other intermediaries, being replaced by electronic commerce). Gains and losses may differ by industry, by geographic area, by skill group. To assess the impact of electronic commerce, it is essential to understand for which industries it is generating or will generate new demand and growth, which types of jobs will be destroyed and which created, and what the overall needs are in terms of skills.

Even if electronic commerce is still quantitatively "small", it is very pervasive. It implies the seamless application of information and communication technology along the entire value chain of a business process that is conducted electronically. It favours the introduction of new business models and entails organisational changes at firm level. It also facilitates international trade and is a means of supplying goods and services across borders (*e.g.* transmission of digital products over the Internet). Moreover, it affects product markets by increasing the efficiency of transactions, by affecting market structure, and by providing more quality and variety. Information and communication technologies (ICTs), organisational change, international trade, and product market competition all have an impact on the labour market, either directly, by acting on skills, wages, and on work organisation, or indirectly, through the effects of productivity and demand on employment. The impact of electronic commerce on the job market is thus the result of a complex balance and many interactions and cannot easily be quantified. However, some lessons can be learned by looking at the various channels of transmission and the literature that examines their impact on employment.

This chapter starts by looking at the employment effects of electronic commerce at the micro, sectoral and aggregate level. First, US firm-level data are used to give an overall picture of e-commerce-related employment. Then, employment trends in related industries, such as those providing online services, audio-visual services, information services, as well as the Internet and the software industries, are examined. As electronic commerce is also likely to displace jobs, especially in retailing, the postal sector, or travel agencies, national statistics (despite the lack of comparability) and data from professional associations are used to quantify the weight of these industries in overall employment, and their potential for employment creation or displacement. Finally, an attempt is made to see how sectoral employment changes might translate to the aggregate level, by drawing lessons from available evidence on the employment impact of the growth of electronic transactions and e-commerce-related industries.

The spread of the Internet and the growth of electronic commerce, together with the substitution of off-line activities by online activities, will also affect the demand for skills. The final part of this chapter tackles the issue of skill needs in e-commerce-related industries and tracks the evolution of occupations affected by the growth of electronic commerce. The Annex presents empirical evidence that complements and substantiates the analysis.

The employment effects of electronic commerce

Electronic commerce affects a wide range of heterogeneous industries

A number of industries are affected by electronic commerce. The distribution sector ("commerce") is directly affected, as electronic commerce is a way of supplying and delivering goods and services. Other industries, indirectly affected via upstream and downstream linkages to e-commerce activities, are those related to ICTs (the infrastructure that enables electronic commerce), content-related industries (information-related goods and services, entertainment, software and digital products), transactions-related industries, *i.e.* those affected by the size and type of economic transactions (*e.g.* the financial sector, the postal sector, advertising, travel and transport). Some of these sectors are quite important in terms of employment; Table 4.1 shows the weight and composition of employment in ICT-related industries and in the finance and business and commerce-related sectors. Together, these industries account for almost one-third and one-fourth of total employment in the United States and the European Union, and roughly one-third of job creation in 1993-96 (28 and 35 per cent in the United States and the European Union, respectively).

Table 4.1. **Contribution[1] of selected industries to average annual employment growth rate, United States and EU-10**

	Percentage of total employment		Percentage contribution to total employment growth	
	United States 1996	EU-10[2] 1996	United States 1993-96	EU-10[2] 1993-96
Hardware and communication equipment[3]	1.4	2.0	0.034	0.002
Computer and data processing services[4]	1.0	0.8	0.090	0.078
Communications[5]	1.0	1.8	0.021	0.017
Financial intermediation[6]	5.7	4.3	0.038	−0.013
Trade[7]	22.6	13.4	0.570	0.094
Total	31.7	22.3	0.751	0.178
Others	68.3	77.7	1.521	0.330
Total employment growth rate			**2.272**	**0.508**

1. Contributions are calculated as the growth rates weighted by average shares in employment.
2. Belgium, Denmark, France, Greece, Italy, Luxembourg, Netherlands, Portugal, Spain, United Kingdom.
3. For the EU, sectors 30 to 33 of NACE Rev. 1, and 357, 365-367, 369 and 382 of the US SIC.
4. For the EU, sector 72 of NACE Rev. 1, and sector 337 of the US SIC.
5. For the EU, sector 64 of NACE Rev. 1, and sector 48 of the US SIC.
6. For the EU, sectors 65-67 and 70 of NACE Rev. 1, and sectors 60-65 and 67 of the US SIC.
7. For the EU, sectors 50-52 of NACE Rev. 1, and sectors 50-52 of the US SIC.
Source: OECD, based on US Bureau of Labour Statistics and Eurostat Labour Force Survey and OECD data.

The sectors affected by electronic commerce are also not homogeneous in terms of growth trends and skill composition. Table 4.2 shows the contribution of the ICT industries, the financial, and the commerce sectors to growth; it also shows that the share of high-skilled workers (defined as the sum of ISCO-88 occupational categories 1, 2 and 3) is typically higher in the financial sector, and that, while trends are similar, sectoral skill shares, as well as the weight of the three sectors in employment, differ widely across countries. Owing to heterogeneity, the impact of electronic commerce may be expected to differ, in both qualitative and quantitative terms, in these three sector.

Table 4.2. **Heterogeneity in e-commerce-related sectors**

Percentages

	Information and communication technologies[1]				
	Share of total employment		Contribution to total employment growth[2]	High-skill sectoral share[3]	
	1980	1995	1980-95	1980s	1990s
United States	2.6	1.9	−0.01	26.4	28.0
Canada	2.7	3.0	0.07	..	..
Finland	2.6	3.4	0.03	14.0	21.6
France	3.1	2.9	−0.01	36.4	44.3
Japan	3.7	4.0	0.05	14.6	16.8

	Finance, insurance, real estate and business services				
	Share of total employment		Contribution to total employment growth[2]	High-skill sectoral share[3]	
	1980	1995	1980-95	1980s	1990s
United States	10.7	14.7	0.46	31.2	32.8
Canada	9.4	12.4	0.36	47.3	53.5
Finland	5.7	8.4	0.11	30.3	36.9
France	7.8	11.3	0.25	43.2	51.6
Japan	4.0	4.7	0.08	32.4	34.9

	Wholesale and retail trade				
	Share of total employment		Contribution to total employment growth[2]	High-skill sectoral share[3]	
	1980	1995	1980-95	1980s	1990s
United States	19.6	20.5	0.37	12.6	11.8
Canada	22.3	23.5	0.42	11.4	12.3
Finland	15.7	14.0	−0.26	24.4	31.9
France	16.7	17.5	0.07	38.4	40.8
Japan	17.8	16.7	0.07	15.8	18.9

	Total economy		
	Total employment 1980-95 AAGR	High-skill share	
United States	1.53	24.3	26.3
Canada	1.49	26.2	31.0
Finland	−1.00	22.9	30.5
France	0.12	28.1	33.2
Japan	0.86	19.1	22.9

1. ICTs are defined as sectors 3825, 3832 and 72 (ISIC Rev. 2). Due to the level of aggregation, software services – part of business services – are not included.
2. Contribution of sectors to total employment growth are calculated as growth rates weighted by average shares in total employment.
3. The high-skill sectoral share is defined as the share of occupational categories (1 + 2 + 3) of the ISCO-88 classification in total employment for the sector.

AAGR = Average annual growth rate.

Source: OECD, based on data from STAN, ISDB and Services and Skills databases, and national sources.

The net direct impact: complementarity, substitution and market size effects

Some activities may increase as a direct consequence of electronic commerce (*e.g.* activities related to the information industries and services). Virtual firms entering the market create new jobs, and, at least initially, online and off-line activities tend to be carried out simultaneously. Nevertheless, this may not translate into increased jobs at a later stage, because of a substitution effect (online activities may replace traditional ones). It is reasonable to expect that the adoption of e-commerce will complement the adoption of ICTs, that it will imply major changes in financial transactions, with electronic financial services replacing traditional financial transactions to some extent, and that, in retailing, there may be employment shedding as electronic transactions and delivery replace physical ones.

Electronic commerce might also create new markets or extend market reach beyond traditional borders. Enlarging the market will have a positive effect on jobs. To understand the direct overall impact, it would be necessary to identify activities that have replaced existing ones, analyse their revenue growth compared with that of the sector as a whole, and identify those whose emergence has led to a readjustment of market share and those whose effect has been to enlarge the market.

Indirect effects on employment

Another important issue relates to interlinkages among activities affected by electronic commerce. Direct and indirect effects must be distinguished and aggregated, and overall, indirect effects may be greater than direct ones. Moreover, indirect effects follow several paths. Expenditure for e-commerce-related intermediate goods and services will create jobs indirectly, on the basis of the volume of electronic transactions and their effect on prices, costs and productivity. Depending on price elasticities, electronic commerce transactions will have a net positive impact on the demand for industries such as software, online services, audio-visual, music, and publishing. Their expansion, in turn, will have a multiplier effect on other industries. Due to intersectoral linkages, growth opportunities in e-commerce-related industries may translate into overall employment growth.

E-commerce players: employment at glance

Where are electronic commerce jobs created, and what are the related industries' employment trends? This section builds a profile from microeconomic market and employment data of individual US firms. The choice of the United States is compelled, first, by the fact that company data are readily available on the EDGAR database,[1] and, second, by the observation that, because of the maturity of the US e-commerce market relative to that of other countries, the US data can be taken as a benchmark for forecasting future trends. A rough estimate of e-commerce-related employment in various industry sectors can be obtained from examining micro data. Then, industry trends and employment projections can be studied.

The sample includes public Internet-related companies that are strongly influenced by electronic commerce developments (for the firm-level employment data and methodological details, see Annex 4.1). One group provides infrastructure for electronic commerce over the Internet, the second provides software and services for electronic commerce, and the third conducts electronic commerce (providing online services, content, selling goods and services). The firms providing infrastructure and software services are part of the computer and office equipment industry (manufacturing) and the communications and computer and data processing services (part of business services). The firms that provide online search/aggregation and information services also belong to the computer and data processing services industry. Electronic commerce content providers cover a wide spectrum of industries, ranging from publication and advertising to business services and financial services.

Most of the employment created by the US Internet/electronic commerce firms in the sample is related to computers (41.5 per cent) and to telecommunications equipment and services (20.3 per cent). Table 4.3 presents estimates (for the methodology, see Annex 4.1) which, while not representing the entire sample of Internet-related firms that conduct e-commerce-related activities, do provide a minimum order of magnitude for employment directly created by electronic commerce occurring over the Internet (approximately 123 000 employees).

Table 4.3. **Estimated electronic commerce full-time employees
in selected US firms**

	Estimated employment
Data networking/telecommunication equipment	6 238
Internet service providers	22 927
Internet security equipment and software	5 057
Total infrastructure	**34 222**
Applications software	19 190
Enterprise and related software	5 327
Commerce enablers	2 487
Internet/on-line consulting and development	2 151
Total software	**29 154**
Organisation/aggregation	2 256
On-line services/information services	9 340
Publication	12 022
Transaction processing, financial services, and on-line commerce	36 354
Total content/aggregation/commerce	**59 971**

Source: OECD estimates, based on data from the US Securities and Exchange Commission.

The firms' employment numbers are very small. Moreover, the sectors to which they belong (Table 4.4) represent a small share of the overall 1997 US employment figures, ranging from a high of 1.4 per cent of a sector's total employment (business services) to a low of 0.04 per cent (services n.e.c.). Employment in some of these industries is projected by the US Bureau of Labor Statistics to grow at below average rates by the year 2006, with computer and telecommunications equipment actually losing employment. Among the industries expected to create employment are those belonging to the financial services sectors, computer services, motion pictures, and other business sectors.

Table 4.4. **Employment in selected e-commerce-related US industries: estimates and projections**

US SIC	Industry	1997		2006		Employment change, 1997-2006	
		Number	Share in total (%)	Number	Share in total (%)	Number	%
357	Computer and telecom. equipment	379 000	0.30	314 000	0.23	−65 000	1.72
481	Telecommunications	922 238	0.74	925 000	0.66	2 762	0.03
272	Periodicals	132 575	0.11	140 000	0.10	7 425	0.56
596	Non-store retailers	341 892	0.27	350 000	0.25	8 108	0.24
621	Security and commodity brokers	590 971	0.47	740 000	0.53	149 029	2.52
720	Personal services	1 220 707	0.98	1 294 000	0.93	73 293	0.60
731	Advertising	255 732	0.21	270 000	0.19	14 268	0.56
733	Mailing, reproduction and stenographic services	313 324	0.25	361 000	0.26	47 676	1.52
737	Computer and data-processing services	1 341 711	1.08	2 509 000	1.80	1 167 289	8.70
738	Miscellaneous business services	1 690 787	1.36	2 086 000	1.50	395 213	2.34
781	Motion picture production and distribution	256 031	0.21	328 000	0.24	71 969	2.81
820	Education, public and private	2 080 994	1.67	2 478 000	1.78	397 006	1.91
890	Services, n.e.c.	48 603	0.04	62 000	0.04	13 397	2.76
	Total economy	**124 470 593**		**139 192 000**		**14 721 407**	**1.18**

Source: OECD, based on data from the US Bureau of Labor Statistics.

Job gains and losses in e-commerce-related industries

The convergence of media, telecommunication and computing technologies is creating a new integrated supply chain for the production and delivery of multimedia and information content. Most of the employment related to electronic commerce evolves around the content industries and communication infrastructure such as the Internet. Both in political circles and in the mass media, these industries often raise great hopes for job creation. What is the relative size of these industries and what are their dynamics?

Previous chapters have dealt with the production function of new firms entering the electronic market and of existing firms that are trying to adapt and move towards electronic commerce activities. As pointed out, changes in the production function tend to mean that production will become less labour-intensive. In addition, electronic markets may partly displace traditional ones, although, eventually, new industries will emerge and the output and employment effects of innovation are expected to be expansionary (see Chapter 1). During the transition, some industries or jobs, *e.g.* travel agents, retailing and postal services, will be particularly hard-hit. This section offers some evidence on the role that electronic commerce may play in direct job creation or displacement in these industries; further details can be found in Annex 4.2. Indirect job creation effects are discussed in the next section.

The "copyright" industry

The "copyright" industry broadly includes information services (mainly software services) and the content industries, such as motion picture, audio-visual and publishing industries. Its share in total employment is estimated at 3 per cent in Canada, Japan, the United States and the European Union (see Annex 4.2). The industry is quite diversified, and the software and computer-related services industry is the main driver of employment growth. In the content industry, job gains will have to be balanced against job declines, as new media activities are likely to replace traditional ones, and new electronic information services will partly replace old ones. A study by DIW, the German economic research institute, carried out projections based on 1995 estimates of the demand for media and communication services in Germany (defined as media, consumer electronics, office machines, computer hardware and software, photo-optical equipment, mail and telecom services).[2] Sectors expected to be affected by substitution, such as postal service and photo-optics were included. Taking into account that growth in demand is partly met by increased imports, overall employment in these sectors was expected to grow only 3.5 per cent by the year 2000 (70 000 additional jobs) and 9.5 per cent by 2010 (about 180 000 additional jobs).

While software is the most dynamic industry in terms of employment growth, it is estimated to represent only about 1 per cent of overall employment (see Annex 4.2). It is very difficult to quantify the impact of electronic commerce on job creation in this sector. Among software and service companies involved with the Internet and multimedia applications, most are not very labour-intensive, and estimates of job creation due to the implementation of Internet Web sites or intranet applications are still very modest (see Annex 4.2).

The move towards network-based (particularly Internet) services will reduce employment for physical delivery systems and stand-alone media, such as printed text and CD-ROMs. However, network-based distribution of content is expected to increase demand for technical, creative, managerial/administrative staff and direct marketing positions (OECD, 1998*b*).

New media content industries are creating jobs in the United States as well as in Europe. One report on electronic publishing (European Commission, 1997*d*), estimates than 1 million jobs will be created in electronic publishing in Europe in the next ten years. These job gains will have to be balanced against job declines in the print media industry. Therefore, opportunities in the new media industries may not translate into net sectoral gains. The traditional US publishing industry, which counted 1.5 million employees in 1996, is projected to see its overall employment share drop from 1.26 per cent (1996) to 1.08 per cent (2006). An interesting feature of multimedia jobs is that, at least in the United States, they often emerge at an extremely rapid pace in specific locations. In the New York metro region, the number of new media jobs jumped by 48 per cent to 105 771 in the period early 1996-mid-1997 (*New York Times*, A30, 23 October 1997); the number of new media companies climbed by 16 per cent and revenue rose by 50 per cent. Surveys of this industry in southern California reveal that its workers are predominantly young, white, highly educated, and well-paid (Scott, 1998).

Some online information services are relatively new and are predicted to grow. Others are replacing existing ones (see the example of electronic mail in Chapter 1). Transaction processing services, such as credit and debit card processing, are expected to migrate to the Internet and may require less labour input; on the other hand, they will require new services, such as security and payment services tailored to Internet transactions.

Evidence of noticeable net job creation in online services is lacking or varies, depending on the sources (see Annex 4.2). The extent to which electronic information services will be a source of job creation will depend on the extent to which there will be substitution between off-line and online services. It will vary across countries on the basis of national development trends and will depend on countries' degree of openness.

The Internet industry

Electronic commerce development is strongly connected with Internet development. Employment related to the Internet industry is fairly difficult to calculate. Amano and Blohm (1996), using some *ad hoc* assumptions, estimated that Internet-related employment amounted to 0.6 per cent of the total US work force in 1996.[3]

Since the Internet is a network of networks, delivery of its services is fairly complex and includes many levels of interconnection among suppliers. Actors involved in Internet delivery and services provision have different sizes and belong to different industries.[4] It can be said that Internet service providers (ISPs) are typically not labour-intensive. A survey of all US ISPs by Commercial Internet eXchange estimates that the 215 providers employed about 5 000 workers in 1997.[5]

Travel agencies

Internet auctions of unsold flight seats by airlines are becoming more frequent, and airlines are effectively eliminating travel agents. In 1996, for example, independent travel agents handled 80 per cent of US airline reservations; in 1998, the share is down to 52 per cent, with airlines dealing directly with customers via the Web or telephone (Kehoe, 1998). On the other hand, virtual travel agencies, which combine price advantages with ready access to a server available 24 hours a day, are emerging. These virtual organisations often take advantage of new niche markets and are able to reach a certain type of customer, *e.g.* a clientele able to travel at very short notice (young people, students or freelance professionals). Initially, therefore, such operators can make it possible to enlarge the market and create demand for new services and therefore have an overall positive impact on employment.

One example is Dégriftour in France. First set up in 1991, it offers discounts, two weeks prior to departure, on tickets that tour operators, airlines and hotels have been unable to sell. Since its creation, its turnover has grown by between 20 and 40 per cent a year. Table 4.5 compares Dégriftour employment and turnover with that of its main competitors in France. In 1998, Dégriftour had 150 employees, 40 involved in updating computer files and 110 in dealing with orders. Nouvelles Frontières, which has focused on both the conventional and virtual markets, has the lowest turnover/staff ratio, while Havas Voyages, which has retained a conventional structure, has the highest turnover/staff ratio. This has not prevented Havas from following its competitors into the virtual market, however, so as to explore new niches and increase market shares. The employment size of Dégriftour seems small compared to that of its major competitors but, in fact, 64 per cent of the French firms providing travel agency services in 1995 employed only up to five people (*effectifs salariés*) (INSEE, 1997).

Post offices

The development of electronic transactions is also threatening revenues and thus employment in post offices (see Chapter 1), and new companies that take advantage of the Internet are emerging. E-Stamp Corp., for example, is a start-up firm that plans to sell postage over the Internet. Potential revenues are very high: in 1996, the US Postal Service had revenues of $56 billion, of which 21.5 per cent from stamps and 37.5 per cent from postage meters (*Financial Times*, 17 April 1998). As mentioned above, e-mail messaging is growing fast and replacing traditional mailing activities.

Table 4.5. **Virtual/conventional forms of organisation: some examples of productivity and profitability**

1997	Type of firm	Year set up	Turnover (FF million)	No. of employees	Turnover/staff ratio (FF 1 000/employee per annum)
Dégriftour	Virtual, all transactions via videotex	1991	350	150	2 333
Nouvelles Frontières	Virtual and conventional 219 agencies	Not known	8 796	4 500	1 954
Havas Voyages	Primarily conventional 220 agencies and two telephone sales platforms (2% of turnover)	Not known	15 000	4 000	3 750
Travel agencies	All travel agencies (1995)	–	44 779	28 405	1 576

Source: Alzon, 1998; Rouland, 1998; Havas, 1998; INSEE, 1997.

On the other hand, electronic commerce will have positive spin-offs for transport activities when it entails a physical delivery. The use of the Internet is resulting in increased competition between the Post Office and actors such as DHL, Federal Express and United Parcel Service. The deregulation of the tele-communications sector may well allow post offices to provide telecommunications services. In France, for example, post offices are equipped with sophisticated IT systems for conducting counter operations and, in one of the latest initiatives, a service, Datapost, was introduced for transforming messages submittd in one form (physical or electronic, Minitel or Internet) into another.

The impact of these developments on employment remains unclear. Productivity gains achieved in postal delivery activities appear to have yielded labour savings that have subsequently been invested in new services as they are developed. These new activities, however, are characterised by much higher labour productivity than mail delivery. Labour adjustments in the post office sector, whose share in employment varies across countries (*e.g.* 0.68 per cent in the United States, 0.81 per cent in Canada and 1.41 per cent in France in 1996) are apparently being made gradually as employees retire or are hired and in accordance with internal training programmes. Figure 4.1 shows that, in the United States, the post office sector's employment share has been declining since 1986; nevertheless, the increase in electronic delivery is likely to exacerbate these trends and require more radical and less gradual adjustments.

Retail

According to a 1997 survey, 52 per cent of European retailers think that electronic customers will cease using traditional outlets, while 35 per cent think that electronic customers will correspond to new demand created by the availability of new shopping channels (Cap Gemini, 1997). The first industry expected to be affected by electronic commerce is traditional retailing. While electronic commerce may lead to expanded employment in the near term, as retailers maintain a presence in both physical and cyber channels, disintermediation and the changes in the value-added chain, discussed in previous chapters, are expected to have a negative impact on employment in this sector.

At 21.6 million and almost 18 per cent of the total work force in 1996, the US retail sector is fairly big in terms of employment and has been increasing over time (Figure 4.2). However, in terms of share in total employment, and taking into account the break in the series, it is forecast by the US Bureau of Labor Statistics to follow a downward trend. Chapter 2 formulates some scenarios on the disintermediation of the US wholesale and retail sectors. Under those assumptions, which were characterised as being opti-mistic, US retail activities may decline by 25 per cent. The extent to which these "guesstimates" may translate into retail sector job losses should be investigated. In particular, the restructuring and reorgan-isation of retail activities, as well as differences in labour requirements implicit in the production function of online and off-line retailers, should be researched. Direct job losses should then be weighed against potential indirect job gains due to efficiency gains and increased demand at the economy level (discussed below).

Figure 4.1.   **Employment trends in the US Post Office**[1]

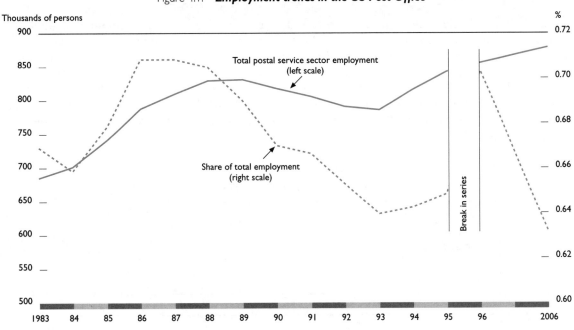

1.   1983-95: national industry-occupation employment matrix 1983-95 time series. 1996-2006: national industry-occupation employment matrix for
     1996-2006.
Source: OECD, based on data from the US Bureau of Labor Statistics.

Figure 4.2.   **US retail trade employment, 1983-2006**[1]

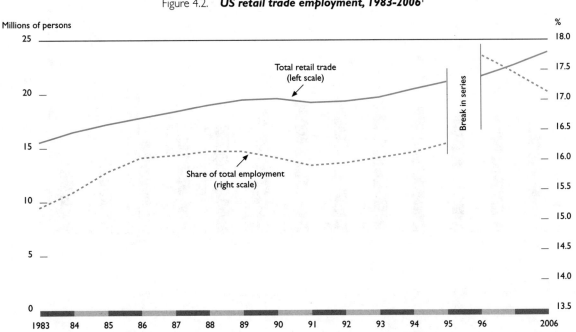

1.   1983-95: national industry-occupation employment matrix 1983-95 time series. 1996-2006: national industry-occupation employment matrix for
     1996-2006.
Source: OECD, based on data from the US Bureau of Labor Statistics.

Finance and banking

Finance is also likely to be significantly affected by electronic commerce. Preliminary results from the Canadian Survey of Innovation (1996) reveal that 82 per cent (representing 99 per cent of the total sample revenues) of the banks (chartered banks, other banking intermediaries, and trust companies) are using the Internet, and that 19 per cent (representing 86 per cent of the total sample revenues) use it to sell goods and services. Shifting from retail to Internet banking has entailed job losses. In moving banking out of branches and onto networks, Finland, a leader in the use of electronic payments (see Table 4.6), has seen a 3.5 per cent annual decline in employment, resulting in a cut of more than a third of the jobs between 1984 and 1996 (Figure 4.3).

Table 4.6. **Indicators of network banking: Finland and EU, 1994**

Indicator	Finland	European Union average
Cash in circulation as % of GDP	2.0	5.5
ATM withdrawals as a % of GDP	6.0	1.5
ATMs per million inhabitants	560	370
Point-of-sale terminals per capita	38	9
% bills paid by ATM	33	n.a.

Source: Kontinen, J. (1998), "Network Banking in Finland", presentation at the OECD, 18-19 February.

Figure 4.3. *Finnish bank employment and transactions, 1984-96*

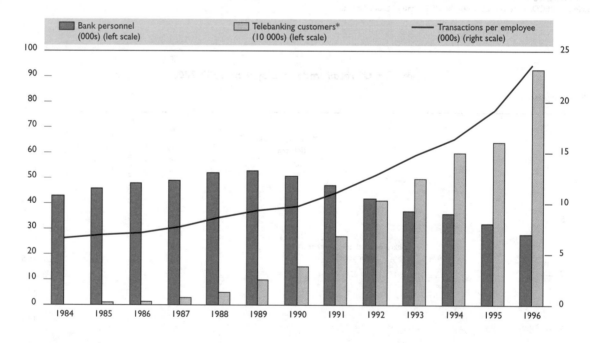

* Includes phone, PC and Internet.
Source: Finnish Bankers' Association, May 1997. Presented at the OECD by J. Kontinen, Merita Bank, 18-19 February 1998.

On the other hand, reorienting activities towards electronic commerce does not always come at the expense of jobs. Charles Schwab & Co. (see Chapter 1) seems to have managed the substantial shift to online transactions not by dismissing brokers (it currently has 5 000 registered brokers) but by redefining brokers' functions (Girishankar, 1998*b*).

It is especially difficult to single out the impact of electronic commerce on banking, a very IT-intensive sector which has undergone a great deal of deregulation and rationalisation. For the banking sector, US data show that employment has been declining since the beginning of the 1990s and its share in total employment since 1986 (Figure 4.4).

Figure 4.4. **US banking sector employment, 1983-2006**[1]

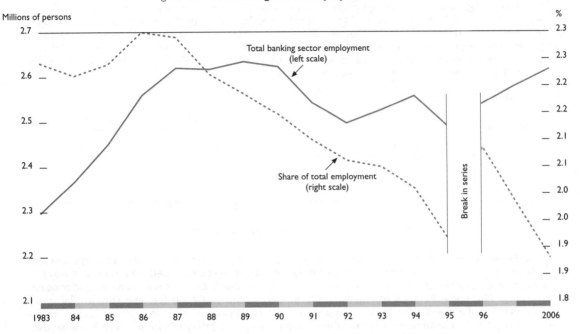

1. 1983-95: national industry-occupation employment matrix 1983-95 time series. 1996-2006: national industry-occupation employment matrix for 1996-2006.
Source: OECD, based on data from the US Bureau of Labor Statistics.

Substitution effects and employment impact: examples from past experience

In order to understand what substitution mechanisms come into play when shifting from off-line to online provision of products and services, and to see whether any employment impacts can be detected and measured, it may be useful to look at past experience in adopting new technologies and delivery channels. For banking, different stories can be told. The example of the Canadian Imperial Bank of Commerce (Box 4.1) shows that while the introduction of automated banking machines (ABM) destroyed CIBC jobs over the years, the shift to new delivery channels, such as telephone banking, has in fact created jobs.

France's Minitel is an interesting case. It was the first large-scale application of electronic commerce and reached a 20 per cent penetration rate (Box 4.2). In order to learn some lessons from this experience, a study was conducted to examine the employment impacts, if any. The study concludes that there were no major impacts on employment as a result of the introduction of the Minitel. Nevertheless, as the report underlines, the same conclusion cannot simply be applied to electronic commerce over the Internet. Unlike the Minitel, the Internet has developed on international markets and has benefited from market deregulation in a favourable economic context.

Box 4.1. Job losses and gains at CIBC (Canada)

The Canadian Imperial Bank of Commerce, Canada's second largest bank, invested heavily in information technologies between 1988 and 1995 (86 per cent increase in IT investment, corresponding to 80 per cent of total investment over the period). Between 1987 and 1996, the number of ABMs grew nearly 310 per cent, with most of the increase (225 per cent) occurring between 1987 and 1991. The number of branches started falling in 1991 and fell by 9 per cent between 1991 and 1996. Both the increasing number of ABMs and the decreasing number of branches played a role in the changes in employment at CIBC (–8 per cent between 1992 and 1995, as opposed to –4 per cent for the banking industry as a whole over the same period). A turnaround was achieved at CIBC in 1996. It was primarily attributable to the creation of nearly 1 000 jobs because of the opening of two new telephone banking centres. The shift to the new delivery channel has meant, however, that occupations such as bank teller are in decline, while customer service representatives are increasing in number and importance.

Source: Conference Board of Canada, 1997.

Box 4.2. Learning from the Minitel experience?

The French videotex industry can be considered an instructive case study of the development and organisation of electronic commerce. The videotex system, which was developed for the mass market as early as the beginning of the 1980s, was for many years the main vehicle for electronic commerce in consumer goods. By 1987, some 3 million terminals had been distributed and 7 000 services were available. By 1994, the number of terminals distributed had passed the 6 million mark (available in 20 per cent of households), and traffic volume amounted to 110 million hours a year, generating FF6 billion of revenue for data traffic alone. In 1994, 1.2 million households used the Minitel to buy a product, whereas in the same year, only 800 000 US households used the Internet to carry out at least one commercial transaction.

None of the existing studies on the Minitel really addresses the issue of net job creation or loss due to its introduction. On the basis of personal opinions collected through interviews, there seems to be agreement that the number of jobs created and lost is more or less evenly balanced. In creating new value added and services, and in developing new strategies, the impact of the electronic commerce generated by Minitel on industry and competition is comparable to that of the Internet. However, unlike the Internet, the Minitel system has not expanded to international level and therefore has not generated one of the most potentially important wealth-creating aspects of the Internet, namely the creation of new markets at international level through the aggregation of dispersed demand. Its growth dynamic therefore cannot be compared with that of the Internet. Moreover, conditions when the Minitel system was launched were not what they are today: the telecommunications market was a monopoly, system convergence and competition between systems were not yet perceived as important, and the economic context was not particularly favourable.

Summary of estimates made or used in reports on videotex services and employment in France

Thousands

Sources	1987	1989	1993	1997
Vidéotex Magazine No. 44 (1990)		+12-13		
Breton (1996)			+15-20	
Ladoux (1998)			+15	
France Télécom (1997)	+40		+15	
Tregouët (1997)				+15

Economy-wide employment impacts of e-commerce-related industries: a review of selected studies

The previous section looked at direct job creation and displacement in sectors related to electronic commerce. This section reviews the literature on the economy-wide impact of the growth of e-commerce-related industries on employment. Most of these studies are based on macroeconomic modelling simulations of different scenarios or on static input-output modelling. They rely on different and often strong assumptions, but, by taking a representative sample in terms of sectors analysed and methodology used, some conclusions can be drawn on the potential aggregate effects of electronic commerce on employment.

Economy-wide impacts of e-commerce

Databank Consulting (1998) has attempted to estimate directly the employment impact of electronic commerce in four European countries. The approach and methodology are interesting (see Annex 4.3), although they are based on a great number of *ad hoc* assumptions, ranging from estimates of electronic transactions and different sectoral business models for electronic transactions *vis-à-vis* traditional transactions, to hypotheses underlying the use of input-output modelling. Overall, the employment effects, calculated on the basis of 1997 electronic revenue estimates, are very small. The four European countries (in which $ 4.53 billion or 60 per cent of European electronic transactions are assumed to take place) see a total gain of 173 000 jobs, of which almost 60 per cent are due to indirect effects. When compared to current employment levels, this very small number is not surprising, given the current size of electronic revenues.

This type of exercise is certainly useful for trying to understand the channels through which electronic transactions affect the economy. More work should be done, however, to understand the source of the different relative impacts across countries. To reduce the size of the cumulative error due to different assumptions and approximations made in the exercise, it would be best to use the wider range of estimates of US electronic transactions. Another convenient feature of US data is that input-output matrices are linked to employment and occupational matrices (hence, the employment impact could be translated into changes in the demand for skills). Finally, as electronic markets are more mature in the United States, the US example could provide a benchmark.

Forecasts of telecommunication, media and Internet-driven employment growth

Cohen (1997) develops three growth scenarios for the US communications and media industry to the years 2000 and 2005. One is a baseline telephony-oriented scenario while the other two are Internet/intranet based scenarios (see Annex 4.4 for the methodology and results). In the Internet/intranet scenarios, the multipliers (hence the impact on employment) are higher than those applied for wired services, owing to the investment in servers, server software, and content needed for the Internet and intranets. Basically, in 2005, the Internet is expected to contribute 50 per cent of jobs created in the US telecommunication sector. Additional jobs created in the Internet/intranet scenarios do not arise from Web usage *per se* but come almost exclusively from the production of Web-related hardware-software content.

This evidence suggests that services diffused via the Internet and intranets generate higher direct and indirect employment growth than traditional telecommunications services. If so, studies on the employment impacts of liberalisation in the telecommunication markets can be used to establish the minimum level of employment gains attributable to Internet and intranet growth. The results of the BIPE-IFO-Lentic study on the employment impact of telecommunication liberalisation in Europe (see Annex 4.4) indicate that, in the best-case scenario of rapid liberalisation and technology diffusion, more than 1.3 million jobs would be created in Europe by the year 2005 (Cohen's baseline scenario for the United States, and for the same year, gives 3 million). Like other macro-modelling exercises such as those that examine the impact of regulatory reform, this study suggests that net job creation usually comes from indirect and secondary effects.

An interesting question is whether the conditions for exploiting the potential of this Internet multiplier are the same across countries, especially given differences in the production of Web-related hardware and software content, which seems to be driving employment gains due to the Internet multiplier. The diffusion of the Internet and intranets in Europe is certainly slower than in the United States. US firms also dominate the development of Web-related hardware and software products. According to the European Commission's Telecommunication Infrastructures Study (1997a), between July 1995 and June 1996, $890 million of US venture capital was invested in Web-related start-ups, whereas European venture capital for such investment was between $10 million and $20 million.

Studies of the impact of Internet revenue streams might give a different result depending on whether telecommunication and backbone operators or simple ISPs are being considered. In Europe, Internet revenues still account for a very small part of the income of the largest telecommunication operators at national and global level (ranging from 5 to 7 per cent of the overall revenues per operator), but they are growing fast with respect to other more traditional sources, such as PSTN (packet switched telephone network) telephony. However, for European operations, the Internet is not yet a profitable activity (European Commission, 1997a).

ICT *diffusion and its impact on jobs*

Electronic commerce contributes to the spread of information and communication technologies (ICTs) which are playing a key role in the transformation of OECD economies. This structural transformation has a number of dimensions linked to employment. One is the shift of economic activities from manufacturing to services and the associated reallocation of jobs. A second is the increased investment in ICTs, with an important impact on productivity and growth (and thus indirectly on employment). A third is the falling cost of telecommunications and the increased availability of ICTs, which has contributed significantly to increased international competition and trade, which in turn constitute another channel affecting the labour market.

The overall impact of ICTs on employment is the result of complex interactions which have been reviewed in detail in a number of OECD studies (OECD, 1996a; 1996b). Much recent research has used firm-level data to investigate the relationship between technology and employment in a number of OECD countries. These studies broadly find a positive relationship between technology adoption and employment at firm level. The impact of technology on employment at industry level, instead, is dependent on the nature of the jobs created, the extent to which they replace other jobs, and the effect on rival firms in that industry as well as in other industries or countries. In turn, sectoral impacts say little about aggregate employment or unemployment. The net outcome for employment depends on the nature of technological advance, the degree of substitution between inputs, the degree of labour market flexibility and mechanisms for upgrading labour skills, and the role of institutions. The evidence on the economy-wide impacts of ICTs on employment is mixed.

Electronic commerce and the skills mix

Jobs are both created and destroyed by technology, trade, and organisational change. These processes also underlie changes in the skill composition of employment and in the importance of different occupational categories to job growth, (OECD 1996a). Beyond the net employment gains or losses brought about by these factors, which occur independently of electronic commerce but are certainly stimulated by its rapid development, it is apparent that workers with different skill levels will be affected differently.

Is electronic commerce generating demand for skills which cannot be met at the rate necessary for its development? Electronic commerce is certainly driving demand for IT professionals but it also requires IT expertise to be coupled with strong business application skills, thereby generating demand for a flexible, multi-skilled work force. Some examples of occupations and underlying skills in the companies performing electronic commerce are provided. Apart from contingent needs for staff implementing Internet/intranet maintenance and development to support electronic commerce transactions and applications, there is a more structural and long-term shift in the skills required to perform economic activities on line. This section also examines those occupations that are most likely to be affected by electronic commerce, such as computer engineers, information-related occupations and commerce-related occupations.

Internet and e-commerce growth are driving demand for IT professionals

As Internet adoption moves to a "transaction" model, there is a growing need for increased integration of Internet front-end applications with enterprise operations, applications and back-end databases. The lack of staff to support ongoing Internet/intranet maintenance and development, coupled with integration problems and cost and time overruns, drives demand for outside services providers to help plan and implement solutions. Activities in demand include security design and firewall implementation, Web page design and creation, and Internet/intranet application development (EITO, 1998).

With the spread of electronic commerce, and the consequent re-engineering of business processes and changes in competitive paradigms (see Chapter 3), software will increasingly be used to create business value. Electronic commerce will thus sustain a high demand for IT personnel. This is expected to exacerbate what has been called a "critical shortage" of IT workers. Such a shortage, which has received great attention in the United States, is not a trend peculiar to that country. Annex 4.5 discusses the issue and presents some estimates of IT skills needs across countries.

Matching network programming activities with business application skills

Many of the IT skill requirements needed for Internet support can be met by low-paid IT workers who can deal with the organisational services needed for basic Web page programming. However, wide area networks (WANs), competitive Web sites, and complex network applications require much more skill than a platform-specific IT job. Box 4.3 provides some examples of employment and skill needs in European innovative firms that provide network applications and consultancy for electronic commerce.

To be effective, electronic commerce requires new generic services as well as competitive operational services. The skills required for electronic commerce are rare and in high demand, as network programming abilities need to be coupled with strong business applications skills (http://www.techworkforce.org/skill.htm). In practice, e-commerce requires people with eclectic skills. Box 4.4 provides a description of some new e-commerce jobs.

In companies that organise and aggregate Internet content, such as those that offer search engines (Excite, Lycos, Yahoo!, Infoseek), the work force seems either to perform research and development activities related to technical networking issues or to be in the marketing and sales area (from 43 to 52 per cent, see Table 4.7). Online and information services providers like America Online and Individual, with the same core business activity (computer and data processing), have a rather different work force composition. America Online employs the bulk of its workers in operations and support activities (73 per cent) while Individual has a more balanced distribution of activities: marketing and sales (36 per cent), research and development (22 per cent), and editorial activities (33 per cent). In the business-to-consumer segment of e-commerce, companies search for managerial, marketing and selling and technical skills, while software and hardware development and maintenance is often contracted out. An example is Auto-By-Tel which provides Internet-based marketing services for new and used vehicle purchase and related consumer services. The company's employment base increased rapidly from 17 employees in December 1995 to 73 in December 1996, plus an additional 19 contractors for software and hardware development. In terms of its employee distribution, 56 per cent are in marketing and sales, while the rest are equally divided among technical, managerial and administrative occupations.

Structural shifts and the need for skills in the e-economy

Electronic commerce might accelerate the existing upskilling trend in the OECD economies by requiring high-skilled computer scientists to replace low-skilled information clerks, cashiers or market salespersons. It would be worth exploring whether such low-skilled workers can be effectively retrained or would be able to find occupations in other growth sectors, such as personal services. This section examines skill trends for sectors and occupations affected by electronic commerce. It relies mainly on US and European data.

Box 4.3.   Skill needs in Internet-/intranet-related European companies

Ex-Novo is a small Italian graphic advertising and communication company (eight employees) which started a new Internet-related activity (multimedia and Internet services) and a more consultancy-oriented activity (intranets and virtual marketing) in 1996. The new Internet activity required three additional full-time external consultants; the consultancy activity is carried out by a virtual company that works on a project basis with temporary staff. In shifting to these activities, Ex-Novo has had to adapt to an environment where the rate of technical change and the related learning requirements for all personnel are much higher. Sales staff and creative designers must be constantly updated on the potential constraints of multimedia tools. The main challenge for the company seems to be the qualifications/skills of staff for the higher-level jobs, rather than finding people for operational jobs.

Informa is an Italian start-up company (established at the end of 1995) which develops Intranet solutions. This is both a consultancy activity and an activity of developing *ad hoc* software tools for SMEs. It also provides networking and "Internetworking" solutions (pure technological consultancy). It also builds Web sites on the Internet. This requires developing solutions for complex databases, research engines, means of carrying out transactions, and advertising. Apart from the managing director who has a commercial and administrative role, 4.5 persons work on Intranet issues, 1.5 on networking, 1.5-2 on WebFrame package development, and 2.5 (including the general manager) perform pure consultancy activity. Almost all Informa employees are engineers, with a background in telecommunications and networking. As this professional profile is not very common in Italy, the company relies on internal training.

Informconsult is a German consulting company that provides intranet solutions. Implementation of an intranet may require anything from a minimum of two to three man-months (software installed by the customer, 200 people connected, building an internal e-mail system, technological know-how transfer) to two man-years (many thousands of people connected in many locations, integration of the customer's network with its subsidiaries or providers, design of work flow and workgroup software). Lack of qualified employees is cited as the major problem for the company's development, as demand for information technology graduates appears to exceed supply in the Cologne area.

Loud-n-clear is a virtual company (no physical office) started as a joint venture by a group of three companies (British and Swedish). It provides Internet services, as well as consultancy and support for the software products developed by one of the group companies. The company started in 1995 with three members and reached eleven in 1997. A number of external consultants work on specific tasks (mostly graphics and research). Employees have professional profiles in: programming/system architecture/communications (three people with an average of ten years' experience); database/data analysis/high-level systems (two people specialised in databases and data description); marketing and market exploitation (one person with more than 20 years' experience); sales (two people with some technical skills); translation (from Swedish to English), copyrighting and proof-reading (one person, with some limited technical experience); two trainees familiar with Web site development. Once it has a core of technical skills, the company expects to recruit in the field of marketing. It will employ more people on a part-time/specific project basis and will only recruit teleworkers.

Source: Databank Consulting, 1997.

Table 4.7.   **The work force in e-commerce-related companies: content aggregation**

Company	Full-time employees	Sales and marketing	Research and development	Administration and finance	Other
Excite	434	43%	35%	15%	7% (operations and support)
Infoseek Corp.	171	44%	26%	29%	
Lycos	137	46%	39%	15%	Contractors (operations and support)
Yahoo!	386	52%	19%	8%	21% ("surfers")

1.   1997 or latest available year.
Source: OECD, based on data from the US Securities and Exchange Commission.

Box 4.4.   Ten new e-commerce jobs

Entrepreneurial consultant: *Pay*: Up to $250 000 a year. *Background*: Master of Business Administration or similar, extensive business management experience, consulting firm experience.

Task: To analyse the overall business case for a project and turn around struggling enterprises. Part merchant banker, part visionary, part technocrat – you force your clients to rethink their place in the world and then re-engineer their business.

Application developer: *Pay*: Up to $150 000 a year. *Background*: Rocket scientist, astrophysicist, pure science researcher, software engineer, Andersen consulting experience, project director, postgraduate degree.

Task: Create new software programmes or online business tools. New businesses require people to create (develop) the structures (applications) to help them succeed. This may be a new Web site selling technique or a way to share company information among employees.

Fulfilment specialist: *Pay*: $60 000-$100 000 a year. *Background*: Logistics and transportation/trucking, military procurement, police services, entrepreneurs.

Task: To get the product to the customer.

Consumer behaviour consultant: *Pay*: $100 000-plus a year. *Background*: Psychologist, writer, journalist, layout designer, magazine editor.

Task: Analyse why people buy things. The AC Nielsens of e-commerce. With so many people using the Web in so many different ways, it is necessary to have adaptive, meaningful measures of success. Someone who can evaluate consumer behaviour can help an enterprise better target its audience.

Broker: *Pay*: $200 000-$2 million a year. *Background*: Merchant banker, ex-employment agency professional, negotiator (*e.g.* police or counsellor), sales.

Task: Find new business opportunities and staff – a recruiter. As an employment broker you can expect to get 20 per cent of the talent's first-year salary in commission. In return, you will find the people from the other nine categories listed here, many of whom will not have direct IT training, but complementary skills that can translate to e-commerce.

Network security specialist: *Pay*: $100 000 a year. *Background*: Intelligence operative ("spooks" or spies), ex-signals directorate officer, "white" hacker, traditional IT security network manager.

Task: Make sure computer systems are safe from prying eyes.

E-commerce business analyst: *Pay*: $60 000-$100 000 a year. *Background*: accountant, auditor, stockbroker, business manager;

Task: A bean counter, a number cruncher.

Internet architect: *Pay*: $100 000 a year. *Background*: Webmaster "with muscle", designer, relational database construction.

Task: Put it on the Web. The people who design the site and conceive concepts. A Webmaster controls the team that puts the pages on line, like an editor for a newspaper or magazine.

Product manager: *Pay*: $60 000 a year. *Background*: Events management, SAP project manager, traditional IT project manager, producer for TV, magazine or radio.

Task: Make sure it stays on the Web. The environment is constantly evolving and e-commerce products need to be kept on track. The day-to-day programming of the Web needs a timekeeper.

Core programmers: *Pay*: $50 000 a year. *Background*: Programming degree and/or extensive low-level skills in SQL, Java, Corba and network operating systems, especially Windows NT and Unix. Communications experience in TCP/IP an advantage.

Task: Take care of day-to-day computer programming tasks.

Source: Cochrane and McIntosh, 1998.

Figure 4.5 breaks down EU white-collar workers into high-skilled and low-skilled on the basis of the ISCO-88 occupational classification. Hardware and computer equipment, financial, and wholesale and retail are blue-collar, white-collar high-skill, and white-collar low-skill "intensive", respectively. This overall sectoral "skill intensity" hides the heterogeneity within sectors affected by electronic commerce. In the financial and wholesale and retail sectors, industries have different mixes within the white-collar category. In the hardware and computer equipment sector, high- and low-skill-intensive industries coexist. Hence, the impact of electronic commerce will not necessarily fall on any one segment or skill level.

Figure 4.5. *Skill shares within selected sectors, EU-10, 1996*

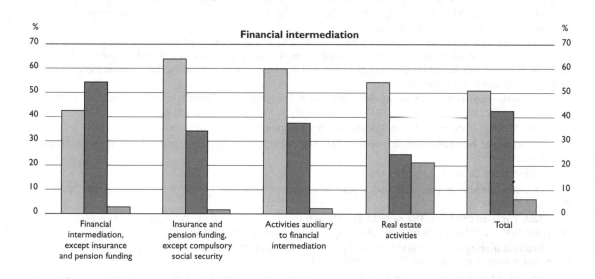

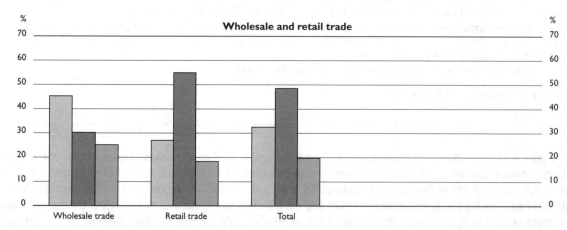

Source: OECD, based on data from the Eurostat Labour Survey.

Box 4.5. **Selected occupations affected by electronic commerce**

ICT-related occupations

Computing professionals (ISCO-88 213): conduct research, plan, develop and improve computer-based information systems, software and related concepts, develop principles and operational methods as well as maintain data dictionary and management systems of databases to ensure integrity and security of data.

Physical and engineering science technicians (ISCO-88 311): perform technical tasks related to the research and the practical application of concepts, principles and operational methods particular to physical sciences including such areas as engineering, technical drawing or economic efficiency of production processes.

Computer associate professionals (ISCO-88 312): provide assistance to users of microcomputers and standard software packages, control and operate computers and peripheral equipment and carry out limited programming tasks connected with the installation and maintenance of computer hardware and software.

Optical and electronic equipment operators (ISCO-88 313): take photographs, control motion picture and video cameras and other equipment to record and edit images and sound, control broadcasting and telecommunication equipment and telecommunications systems, as well as technical equipment used for medical diagnosis or treatment.

Information-related occupations

Office clerks (ISCO-88 411-4 + 419): record, organise, store and retrieve information related to the work in question and compute financial, statistical and other numerical data. The group includes secretaries and keyboard-operating clerks, accounting, bookkeeping, statistical and finance clerks, material-recording and transport clerks, library, mail and related clerks.

Customer services clerks (ISCO-88 421 + 422): deal directly with clients in connection with money handling operations, travel arrangements, requests for information, appointments and by operating telephone switchboards. The group includes cashiers, tellers and related clerks, client information clerks (*e.g.* travel agencies, receptionists, telephone switchboard operators).

Commerce-related occupations (ISCO-88 522)

Shop salespersons and demonstrators: sell goods in wholesale or retail establishments and demonstrate and explain the functions and qualities of these goods.

Stall and market salespersons: sell various goods (*e.g.* newspapers, periodicals) in open spaces or sell food-stuff in markets.

Owing to sectoral heterogeneity, it seems more useful to track those occupational categories that are more likely to be affected by electronic commerce: ICT-related occupations, information-related occupations, and commerce-related occupations. An *ad hoc* non-exhaustive classification for these three groups has been constructed (see Box 4.5), based on the ISCO-88 classification, and Table 4.8 provides a list of the occupational categories chosen for the EU and US comparisons.

Figure 4.6 provides a snapshot of the three broad trends in e-commerce occupational categories in the United States and the European Union. ICT occupations are the smallest category, with 2.4 per cent in the former and 3.8 per cent in the latter in 1995. In the same year, information workers represented 12.9 per cent in the United States and 16.1 per cent in the European Union. Although the EU and US classifications are not strictly comparable, Figure 4.6 shows that ICT occupations are growing everywhere and that the number of information- and commerce-related workers were declining in the European Union but rising in the United States in that time span. The underlying data also show wide differences in these occupational trends within Europe. Even if the role of electronic commerce cannot be separated from that of other structural or cyclical factors, electronic commerce will exhibit country-specific impacts that should be investigated case by case.

The positive growth rates in US e-commerce occupations (Figure 4.6) are confirmed by a general long-run positive trend (Figure 4.7). The growth in ICT occupations, also stressed in a US Department of Commerce report (Margherio *et al.*, 1998), is less spectacular in relative terms. Figure 4.8, which shows ICT-related occupations as a share of the overall US work force, makes it clear that the increase begins to be

Table 4.8. **Occupational categories used in the EU-US comparisons**

Definitions
ICT-related occupations include the following categories:

For EU countries (ISCO 88):	**For the United States (US Standard Occupational Classification):**
ICT-related occupations	**ICT-related occupations**
213 Computing professionals	22126 Electrical and electronics engineers
311 Physical and engineering science technicians	25197 Computer engineers, scientists, and systems analysts
312 Computer associate professionals	35101 Engineering technicians
313 Optical and electronic equipment operators	34028 Broadcast technicians
	25109 Computer programmers
	25111 Programmers, numerical, tool, and process control
	57100 Communications equipment operators
	56100 Computer operators and peripheral equipment operators
Information-related workers	**Information-related workers**
411 Secretaries and keyboard-operating clerks	55700 Information clerks
412 Numerical clerks	59900 Other clerical and administrative support work
413 Material-recording and transport clerks	57323 Mail clerks and messengers
414 Library, mail and related clerks	53200 Records-processing occupations
419 Other office clerks	This category includes:
421 Cashiers, tellers and related clerks	Brokerage clerks
341 Finance and sales associate professionals	Correspondence clerks
342 Business services agents and trade brokers	File clerks
343 Administrative associate professionals	Financial records processing occupations
Commerce-related occupations	**Commerce-related occupations**
522 Shop, stall and market salespersons and demonstrators	40 000 Marketing and sales occupations

Figure 4.6. *Average annual growth rates in selected occupations, EU-10 and United States, 1993-97*

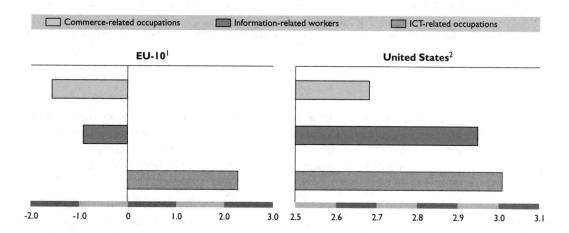

1. Belgium, Denmark, France, Greece, Italy, Luxembourg, Netherlands, Portugal, Spain and United Kingdom.
2. 1993-95 only for United States, due to break in series in 1996.
Source: OECD, based on data from Eurostat and the US Bureau of Labor Statistics.

noticeable in 1995. The OECD selection of ICT-related occupations is based on the US occupations listed in Table 4.8, while the US selection is based on the IT-related occupations used by the Department of Commerce (Margherio *et al.*, 1998).

A closer look at US ICT occupations over time reveals that what is really growing within the ICT category is "computer engineers, scientists and system analysts" (Figure 4.9). This category is expected to be in greater demand as electronic commerce develops.

Figure 4.7. **Share of e-commerce-related occupations within the US economy, 1983-95**[1]

As a percentage of total US employment

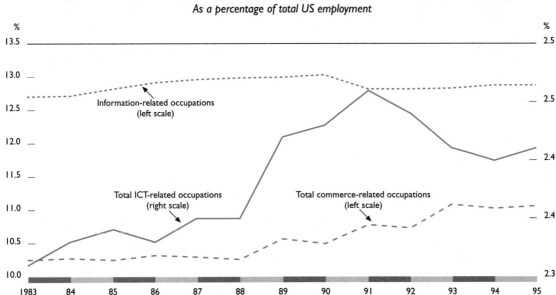

1.   See Table 4.8 for the definition of occupational categories.
Source: OECD, based on data from the US Bureau of Labor Statistics.

Figure 4.8. **Share of ICT-related occupations in the United States and the OECD, 1983-2006**

As a percentage of total employment

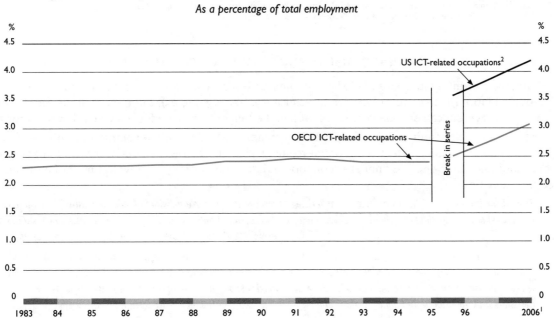

1.   2006 forecast.
2.   Data only available for 1996.
Source: OECD, based on data from the US Bureau of Labor Statistics.

Figure 4.9. **Share of ICT-related occupations within the US economy, 1983-2006**
As a percentage of total US employment

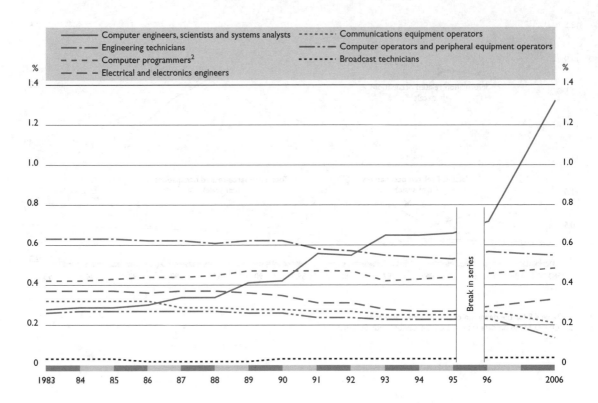

1. 1983-95: national industry-occupation employment matrix 1983-95 time series. 1996-2006: national industry-occupation employment matrices for 1996-2006.
2. The category "Computer programmers" (25109) includes the category "Programmers, numerical, tool and process control" (25111).
Source: OECD, based on data from the US Bureau of Labor Statistics.

CONCLUDING REMARKS AND FUTURE RESEARCH AGENDA

Given the current relative size of electronic commerce with respect to other factors that may contribute to overall labour market turbulence (*e.g.* technology, trade, policies), the impact of electronic commerce on employment can only be very small, but, in the longer term, its effect may be felt more strongly.

The direct employment impact of electronic commerce will depend on complementarity, substitution and market-size effects. Electronic commerce may also create new markets or extend market reach beyond traditional borders. The final effect on jobs will depend crucially on development of demand for electronic activities.

- *The labour intensity and the work force characteristics of electronic commerce activities should be analysed on the basis of micro-level data. A special focus should be placed on firms that carry out online and off-line activities simultaneously in order to determine in which cases electronic commerce offers "intermodality" and "complementarity" in business processes.*

- *Research is also needed to identify activities that have replaced existing ones, analyse their revenue growth compared with that of the sector as a whole, and identify those whose emergence has led to a readjustment of market shares and those whose effect has been to enlarge the market. Given the crucial role played by demand, demand trends for these new activities should be monitored and policy makers should be made aware of the factors underlying country-specific differences.*

Direct job creation associated with electronic commerce is still fairly small and mainly driven by employment growth in the software sector. Evidence of substantial direct job displacement by e-commerce is lacking at this stage but it is most likely to occur in the retail, post office and financial sectors. In particular, electronic commerce is likely to cause a radical transformation of the distribution sector, whose share in total employment varies in the OECD countries from a minimum of 10.8 per cent in Denmark to 22 per cent in Korea.

- *Case studies are needed to better understand impacts on sectoral employment. In particular, as the employment potential of electronic commerce is not the same across countries, the differences among countries in the production of Web-related hardware and software content, which seems to be driving employment gains from electronic commerce, should be explored. Also, the impact on employment in the distribution sector, which will depend on differences in the sector regulatory and organisational structure across countries, should be investigated.*

Indirect/long-term employment effects driven by demand and productivity growth are likely to offset shorter-term/job destroying effects, depending on the country and the assumptions made about the size and structure of electronic transactions.

- *Research on country-specific differences in the size and growth potential of electronic transactions, as well as on countries' differences in online organisational models, is essential in order to evaluate the long-term impact on employment.*

Electronic commerce is driving demand for IT professionals but it also requires IT expertise coupled with strong business applications skills. Therefore, it generates demand for a flexible, multi-skilled work force. Apart from contingent skill needs to support electronic commerce transactions and applications, there will be a more structural and long-term shift in the skills required to perform economic activities online. E-commerce is likely to accelerate existing upskilling trends in the OECD work force.

- *Work to identify specific skill needs for e-commerce and opportunities for worker requalification is needed. Policies to cope with skill mismatches will have to be reinforced as the volume of electronic transactions increases.*

Annex 4.1

E-COMMERCE-RELATED EMPLOYMENT IN US FIRMS

Morgan Stanley reports a list of public Internet-related companies that comprises those providing infrastructure (among which are companies providing data networking and telecommunication equipment, Internet service providers, and Internet security equipment and software providers), those providing software and services (application software companies, enterprise and related software companies and commerce enablers), and those companies providing content, aggregation and commerce (Morgan Stanley Dean Witter, 1997). This taxonomy is very useful for looking at Internet-related companies that are strongly influenced by electronic commerce developments. While the third category represents firms that conduct electronic commerce (providing online services, content, selling goods and services), employment opportunities also need to be assessed with respect to industries that enable electronic commerce. The data were collected for a sample of the firms given in the Morgan Stanley list.

Annex Tables 4.1, 4.2, and 4.3 show selected Internet-related firms' market capitalisation and number of full-time employees in 1997 or latest year. Market capitalisation bears the same relation to GDP contribution as an individual firm's return on sales does to its return on equity market value (Amano and Blohm, 1997). This variable is supposed to give a real-time measure of the economic impact of those firms. The share of Internet-related employment is obtained by using Amano and Blohm's estimates of the share of firms' Internet-related activities. Where these estimates were not available, it is assumed that employment is entirely related to Internet/electronic commerce activities.

Annex Table 4.1. **Selected US Internet-related firms' market capitalisation and number of full-time employees**

Infrastructure providers, 1997[1]

Company	Industry	US SIC	Market capitalisation (1997) (US$ million)	Internet-related market capitalisation (%)	Full-time employees	Internet-related employment
Data networking/telecommunication equipment						
Ascend	Computer communications equipment	3 576	6 768	50	1 644	822
Cisco	Computer communications equipment	3 576	50 735	25	3 500	875
3Com	Computer communications equipment	3 576	8 880	20	7 109	1 422
Internet service providers						
PSINet	Computer programming, data processing, etc.	7 370	360	100	775	775
Earthlink	Prepackaged software	7 372	190	*	785	785
IDT	Computer-integrated systems design	7 373	396	*	360	360
WorldCom	Telecommunications	4 813	35 261	30	20 300	6 090
Concentric Network	Telecommunications	4 813	182	100	387	387
Internet security equipment and software						
Cylink	Computer peripheral equipment, n.e.c.	3 577	405	*	432	432
Security Dynamics	Computer peripheral equipment, n.e.c.	3 577	1 332	*	610	610
Total infrastructure						**12 558**

* Estimates are not available. It is assumed that 100% of market capitalisation is related to the Internet.
1. Or latest available year.
Source: OECD estimates, based on data from the US Securities and Exchange Commission.

Annex Table 4.2. **Selected US Internet-related firms' market capitalisation and number of full-time employees**

Software and services providers, 1997[1]

Company	Industry	US SIC	Market capitalisation (1997) (US$ million)	Internet-related market capitalisation %	Full-time employees[2]	Internet-related employment
Application software						
Accent Software	Prepackaged software	7 372	36	35	88	31
FTP Software	Prepackaged software	7 372	136	50	350	175
Microsoft	Prepackaged software	7 372	179 145	25	22 232	5 558
NetManage	Prepackaged software	7 372	172	50	440	220
Netscape	Prepackaged software	7 372	3 813	100	2 310	2 310
Spyglass	Prepackaged software	7 372	120	100	162	162
Enterprise and related software						
Business Objects	Prepackaged software	7 372	153	*	757	757
Versant Object Tech. Corp.	Prepackaged software	7 372	238	*	196	196
Verity	Computer processing and data preparation	7 374	55	50	311	156
Commerce enablers						
Broadvision	Prepackaged software	7 372	140	*	188	188
Cybercash	Computer integrated systems design	7 373	220	100	227	227
Edify	Prepackaged software	7 372	270	*	349	349
Open Market	Prepackaged software	7 372	434	60	527	316
Premenos	Prepackaged software	7 372	180	35	254	89
Internet/on-line consulting and development						
CKS Group	Business services	7 389	630	*	580	580
Eagle River Interactive	Business services	7 389	165	*	463	463
Total software and services						**11 777**

* Estimates are not available. It is assumed that 100% of market capitalisation is related to the Internet.
1. Or latest available year.
Source: OECD estimates, based on data from the US Securities and Exchange Commission.

Annex Table 4.4 shows sample totals by sector. Most employment created by US Internet/electronic commerce firms in the sample is related to computers (41.5 per cent) and telecommunications equipment and services (20.3 per cent).

Given that data were collected from selected firms in the Morgan Stanley list, Internet-related firms' employment was then scaled up to represent the complete sample. Total employment in each segment (infrastructure, software, etc.) was increased proportionally to the weight of the chosen firms in total market capitalisation for the whole sample. Therefore, a one-to-one correspondence between market capitalisation and employment was assumed within each segment.

Moreover, these are public firms and, according to Amano and Blohm (1997), employment in publicly traded firms in the United States represents about 50 per cent of total employment. The estimates obtained were thus doubled to represent overall (private and public) employment. The second column in Table 4.4 presents the estimated number of jobs resulting from both scaling up to the complete sample and scaling up to the total economy.

Annex Table 4.3. **Selected US Internet-related firms' market capitalisation and number of full-time employees[1]**

Content/aggregation/commerce providers, 1997

Company	Industry	US SIC	Market capitalisation (1997) (US$ million)	Internet-related market capitalisation (%)	Full-time employees	Internet-related employment
Organisation/aggregation						
Excite	Prepackaged software	7 372	377	*	434	434
Infoseek Corp.	Prepackaged software	7 372	234	*	171	171
Lycos	Miscellaneous business services	7 380	518	100	137	137
Yahoo!	Computer-integrated systems design	7 373	2 448	100	386	386
On-line services/information services						
America Online	Computer programming, data processing, etc	7 370	7 425	30	7 371	2 211
Compuserve	Computer programming, data processing, etc.	7 370	1 302	30	3 050	915
Individual	Computer processing and data preparation	7 374	112	*	176	176
Infonautics	Computer processing and data preparation	7 374	27	*	177	177
Publication						
CMG Information Services	Direct mail advertising services	7 331	270	25	912	228
CMP Media	Publishing and printing	2 721	638	*	1 720	1 720
Mecklermedia	Publishing and printing	2 721	216	*	182	182
CNET (4)	Motion picture and videotape production	7 812	533	*	581	581
TMP Worldwide	Advertising agencies	7 311	576	*	3 300	3 300
Transaction processing, financial services, and online commerce						
Amazon.com	Publishing and printing	2 721	1 128	*	614	614
CheckFree	Business services	7 389	1 050	*	1 444	1 444
CUC International	Personal services	7 200	13 140	*	15 000	15 000
CyberCash	Computer-integrated systems design	7 373	220	100	227	227
E*Trade	Security brokers, dealers and flotation companies	6 211	1 394	100	245	245
First Virtual	Services	8 900	54	100	77	77
iMall, Inc	Educational services	8 200	57	*	65	65
Onsale	Retail catalogue and mail-order houses	5 961	464	*	129	129
Peapod	Business services	7 389	170	*	285	285
Total content/aggregation/commerce						**28 704**

* Estimates are not available. It is assumed that 100% of market capitalisation is related to the Internet.
1. Or latest available year.
Source: OECD estimates, based on data from the US Securities and Exchange Commission.

Annex Table 4.4. **E-commerce-related jobs by industry in the United States**

US SIC	Industry	Number	%
737	Computer and data processing services	42 303	41.5
481	Telecommunications	20 687	20.3
720	Personal services	15 000	14.7
357	Computer and telecommunication equipment	13 295	13.0
731	Advertising	3 300	3.2
738	Miscellaneous business services	2 909	2.9
272	Periodicals	2 516	2.5
733	Mailing, reproduction and stenographic services	912	0.9
781	Motion picture production and distribution	581	0.6
621	Security and commodity brokers	245	0.2
596	Nonstore retailers	129	0.1
890	Services, n.e.c.	77	0.1
820	Education, public and private	65	0.1
	Total selected industries	102 019	100.0

Source: OECD estimates, based on data from the US Securities and Exchange Commission.

Annex 4.2.

JOB OPPORTUNITIES IN E-COMMERCE-RELATED INDUSTRIES

The "copyright industry"

The computer software, motion picture, audio-visual and publishing industries have been defined as the "copyright industry" (Economist Incorporated, 1996). In the United States, the industry's employment share grew from 1.60 per cent in 1977 to 3.08 per cent in 1996 and is forecast to generate 1.4 million new jobs in the period 1996-2006 (Annex Table 4.5). The industry is quite diversified, with software services a fast-growing component (see below); employment in the advertising and publishing industries is forecast to lose share.

Annex Table 4.5. **Employment in the US copyright industries**

	US SIC	Employment (thousands)				Share of US workforce (%)			
		1977	1987	1996	2006	1977	1987	1996[1]	2006[1]
Publishing-related industries	2711, 2721, 2731, 2741, 277, 2732, 2789, 2791, 2796	697.3	884.5	1 537.7	1 501	0.76	0.79	1.26	1.08
Computer programming and software	737	186.6	630.5	1 208	2 509	0.20	0.56	0.99	1.80
Radio and TV broadcasting	483	162.2	225.4	242.8	245	0.18	0.20	0.20	0.18
Advertising	731	131.5	216.8	242.4	270	0.14	0.19	0.20	0.19
Motion picture	78	214	235.7	522.4	628	0.23	0.21	0.43	0.45
Theatrical production	792	65.5	117	n.a.	n.a.	0.07	0.10	n.a.	n.a.
Records and tapes	3652	26.5	21	n.a.	n.a.	0.03	0.02	n.a.	n.a.
Total		**1 484**	**2 331**	**3 753**	**5 153**	**1.60**	**2.07**	**3.08**	**3.70**

1. Total excludes theatrical production and records and tapes.
Source: Economist Incorporated for the years 1997; US Bureau of Labor Statistics for the years 1996 and 2006.

In Europe, there seem to be no consistent source of data to estimate employment for this industry. Adding estimates of the publishing, audio-visual and software industry, Databank Consulting (1997) obtained an estimate of around 5 million people (*i.e.* 3 per cent of overall employment). The main difficulty is estimating software programming and computing services in Europe. The Community Labour Force Survey reports an estimate of about 1 million employed in software companies in 1995 (excluding software personnel in hardware manufacturers and user companies). Another survey reports 2 million employees for the same year and for a wider definition. A third survey reports an estimate of 1.5 million employees only for Germany, France and Italy (Databank Consulting, 1997). Japan carries out a special survey on information services; for 1996, it gave a total of 417 087 employees. In addition, employment in the publishing industry and the audiovisual sector is estimated at 2 million for the year 1996 (*i.e* 3 per cent of total employment). Annex Table 4.6 summarises estimates of the copyright industry for Canada, Japan, the United States and the European Union. The industry's share in total employment averages 3 per cent.

Employment growth in the content industry is driven by information services, and particularly by professional computer services (which represent 58 per cent of information services in the United States), data processing and network services (28 per cent in the United States), and electronic information services (14 per cent in the United States). Annex Table 4.7 shows the trends in software and computer-related services in a sample of selected countries. While the number of jobs differs greatly among countries, employment in this fast-growing industry represents only about 1 per cent of overall employment across countries.

Annex Table 4.6. **Estimates of the copyright industry (Canada, Japan, United States and European Union)**

	Year	Copyright employment (millions)	Share in total employment (%)
Canada[1]	1994	0.22 million	2
European Union[2]	1995	5 million	3
Japan[3]	1996	2 million	3
United States[4]	1996	3.8 million	3

1. Includes print and publishing, audio-visual, new media content, and software and computer services.
2. Includes computer software, motion picture, audio-visual and publishing.
3. Includes print and publishing, information services and broadcasting, movies and entertainment.
4. Includes print and publishing, information services, computer programming and software, radio and TV programming and motion picture.
Sources: OECD, based on data from Databank Consulting for the European Union, US Bureau of Labor Statistics for the United States, Industry Canada for Canada, and MITI and various sources for Japan.

Quantifying the impact of electronic commerce on job creation in the software sector is very difficult. According to the estimates presented above, US Internet-related companies to the computer services sector employ more than 42 000 full-time employees. According to the European Commission's *Panorama of EU Industry* (1997e), western Europe has more than 16 000 software and services companies with over 300 000 employees. In terms of employment evolving from software and services in the context of Internet and multimedia applications, however, most of these companies have less than 20 employees, and several not more than five. Databank Consulting estimates, on the basis of case studies, that Internet activities such as the implementation of Web sites only created about 6 000 man-years of additional work in Europe (Databank Consulting, 1997). As of September 1997, 59 per cent of US companies and 38 per cent of European companies have an intranet. In 1998, these percentages are expected to increase to 77 per cent and 75 per cent, respectively. By the year 2001, it is expected that there will be 133 million intranet users around the globe (Mecklermedia Corp., financial statement, 1997). According to Databank Consulting, the adoption of an intranet for internal communication in large corporations does not seem to have a positive impact on employment.

Electronic or online information services include companies that provide proprietary databases and information either on line, via CD-ROM, or on other media (*e.g.* magnetic tape, floppy disks or audiotext). Online services still represent a small portion of information services, but employment that is strictly related to electronic commerce partly depends on their development. Booz-Allen & Hamilton provides a useful taxonomy of online services and distinguishes among services supplied for *information* (news, information, online databases, search engines), *communication* (e-mail, video conferencing, direct marketing, PC-fax, discussion groups, bulletin boards), *transactions* (EDI, telemedicine, teleworking, training, telediagnosis, e-banking, e-brokerage, e-insurance, e-shopping, travel, cultural, telelearning) and *entertainment* (music, video, games, etc.).

Data on online services are difficult to find and are based on ad hoc surveys which are often out of date. According to European Commission (1996) (Annex Box 4.1), there were only about 60 000 employees in the European electronic information industries in 1994, and given that these services are in part replacing off-line services, there does not seem to be much hope of net job creation. However, a report prepared by Booz-Allen & Hamilton (1997) for the Dutch Economics Ministry, which also takes into account the potential "linkages" in job creation due to the openness of the Dutch economy, estimates the new online services to have created 6 800 full-time equivalent jobs in 1997 (about 1 per cent of 1997 total employment) and forecasts 40 000 more full-time equivalent jobs by the year 2001.

Annex Table 4.7. **Software and computer-related services employment: international comparisons**

	1975	1980	1985	1990	1991	1992	1993	1994	1995	1996
United States[1]	..	363 549	637 409	779 656	791 031	838 334	894 256	955 094	1 083 977	1 223 263
As % of business services	..	13.3	15.4	15.3	15.5	16.3	16.1	16.0	16.4	17.5
As % of services	..	0.6	0.8	0.9	0.9	1.0	1.0	1.1	1.2	1.3
As % of total employment	..	0.4	0.6	0.7	0.7	0.8	0.8	0.9	0.9	1.0
Canada[2]	..	..	..	71 660	90 015	72 024	79 021	99 056	123 312	..
As % of business services	..	..	..	..	..	..	..	..	..	..
As % of services	..	..	..	..	..	..	..	..	..	..
As % of total employment	..	..	..	0.5	0.7	0.6	0.6	0.7	0.9	..
Japan	57 164	93 271	162 010	458 462	493 278	488 469	445 662	424 867	407 396	..
As % of business services	..	..	..	6.7	..	..	..	5.4	..	..
As % of services	..	..	..	0.9	..	..	..	0.8	..	..
As % of total employment	..	..	..	..	..	..	..	..	..	..
France[3]	..	62 509	100 181	144 766	146 220	151 347	147 881	153 329	158 544	..
As % of business services	..	6.2	9.0	8.7	8.7	8.8	8.6	8.3	8.4	..
As % of services	..	3.1	4.6	5.0	5.0	5.1	4.9	4.8	4.9	..
As % of total employment	..	0.3	0.5	0.6	0.6	0.7	0.7	0.7	0.7	..
Finland	4 800	8 200	14 100	18 000	17 500	16 200	17 000	16 500	17 400	..
As % of business services	10.9	15.2	18.6	15.9	16.0	16.3	17.6	16.4	15.9	..
As % of services	0.4	0.7	1.1	1.3	1.3	1.2	1.4	1.3	1.4	..
As % of total employment	0.2	0.4	0.6	0.8	0.8	0.8	0.9	0.9	0.9	..

1. 1982 instead of 1980, 1987 instead of 1985.
2. Including self-employment.
3. Wage earners as of 31 December. 1981 instead of 1980.
Industry definition: United States (US SIC 737); Canada (Canadian SIC 7720); Japan (Japan SIC 84); France (NAF 72); Finland (NACE 72).
Source: OECD, 1997.

Annex Box 4.1.   Jobs and online services in Europe

The MSSTUDY on the markets for electronic information services in the European Economic Area surveyed both suppliers and users of electronic information. It therefore combines a market approach, measuring expenditure for electronic information services, with a supplier approach, measuring the world-wide revenues of suppliers.

According to the study, 60 639 full-time equivalent professionals were employed in the European information industry in 1994. Almost 40 per cent of all jobs on the supplier side were in British companies. Job creation due to the growth of the UK information industry also benefited export countries. Of the 24 000 employees, approximately 25.8 per cent were employed in the United Kingdom. The rest were employed in other countries of the European Economic Area (28 per cent), in the United States (28 per cent) and in the rest of the world (18.2 per cent).

While employment in the information industry is increasing at a rate of 10 per cent a year, qualitative information points to the fact that electronic information services are also an instrument of rationalisation and reduce the number of information professionals, for example in paper-based archives.

Employment in the European information industries, 1994

Region country	Full-time equivalents	Country share (%)
United Kingdom	23 910	39.5
France	7 532	12.4
Germany	7 500	12.4
Italy	6 500	10.7
Netherlands	3 001	4.9
Sweden	880	1.5
Denmark	1 937	3.2
Norway	2 100	3.5
Finland	628	1.0
Belgium	763	1.3
Spain	1 449	2.4
Portugal	2 090	3.4
Austria	629	1.0
Luxembourg	65	0.1
Greece	1 367	2.3
Ireland	185	0.3
Iceland	106	0.2
EEA	60 639	100.0

Source: European Commission, 1996.

Annex 4.3

THE EMPLOYMENT EFFECTS OF ELECTRONIC COMMERCE: ESTIMATES OF THE IMPACT MULTIPLIERS

Databank Consulting (1998) estimates the impact multipliers of electronic commerce on employment in four European countries. The multipliers take into account the direct effects on employment generated by electronic commerce revenues in the industries directly involved in electronic transactions, the indirect effects generated by inter-industry linkages, and the secondary effects originating from the consumption-income link. The methodology used can be summarised as follows:

1. 1997 electronic commerce forecasts (from the European Information Technology Observatory) for France, Germany, Italy and the United Kingdom were broken down by Web-generated revenue segment (see Annex Table 4.8).

2. Different business models for electronic commerce were studied in order to choose a limited set of models to be applied to the revenue segments.

3. It was assumed that electronic transaction revenues replaced about 96 per cent of traditional ones.

4. Input-output multipliers, taking into account direct, indirect and secondary effects, were calculated.

Annex Table 4.8. **Revenue generated by commercial Web sites in Europe, 1998**

Percentages

Segment	France	Germany	Italy	United Kingdom	Average of the four countries
Computers and softwares	25	25	26	25	25
Consumer products	17	20	10	13	15
Finance and insurance	4	4	4	4	4
Manufacturing industry	7	6	8	8	7
Publication and information	10	10	11	10	10
Travel	5	4	6	5	5
Business and professional	18	18	20	20	19
Advertising	12	11	12	12	12
Other	3	3	4	4	4
Total	**100**	**100**	**100**	**100**	**100**

Source: Databank Consulting, 1998.

The exercise required many assumptions, some of which may be questioned. Among these is the assumption of the degree of substitution between off-line and online activities, which is crucial for estimating net job creation. Interestingly, the study adopts the worst-case scenario, in which about 96 per cent of electronic commerce revenues replace traditional ones. As expected, first-order effects are negative; labour-intensive activities, such as retail and wholesale, are assumed to be completely replaced by electronic ones. However, indirect and secondary effects more than compensate the negative first-order effects (except for Germany). 1997 electronic revenues in the four European countries are estimated to have generated about 173 000 jobs in 1998. Annex Table 4.9 presents the net gain in the number of jobs obtained by substituting electronic transactions for traditional ones (the difference between the jobs that would have been created by electronic revenues and those that would have been created by traditional revenues).

Annex Table 4.9. **E-commerce fully replacing traditional commerce: number of jobs created or lost**

Multipliers	France	Germany	Italy	United Kingdom
Primary: direct (industry direct requirements)	−169	−520	−109	−76
Primary: indirect (inter-industry linkages)	44	20	53	680
Secondary (consumption-income linkage)	322	324	851	3 062
Total	**+197**	**−216**	**+795**	**+3 666**

Source: Databank Consulting, 1998.

Annex 4.4.

FORECASTS OF TELECOMMUNICATION, MEDIA AND INTERNET-DRIVEN EMPLOYMENT GROWTH

Three scenarios for the development of the US communications and media industry

Cohen (1997) develops three scenarios for the development of the US communications and media industry to the years 2000 and 2005. One is a baseline telephony-oriented scenario which assumes that current development trends in telecommunications continue and incorporate the further liberalisation of services expected to follow the 1996 Telecommunication Act. This scenario makes use of predictions by Wall Street analysts and the Federal Communications Commission on the growth of the (narrow and broadband) wireline business, cable operators, wireless companies and satellite service providers. The second and third are more Internet-based scenarios and reflect Massachusetts Institute of Technology predictions that the bandwidth required for data, much of which are in intranets and on the Internet, will equal the bandwidth used for telephony by the year 2000 and will substantially overtake it by 2005. The third Internet-intranet scenario is the most dramatic and assumes that 60 per cent of leased lines will be replaced by Internet and intranet infrastructure. Scenario 2 (also intranet/Internet-based) is intermediate and assumes the share to be 20 per cent.

To measure employment impacts, Cohen used estimates of thousands of jobs created for each billion dollars of revenue in some of the main industries affected by the growth of the Internet and intranets, such as communication services, software services, computer equipment and motion picture content. Employment estimates were then corrected using revenues adjusted for substitution effects. Parts of the sales of products and services on the Internet and corporate intranets replace sales through traditional retail channels, such as retail stores, software firms, business service companies, and firms that sell different types of content. Between 25 and 40 per cent of the revenue gains due to sales of content and transactions on the Internet and intranets were subtracted from the original estimates. Annex Table 4.10 shows the estimated impact on jobs. The first (baseline) scenario estimates a contribution of 3 million new jobs in wireline services by the year 2005. The two Internet/intranet-based scenarios have a different impact depending on the assumption of substitution of Internet/intranet jobs for jobs lost in the wireline sector (lower impacts correspond to a higher substitution rate, *i.e.* 40 per cent, higher ones to a 25 per cent substitution rate).

Annex Table 4.10. **The impact of the development of the US telecommunications and audio-visual industry on employment, 2005**

	Scenario		Employment impacts (thousands of jobs)
1. Telephony-oriented	Baseline		2 961
2. Internet/intranet-oriented	Intermediate	40% substitution	3 648
		25% substitution	3 939
3. Internet/intranet-oriented	Radical	40% substitution	4 391
		25% substitution	5 138

Source: Cohen, 1997.

In the Internet and intranet scenarios, the multipliers (hence the impact on employment) are higher than the ones applied for wired services, owing to the investment in servers, server software, and content needed for the Internet and intranets. In the third scenario, the much greater use of content and software for the Internet and intranets results in the creation of an additional 1.4 to 2.2 million jobs in content-related industries in 2005 as compared to the baseline scenario (where content growth is driven by cable and satellite distribution only). The additional increases in GNP and jobs created in the third scenario do not arise from Web usage *per se*, as the direct impact on GNP of Web usage is more or less nullified by the loss of revenues from other existing wired services (broadband, leased lines, etc.). They come almost exclusively from the production of Web-related hardware-software content (Databank Consulting, 1997).

The BIPE-IFO-Lentic study of EU-15 countries

The BIPE-IFO-Lentic study adopts an integrated methodological approach, which includes country studies and macroeconomic modelling, to forecast the effects on employment of the liberalisation of the telecommunications sector in the EU-15. Four different liberalisation scenarios (against the baseline scenario of no liberalisation) were distinguished, based on the combination of the pace of liberalisation and technology diffusion (see Annex Table 4.11). The study includes all telecommunications sector technologies: radiotelephone communication, mobile telephony, cable telephony, satellite telephony, data transmission and value-added networks and services.

Annex Table 4.11. **Liberalisation of the telecommunications sector: economy-wide gains in employment in the EU-15**

	Technology diffusion			
Liberalisation	Slow		Rapid	
	2000	2005	2000	2005
Gradual	121 000	228 200	374 500	834 000
Rapid	291 700	641 800	49 020	1 300 300

Source: European Commission, 1997f.

The overall impact was estimated through four stages:
– job destruction at dominant operators;
– job creation at other providers of telecommunication services (emergence of new operators and services);
– jobs generated by purchases of intermediate goods and equipment by the rest of the economy (rise in the volume of telecommunication activity, price reductions that translate into higher consumer purchasing power, and lower cost/higher productivity for companies, investment and productivity gains and greater competitiveness);
– macroeconomic benefits via the improvement in employment and corporate investment.

Figure A4.1. **Job creation is due to indirect and secondary effects**

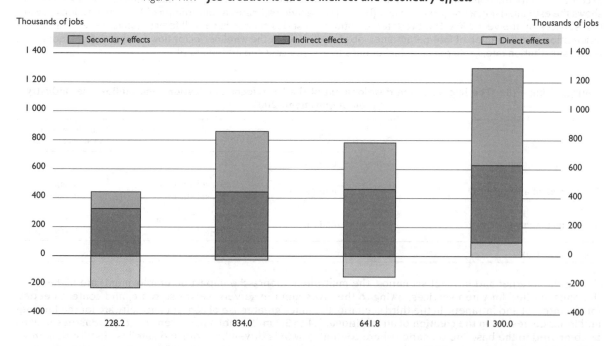

Source: European Commission, 1997f.

Annex 4.5.

THE "SKILLS SHORTAGE"

This section first attempts to assess whether electronic commerce is generating demand for skills or for new skills which cannot be met at the rate necessary for its development, thereby generating or exacerbating what is currently seen as a critical shortage of information technology (IT) workers.

In 1996, 4.2 million people worked in IT-related occupations in the United States, and the number is expected to reach 5.6 million by the year 2006.[6] A survey of medium-sized and large US companies by the Information Technology Association of America (ITAA) concluded that there are about 346 000 unfilled IT jobs in the United States today owing to a shortage of qualified workers (ITAA, 1998). In another study, conducted by Coopers and Lybrand, nearly half of the chief executive officers (CEOs) of America's fastest-growing companies reported that they had inadequate numbers of IT workers. According to an *Information Week* survey of 400 top-level managers, the jobs in shortest supply are IT professionals, followed by network administrators, database administrators, and system administrators. Some 80 per cent of managers said that they currently have IT job vacancies, and nearly a quarter said that the vacancy rate reaches 10 per cent of all IT jobs in their organisations. Wages in US ICT industries are 73 per cent higher than in other private industries (American Electronics Association, 1997) and have been growing at higher than average rates over the period 1985-96 (Annex Table 4.12). The US Bureau of Labor Statistics estimates that an additional 1.3 million workers will be needed in the period 1996-2006 (Margherio *et al.*, 1998).

Annex Table 4.12.   **US workers' annual wages in ICT industries**

Average annual growth rate, 1985-96 (%)

Average of all private industries	3.8
ICT industries	**5.2**
Hardware	5.1
Software/services	6.6
Communications equipment	4.1
	4.3

Source: Margherio *et al.*, 1998.

This has been called a "critical shortage" of qualified IT personnel and has received great attention in the United States, but it is not a trend peculiar to that country. Annex Table 4.13 presents some estimates of IT skills needs across countries.

Annex Table 4.13.   **IT jobs unfilled owing to skill shortages**

	Current estimate of unfilled jobs	Source
World	600 000	European Information Technology Observatory
United States	190 000	Information Technology Association of America[1]
United States	346 000	Information Technology Association of America[2]
United States	450 000	Microsoft
Germany	60 000	European Information Technology Observatory
Canada	20 000/30 000	US Office of Technology Policy
United Kingdom	20 000	European Information Technology Observatory

1.   February 1997 survey.
2.   January 1998 survey, with a different sample including small business and definition of the "core" IT workers.
Source: OECD, compiled from various sources.

Employment in the European IT industry declined from 940 000 in 1995 to 935 000 (1.1 per cent of total employment) in 1996. The hardware sector was particularly affected (–7 per cent), while the software, services and distribution sectors showed a slight increase (10 000 more employees in 1996 than in 1995). This was due to the Year 2000 problem and to the deployment of Internet-based hardware and software technology which generated both demand for staff skilled in Internet technology, who are rarely available in IT departments, and increased outsourcing of functions (EITO, 1998).

Germany seems to have more than 50 000 ICT jobs for which there is no skill match, and UK industry needs 30 000 IT recruits (while only 10 000 computer science and information systems graduates leave UK universities yearly) (EITO, 1998). In Birmingham, the second largest city in the United Kingdom, one recruitment agency reports that it cannot find computer programmers for less than £80 ($133.80) an hour. Pertemps, a national UK recruitment agency, is spending more than £1 million on IT recruitment this year; however, it still cannot fill 4 500 vacancies for jobs paying up to £1 000 a day. The shortage is driven by demand for programmers using new-generation information systems and for solving the Year 2000 problem (*Financial Times*, 30 March 1998).

Some developing countries may also soon experience a shortage of IT skills. India has a work force of approximately 160 000 high-skilled software professionals (1996-97). Although it supplies graduates at a pace of about 55 000 a year, this may be insufficient to keep pace with a software industry that is growing at over 40 per cent a year (ITAA, 1997).

In other countries, local IT development strategies can create skill shortages. As an essential part of its long-term development strategy, Malaysia is creating a "multimedia supercorridor" (a 9 x 30 mile IT centre) that is expected to boost the country's technological development. At the moment, however, Malaysian universities are producing less than 6 000 IT engineers a year for an estimated annual demand of 10 000.

"If the information technology industry were experiencing shortages, market pressure would be likely to raise salaries for IT workers more rapidly than for other professional workers" (Lerman, 1998). However, Lerman shows that the pattern of US median salary levels for computer scientists, operations researchers, and computer programmers has been essentially flat and not very different from that of US professionals overall through 1996, thereby calling into question the existence of a real shortage and attributing the 1997 median wage rises to the Year 2000 problem. Nonetheless, there is evidence that demand is growing much faster than educational capacity (ITAA, 1997), but increased demand for software professionals may not translate promptly into increased average wages, owing to the specificity of the software industry labour market.

Barr and Tessler (1998) segment the software industry into three tiers characterised by different labour dynamics (Annex Table 4.14). In the top tier, higher wages are matching increased demand for software professionals; however, this segment only employs about 10 per cent of overall software personnel. The third tier does not seem able to deal with the skills shortage. It is in the second that almost all the dynamics are to be found. According to the authors, some firms in this tier are able to offer higher salaries for small, specially recruited teams of software programmers, but most software-related positions are filled by those willing to accept the salaries offered. Some of these firms, because they do not recognise the key role of software personnel, incur massive losses. Data shows that 33 per cent of projects are seriously delayed and/or over budget and that another 40 per cent are abandoned completely (Barr and Tessler, 1998).

Annex Table 4.14. **Different labour dynamics within the software industry**

Segment	Users of software professionals	Market dynamics	Response
1	Venture-capital-funded software start-ups, "boutique" software service firms, software publishing houses	Attract best software talent, shortage felt only recently	Dramatic salary increases, aggressive recruiting practices
2	Computer and other high-tech equipment manufacturers, communication companies, financial services, and other IT-intensive industries	Shortage apparent for many years, outdated management practices give software talent lower status and wages	Hire less experienced software personnel to contain wages, projects are delayed or abandoned
3	Manufacturing, government	No executive-level awareness of the key role of software	No response to labour market changes

Source: Adapted from Barr and Tessler, 1998.

Is the skills shortage a lasting trend or a cyclical peak exacerbated by the Year 2000 problem? According to the Stanford Computer Industry Project (SCIP), the shortage of software talent is universal, is not limited to any specific technology, such as Java, SAP or Year 2000 workers, and extends to all industries (Barr and Tessler, 1998). Certainly the Year 2000 problem increases the need for workers with IT skills, and analysts report that the United States is only prepared for about 10-20 per cent of the workload, while world-wide preparation is minimal. Demand for software professionals nonetheless seems to be driven by the Internet (Joyce Plotkin, Executive Director of the Massachusetts Software Council, http://www.techworkforce.org/skill.htm).

NOTES

1. A database with financial income statements of publicly traded firms (US Securities and Exchange Commission).

2. DIW, German Institute for Economic Research, "Multimedia: Forecasts of Employment Growth in the Media and Communications Sectors Often Exaggerated", as reported in Databank Consulting (1997).

3. Amano and Blohm measure the US market capitalisation of 65 publicly traded leading Internet-related firms at the end of 1996. An "Internet weight" is attributed to each of these firms in order to roughly measure their related Internet value and employment. According to their calculations, US Internet-related jobs in 1996 amounted to approximately 760 000.

4. According to a recent survey of Internet service providers (ISPs) in Europe, carried out by Databank Consulting, IDATE and TNO for the European Commission, about 34 per cent of the sample originates from the telecommunications industry, 33 per cent from the IT industry, about 10 per cent is related to a scientific community, only one explicitly originates from the marketing sector, and only about 8 per cent are start-ups. About 38 per cent of the ISPs interviewed had less than 10 employees, 25 per cent of the sample had between 10 and 20 employees; another group had between 20 and 100, and only a minority had over 100.

5. The survey (March 1997) defined ISPs as any organisation that uses the TCP/IP networking protocol and offers services to the general public; it did not include online service providers such as America Online, which uses proprietary networking protocols.

6. Department of Commerce (Margherio *et al.*, 1998) definition of IT-related occupations; US Bureau of Labor Statistics data and employment forecast.

Chapter 5

SOCIETAL IMPLICATIONS OF ELECTRONIC COMMERCE

Although primarily an economic phenomenon, electronic commerce forms part of a broader process of social change, characterised by the globalisation of markets, the shift towards an economy based on knowledge and information, and the growing prominence of all forms of technology in everyday life. These major societal transformations are now under way and will probably continue far into the foreseeable future. As both a product and manifestation of such transformations, electronic commerce is being shaped by, and increasingly will help to shape, modern society as a whole. Societal factors will thus have a profound influence on its future development. They will also merit attention from a public policy standpoint, both to establish the social conditions that allow electronic commerce to reach its full economic potential and to ensure that its benefits are realised by society as a whole. It is therefore vital to understand the social processes that will inevitably influence how electronic commerce evolves and how quickly it can grow, as well as the areas where, through externalities of various kinds, it may profoundly affect society. In the latter category, distributive effects may have direct economic relevance of considerable interest to policy makers.

Analysis of the social dimensions of electronic commerce is hindered, however, both by the rapidity of change, which limits the collection of quantitative data on the growth and implications of new forms of electronic business (see Chapter 1), and by the difficulty of isolating electronic commerce from ICTs more generally. Many of the effects of the latter are well documented in studies and reports on the information society, such as those of the OECD on the GII-GIS (1997h), of the High Level Advisory Group of the European Union and of Canada's Information Highway Advisory Council (IHAC). This work illustrates some of the social dimensions of the shift to an information-based economy, but is not designed to isolate the place of electronic commerce *per se* in the information society. Research is also hampered by the pervasiveness of electronic commerce in the economy and the consequently diffuse nature of its linkages to broader social, institutional and cultural factors. Within these limitations, this section reviews literature and evidence from a variety of disciplines to point to areas where a significant relationship appears to exist between social and economic considerations and which consequently may merit attention in terms of public policy.

Social enablers of electronic commerce

It has long been established that social processes of various kinds, including some that are cultural and attitudinal in nature, enable and support efficient markets and economies. Consequently, to understand which environments favour electronic commerce, it is important to identify the social processes that underlie electronic markets and determine their viability. Knowledge of these enabling factors could inform public policies for promoting the growth of electronic commerce nationally and internationally. Two such elements are identified and briefly explored here – first, access and its determinants and constraints and, second, confidence and trust.

Access to the digital economy

The "death of distance" (Cairncross, 1997) that is intrinsic to information networking is probably the single most important economic force shaping society at the dawn of the 21st century. Both for individual citizens and for businesses, affordable access to the information infrastructure has become a necessity for effective participation in a knowledge-based economy and society (IHAC, 1997). Access to the Internet in particular has become a critical enabler of electronic commerce, since it has emerged as the dominant platform for a wide range of information and transactional services associated with business-to-business as well as business-to-consumer applications (see Chapter 1). As a result, several aspects of access are important: the availability of advanced networks able to support the provision of Internet services; consumers' and businesses' ability to connect to digital networks and services; and the existence of the skills and capabilities necessary to use the information networks.

Network availability

Physical access to a telecommunications network capable of supporting data traffic at an adequate bandwidth, along with access to a computer equipped with a modem and the necessary software, are currently the necessary pre-conditions for accessing the Internet and engaging in Internet-based electronic commerce. In many developed countries, universality has essentially been achieved with respect to off-air broadcast services (*i.e.* radio and television), public network access, and basic telephone service (ITU, 1997; Stentor, 1997). In 1996, teledensities (*i.e.* number of main telephone lines per 100 persons) for developed countries were in the 45-65 range, and 90 per cent or more of households had telephone service. Telecommunications networks are increasingly being digitised and made capable of supporting higher bandwidth access. In addition, wireless networks and cable-TV networks are capable of providing high bandwidth access (high bandwidth, two-way or interactive access is often limited to urban areas, for a variety of technical and economic reasons).

Access to the physical network and high bandwidth capabilities will clearly affect the take-up and implementation of electronic commerce activities, particularly for consumers and small and medium-sized enterprises (SMEs) located outside urban centres in the developed world. Therefore, governments might well look at ways to promote the development and availability of advanced networks, either by means of conventional telecommunications policy measures or through other appropriate policy instruments. These are discussed in greater detail in the OECD background paper, "Infrastructure Requirements for Electronic Commerce".

Connectivity

To participate in electronic commerce as consumers, most people use dial-up access to the Internet from their homes. Access implies the cost of a subscription to an Internet service provider (ISP), the usage cost of a network connection, hardware costs (usually a PC and modem), and skills acquisition and support costs. For many households, such expenses may not be trivial. According to available data, Internet users are well-educated and tend to have above-average household incomes and even ownership of personal computers is highly correlated to income (OECD, 1997c; IDC, 1998; Dickinson and Sciadas, 1997); it is therefore reasonable to assume that the total cost of access will significantly affect consumer involvement in electronic commerce.

Data compiled by the OECD indicate that connectivity costs vary considerably across countries and in some cases within countries as well (OECD, 1997a). Although hardware costs are relatively constant and declining, others, such as charges by ISPs and network providers, may differ widely for different consumers. Local telephone access costs largely account for these variations, but any long-distance charges needed to reach an Internet node can also involve substantial costs. As a result, where circumstances keep these costs fairly low, as in North America and the Nordic countries, the rate of Internet connectivity has generally been high. Pricing trends appear to be moving towards lowering the overall levels and variations in access costs in order to maximise network usage and thus capture network externalities. Telecommunications policy and regulations could favour growth prospects for electronic commerce by encouraging telecommunication supplier prices to move in this direction.

Another set of issues surrounds the connection of businesses and institutions to the Internet. Engaging in electronic commerce as a supplier, either of Web-based information or of services, requires a higher level of connectivity in terms of bandwidth and reliability. The costs of equipment and networking are therefore more substantial, and may vary even more, depending on location, telecom provider, and the applicable regulatory arrangements. Small businesses and businesses operating in rural and remote areas in particular may be particularly disadvantaged. In terms of policy, connectivity issues may be more crucial to the development of electronic commerce than consumer access since they determine the degree to which a viable and competitive industry can emerge on an economy-wide basis in OECD countries.

Skills and digital literacy

Familiarity with and basic competence in the use of computers and networks like the Internet are necessary for involvement in electronic commerce and in the digital economy in general. Becoming computer literate can be a significant additional cost, one which is likely to vary as a function of age and educational background. A system of education that familiarises young students with the technology of the Internet can greatly reduce skills acquisition costs and decrease differences in participation rates in electronic commerce in the various segments of a society's population (Mansell *et al.*, 1998; Saint Clair-Harvey and Rapp, 1998).

It is widely recognised that emphasis must be placed on ensuring a solid universal base for developing computer skills and Internet awareness among grade school students. In the United States, President Clinton has proposed a far-reaching initiative to close the gap between those with access to Internet technology and those without. He has called on all state governments to require computer literacy of all 12-year-olds as a requirement for entering high school and encouraged the private sector to boost efforts to hook up schools so that every classroom has access to the Internet (Griffith, 1998). These and other national initiatives launched in OECD Member countries are indicative of the paramount importance of digital literacy.

Confidence and trust

Most business relationships, whether between a company and a consumer or among firms, exhibit a strong element of confidence and trust. While both conventional and electronic markets rely on high levels of mutual trust, electronic transactions create specific challenges for both businesses and individuals. Because they are impersonal and remote, these exchanges make mechanisms that reduce or eliminate risk especially important. In particular, the potential for anonymity can pose greater risks of fraud for parties engaged in an electronic transaction than for those involved in more traditional forms of commerce.

A specific form of risk is the possibility that personal or corporate information may be revealed or misused. While such issues are not restricted to electronic commerce, they take on special significance in an environment based on the use of sophisticated computer and communications technologies (for early recognition of these problems, see Government of Canada, 1972). Internet-based technologies make it possible to keep, update, and give third-party access to detailed profiles of individuals. Better information means, for example, that sales promotions can be targeted to those interested in the product, so that those who would find the information intrusive will be spared unnecessary communications. On the other hand, the potential for technological monitoring of personal lives and activities prompts many to resist providing personal information or to supply inaccurate information, for fear of misuse.[1] In a recent World Research Survey, 13 per cent of respondents who said they would not buy over the Internet cited the need to reveal personal information as their reason for not doing so.[2]

Concerns over the security of transactions are also a barrier to the growth of Internet commerce. Consumers fear that their financial information may be manipulated and misused either by the intended recipient of a credit card number or by a hacker who intercepts the card number before it reaches its final destination. In the World Research Survey mentioned above, 21 per cent of respondents who had not bought on line cited fear of hackers as their reason. Another 12 per cent cited distrust of Internet companies or a fear that money or merchandise would be lost.[3] A similar survey found that 15 per cent of respondents feared misuse of information by the intended recipient while 7 per cent feared hackers.[4]

Issues of confidence and trust are also relevant for business-to-business electronic commerce. As discussed in Chapter 2, the creation of extranets to facilitate supplier-seller relationships is largely seen as a positive development in terms of maximising efficiency, although security concerns remain prevalent. Proprietary information sent over networks, including trade secrets and company strategies, may be stolen. More than 80 per cent of companies say security is the leading barrier to expanding electronic links with customers and suppliers. *Business Week* reports that in 1997, a single group of Texas hackers was able to penetrate the security of the telecommunication companies SBC, GTE, MCI and Sprint. The result was $500 000 worth of damage and the rerouting of calls from FBI crime centres to international sex lines.[5]

Businesses that expand their internal networks to include linkages with other firms typically need to develop strong trust relationships. Security concerns, as well as the sensitivity of information transmitted over company networks, prompt many firms to forge alliances with partners they trust. Such alliances create co-operation based on personal relationships and mutual confidence which can lead to greater efficiency but may result in closed market structures. These may tend to restrict market entry for competing firms that lack such close relationships (Hawkins, 1998).

Benefits and social impacts

The rapid diffusion of electronic commerce and its growing importance in economic life can dramatically affect social relationships at many levels. Like all other technology-based change, significant social benefits will be counterbalanced by less positive effects brought about by externalities and various spillover effects. Owing to the speed of the information technology revolution, it is impossible to gauge the full range of social impacts and their net effect on the basis of the situation at a single point in time. From developments observed to date, however, the societal outcomes of electronic commerce appear to be of substantial interest to policy makers in several areas. For instance, some electronic commerce applications are emerging as effective means of enhancing the social infrastructure. Moreover, like other aspects of information technology, electronic commerce may affect the individual and society in a more general way. One of the more important of these broader social impacts, the effect on the use and management of time, is discussed below.

Strengthening the social infrastructure

Computer and information technologies have begun to make a significant contribution to strengthening the social infrastructure through improvements in education, health, and other aspects of human resource development, including the sense of community. The technologies and applications associated with electronic commerce, such as "smart cards", automated payment systems, and electronic information, can play an important role in the organisation and delivery of such services. These tools will increasingly be used by both the public and private sector as a means of improving and expanding services to the public.

Education and training

As shown in Chapter 4, high skill levels are vital in a technology-based and knowledge-intensive economy. Changes associated with rapid technological advances in industry have made continual upgrading of professional and vocational skills an economic necessity, whence the almost universal priority assigned to lifelong learning as a component of national development strategies. This places severe demands on established educational institutions and on traditional professional and vocational training. It is now generally acknowledged that the goal of lifelong learning can only be accomplished by reinforcing and adapting existing systems of learning, both in the public and private sectors.

The demand for education and training concerns the full range of modern technology, including robotics, biotechnology, and communications and computer technologies, which involve virtually all economic sectors. Information technologies are uniquely capable of providing ways to meet this demand. For instance, the Internet is at the centre of a learning revolution that is rapidly being adopted by many business entities. Online training via the Internet ranges from accessing self-study courses at a supplier's Web site to complete electronic classrooms. These computer-based training programmes provide flexibility in skills acquisition and are more affordable and relevant than more traditional seminars and courses. There is no need to "go away on a course, paying three-figure sums per day, plus accommodation and travel…" (Kavanagh, 1998).

Computer-based training has clear advantages over traditional training programmes in terms of providing information when it is most relevant and immediately applicable. For instance, Oracle, the database software giant, is building a "virtual campus". This educational application is meant to assist staff in determining which skills are currently needed for particular aspects of their work and how their current capabilities can be most effectively upgraded with courses available on line. This kind of flexibility allows for "just-in-time" learning, which makes it possible to learn the specific characteristics of a particular software product just before using it (Manchester, 1998).

In addition to enhancing the possibilities for lifelong learning, the Internet can make a second important contribution to long-term vocational development. In OECD economies, applications aimed at matching people's skills more effectively with the needs of the labour market are emerging. They improve the ability of employees and employers to meet the specific needs of a complex, sophisticated economy and labour market (Dyson, 1997).

Health

In 1990, world-wide public and private expenditures on health services amounted to about $1 700 billion, approximately 8 per cent of total world product. This expenditure is under increasing pressure, owing to government cutbacks and downsizing. At the same time, however, populations are demanding a higher quality and level of health care. It is well established that a population's overall health is closely related to its economic prosperity. Improved health conditions and access to health information contribute significantly to economic growth, because healthier workers are more productive. Government policies that promote health education help people lead healthier lives by increasing their access to and use of relevant information. When combined with policies to ensure effective and accessible health services and those that generate income growth, a virtuous cycle is created in which economic growth and improvements in health reinforce each other (World Bank, 1993).

Information technologies and electronic commerce health-care applications can play an integral role in the promotion of this virtuous cycle. They can help realise cost savings while broadening the reach of the health-care system (Industry Canada, 1998). In addition, ICTs can assist the overall health system to become "more cost-effective through structural and functional rationalisation of the delivery system, and the wide-scale implementation of ICTs… will result in improved availability and quality of health services" (European Commission, 1996). Information technology can play a positive role in expanding services and service delivery options while creating cost efficiencies in the administration and management of health services and therefore lead to greater economic prosperity. This is particularly true if access to these new and better services is extended to the most disadvantaged segments of society, as they have the most to gain from improved health conditions.

A sense of community

Electronic commerce and ICTs abolish distance and alter the concept of community. Many of these changes are positive – creating links with new people, maintaining closer ties with far-flung friends and family members,[6] and creating new online communities with potentially global membership. There are potential costs as well, such as those incurred in some countries with the arrival of automobile-dependent suburban shopping malls and the demise of urban pedestrian shopping. Likewise, as firms' production facilities and customer base become global, their loyalty to a particular area is likely to erode. There are concerns that because of the new technology, people will no longer have to live in built-up regions and urban centres will decline (ActivMedia, 1998). However, as much of the infrastructure for effective high-bandwidth communication is found in the traditional built-up areas, a technology-driven exodus from the city is unlikely in the near future. Cyber-links may allow some rural communities to strengthen their social and economic situation and reverse lower growth trends and shrinking populations. In general, electronic commerce and ICTs tend to reduce the need for direct physical interaction between people. More time and research will be needed to see to what extent people are willing to forego such interaction and to see the broader economic and social implications.

General social effects: time

Time affects all interactions and activities in the business as well as the social realm. Developments such as shorter product cycles, Moore's Law, and the rise of 24-hour, seven days a week service delivery are transforming business, but they will also affect the behaviour of individuals, communities, governments and social organisations. These changes will improve the competitiveness of global firms and will give consumers greater convenience and flexibility. In many ways, the shrinking of delays brought about by electronic commerce will lead to similar efficiency gains in the management and operations of public sector organisations such as health and educational institutions. The effect of such developments on the individual and on smaller organisations is less clear.

Issues of time concern individuals, organisations and society. Time management has always been a key component of efficient behaviour, but the requirements of modern business, transformed by technology and globalisation, may increase the demands, in terms of time and stress, placed on managers and senior personnel.[7] While compressed time frames may get products to market quickly and more effectively and may reduce the time spent on mundane, repetitive tasks, these benefits are accompanied by pressures on the decision-making process stemming from the rapid pace of technology change. Articles in magazines and newspapers describe demands for instant information, rapid decisions, and continuous adoption of new, complex technologies. Workers may be expected to be available or on call for longer periods of time, as there may be increased need for shift work outside normal waking hours to co-ordinate activities and keep systems running. This may increase the percentage of the work force required to adapt to non-standard working hours. In addition, the need to upgrade skills to accommodate technological change requires more time from workers, many of whom feel compelled to acquire these skills outside working hours. While e-commerce may help drive this change in the supply of labour, its growth is also in many cases a function of consumer demand, as many e-commerce products (*e.g.* entertainment) are interactive and require immediate consumption (European Commission, 1997c). In this sense, available time both drives and inhibits the growth of electronic commerce.

Whereas technological development is taking place at an astounding and accelerating speed, reaching understanding and consensus, especially on social issues, is typically time-consuming. The nature of the Internet forces a reconsideration of the most effective way to govern and of whether centralised decision making can keep up with the speed and fluidity of the Internet. This suggests the need to consider decentralised modes of decision making, such as self-regulatory mechanisms. Another option may be to consider methods of controlling speed by "throwing sand into the wheels" (Eichengreen *et al.*, 1995). This idea is the basis for limiting programme-trading on the New York Stock Exchange and has received further attention in light of the recent currency fluctuations associated with the Asian crisis (Stiglitz, 1998; Baker, 1997). Recent work by IBM on the potential impact of e-commerce intelligent agents suggests that e-commerce could increase economic volatility (Ward, 1998). It remains to be seen whether technologies such as e-mail, Internet discussion groups, and other technological aids to communication can assist in the decision-making process. Ultimately, however, biological constraints will allow only so much compression of the process of communication and understanding. This points to the need to develop a deeper understanding of how "cyber time" and biological time will mesh and of what the impact is on individuals, organisations and communities. More narrowly, it is necessary to analyse the net impact of e-commerce, as one of its key features is the compression of response times, while it may also free up time previously spent shopping.

Distributive effects

A central question for research into the societal effects of electronic commerce concerns its short- and longer-term implications for the distribution of income and opportunities in an information society. Currently, there is considerable debate regarding the scope and incidence of market failures in emerging information industries and the nature of biases that might prevail in information markets. Data now being collected may give some indication of where electronic commerce may have distributive effects that affect individuals, the workplace, and small business, as well as geo-political relationships.

Individuals

Because of the unique nature of information-based products and services, there are specific outcomes for market participants which are without obvious parallels in the conventional commodity or industrial marketplace. The positive externalities that accrue to public telecommunications networks offer one well-documented example of an effect that derives specifically from the informational nature of the activity. Similarly, many other social effects result from the close relationship between information and social, cultural and attitudinal variables. This relationship merits close examination to determine whether there may be a bias that might favour a particular group over others or which might exclude certain segments of society or make it difficult for them to access and benefit from the market.

The possibility of negative externalities has led to considerable speculation and concern regarding the possible creation of "information haves and have nots" and provoked policy discussions in a large number of OECD countries. Speaking of a "digital divide" between poor and wealthy households, President Clinton has pointed to other technology revolutions, such as the mechanisation of agriculture, that have expanded the gap between the rich and the poor and has warned that, in the absence of corrective measures, this could also happen in the information age (Griffith, 1998). Many national leaders in North America, Europe and Japan have also expressed their commitment to addressing these concerns. In this respect, attention is warranted to variables such as income, ethnicity and race, language and disability, which appear to affect individuals' participation in the information economy and by extension their involvement in electronic commerce.

Income

One consistent finding across many countries is that intensive users of information technology tend to be well-educated and to have higher than average household incomes (IDC, 1998) (Figure 5.1). For every $10 000 increase in income, the likelihood of a household owning a computer increases by 7 percentage points.

Internet penetration rates show a similar pattern. Canadian figures on households' access to the Internet segment Internet use by income (Table 5.1). While use is subject to variables other than income, it is apparent that as household income increases, so does the likelihood of Internet access. The data clearly support the view that, at least for now, households with higher incomes have more opportunity to benefit from electronic commerce than those with lower incomes. While this phenomenon is common to the introduction of most new technologies (*e.g.* electricity, telephone, TV), it is certainly of policy interest to OECD countries. There is reason to believe that the correlation between income levels and Internet usage may weaken, as lower-cost alternatives to the traditional personal computer become available, as the price of personal computers continues to fall, and as telecommunications markets are liberalised, although the fact that recent longitudinal work carried out in the United States between 1994 and 1997 reveals a widening gap between upper and lower income groups also needs to be taken into account.[8] Governments may wish to consider what policies, if any, might encourage the trend towards lower prices and thus accelerate connectivity.

Ethnic and race

Ethnic and racial origin is commonly associated with disparities in income and education, and there appears to be a similar correlation in use of information technology, the Internet and, by extension, electronic commerce. A recent survey comparing Web ownership and use by African Americans and whites in the United States (Hoffman and Novak, 1998) speaks of a "digital divide". The survey found that while home computer ownership among African Americans and whites is roughly equal at high income levels (over $40 000), whites were twice as likely to own a computer and six times as likely to have recently used the Web in low-income families. Although the results were found to be significantly related to income and education levels, the study concluded that, even after correcting for income, there were significant differences between the two groups. Statistical evidence from other countries suggests similar ethnicity-related differences in IT use, although links to factors such as economic status and language are less clear. The implications are obviously important for policy makers. The mutual reinforcement of income, education, and ethnicity/race as determinants of participation in electronic networks represents a serious challenge, both from an economic and social policy perspective.

Figure 5.1. **Computer penetration rates, by household income, in Australia, Canada, Japan and the United States**

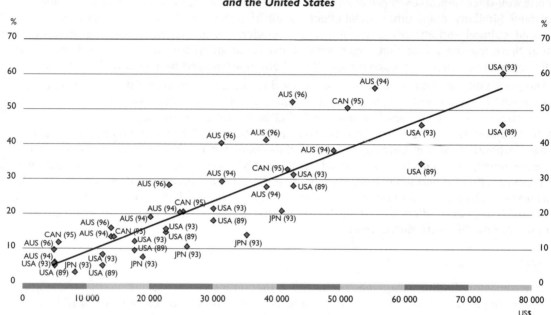

1. Household incomes were converted to US$ using PPPs. Income values were obtained by taking the midpoint of each income bracket except for the upper open-ended ranges where the lower bounds were used.
Source: OECD, 1997c.

Table 5.1. **Technology penetration rates and income levels of Canadian households, 1996**

Canadian dollars and percentages

	< $22 164	$22 165-$40 000	$40 000-$64 280	> $64 280	All
Telephone	96.7%	98.8%	99.6%	99.9%	98.7%
Computer	13.9%	22.2%	35.9%	54.2%	31.6%
Modem	6.1%	9.8%	16.3%	29.8%	15.5%
Internet	2.7%	4.4%	7.3%	15.2%	7.4%

Source: Dickinson and Sciadas, 1996, p. 79.

Language

Owing to its early establishment and current strength in North America, the English language dominates Internet-based electronic commerce. Its dominance reflects its status as the current *lingua franca*, the wealth of American society, and the position of the United States as the originator of Internet technology. A variety of international bodies, including the G7 and the European Union, have stressed the importance of multilingual access to the Web. As the North American share of Internet sites declines, greater multilingualism is likely to appear. Moreover, as world trade barriers are reduced, firms seeking to expand into new markets will offer Web sites in a variety of languages. Combined with innovative translation software, these market developments could well enable a more balanced participation of linguistic communities in global electronic commerce.

Gender

Since recent studies indicate that Internet use by men and by women may soon approach equality,[9] gender is becoming less of an issue. Electronic commerce in particular has already provided its value from the gender standpoint. E*Trade, an online stock trader, reports that half of its customers are women, far in excess of the average for e-commerce shopping.[10] It attributes this to the fact that women prefer online trading to traditional trading, where they may feel pressured or intimidated by male brokers. A similar dynamic appears to be unfolding at online car sites. NetGrocer, an online grocery delivery service, reports that many of its orders are from stay-at-home or single parents who can therefore better manage time with their children (Tanaka, 1998). However, the dissemination of pornographic material, which remains a significant portion of the electronic marketplace, represents a possible source of negative externalities. Not only may the perceived prominence of such material significantly discourage participation in online activities, it may more generally lower participation by women.

Disability

Both the biases of the Internet market and the capacity of the Internet to reduce these biases are well illustrated by the case of individuals with disabilities. Individuals with special needs could be among the greatest beneficiaries of electronic commerce and information technologies generally. Using advanced computer software, information can be easily translated from one format to another: texts can be converted to the spoken word or to Braille for the visually impaired; closed captioning allows the hearing-impaired to understand television transmissions better. Also, electronic commerce itself promises to allow individuals with restricted mobility to participate more effectively in the economy, both as individual consumers and in the work place. The Web can bring information, contacts, products and services from around the world to their desktops in an accessible form. However, many of these advantages are linked to text-based content. When pages are text-based, software allows the pages to be read or converted to Braille, thereby opening up vast areas of information to the visually impaired. Now, however, Web pages are increasingly graphics-based, and provision of plain text versions of information is falling behind. Even though the technology required to generate parallel text versions is inexpensive and simple, many organisations fail to provide information in this format. Moreover, the technology required to access the Internet, while dropping in price, can still be an expensive burden for groups that tend already to be economically marginalised. In short, the technology has the potential to help many individuals, but these benefits will only be generated if the issues of design and access are explicitly addressed.

The workplace

As the driving force in the knowledge-based economy, electronic commerce will have a variety of effects on the composition and skill mix of employment opportunities, the level of employment and the nature of work. The nature and scope of these impacts are discussed in Chapter 4. For example, through disintermediation, e-commerce has the potential to generate structural changes that will affect current manufacturing and services employment. Apart from the economics of these trends, there would be a significant social dimension to any changes involving substantial employment displacement, even if it is short-term in nature (European Commission, 1996).

In addition to aggregate employment effects, information technologies and electronic commerce have the potential fundamentally to alter the work environment and work experience. Telework and home businesses are two phenomena that are closely tied to the capabilities of information technologies and the growth of electronic commerce. Both result in significant changes in the nature of employment and the workplace. On the positive side, reduced travel time and flexible hours offer personal and environmental benefits, as do the lower costs of office space, a greater ability to avoid workplace distractions, and the ability to co-ordinate work projects over greater distances (Box 5.1). In Canada, nearly a quarter of workers had flexible schedules in 1995, compared to 17 per cent in 1991 (Statistics Canada, 1998). However, work tends to increase as these technologies are introduced. In one large computer firm, where 20 per cent of the staff teleworked, telecommuting resulted in a voluntary 20 to 25 per cent increase in the number of hours worked (cited in Breault, 1997). A recent Harris poll found that in the United States, the median number of hours worked per week increased between 1973 and 1995; leisure time fell from 26.2 to 19.2 hours over the same period. These data tend to suggest that some of the gains in corporate productivity may come at the expense of personal productivity.

Box 5.1.   **Examples of competitive advantages from teleworking**

Costs	– Up to 50 per cent savings in office overheads, relocation costs, etc.
	– Up to 40 per cent improvement in managerial and professional productivity
Business opportunities	– Better retention of experienced staff
	– Extended geographic scope for recruitment
	– Wider outsourcing opportunities
	– Access to scarce skills and to high-value people who have opted out of the conventional career environment
Innovation	– Refocusing enterprise geography around access to best work forces
	– Assembly of best know-how in multi-site project teams free of geographic constraints
Organisation and management	– Greater flexibility in organising and managing work when, where and how it appears best to do so
Quality	– Empowerment of employees to determine optimum work/lifestyle
	– Reduction of time, costs and frustration of peak-hour travel and the disruption of career relocations
	– Better access to the skills of excluded groups – disabled, single parents, dispersed communities

Source: EITO, 1998.

Small businesses

The effect of electronic commerce on SMEs has received much attention from policy makers and the media in OECD countries, a sign of the economic importance of small firms. In Canada, for example, 57 per cent of economic output is generated by an SME sector consisting of more than 2.2 million firms. Aside from the economic significance of SMEs, the sector's social significance is widely recognised. In many cases, SMEs reflect the more personal and unique characteristics of a community than larger firms. They also often serve specific market niches, the very presence of which can be a manifestation of special social and cultural characteristics. The greater independence and entrepreneurial nature of SMEs are thought to embody desirable social values and their presence is regarded as an important source of social stability (IHAC, 1997).

The Internet and the transactional tools associated with electronic commerce provide means that allow SMEs to collaborate and to access important information they previously found difficult to acquire. Many Web sites are targeted specifically to SMEs and provide information on venture capital, market information, specialised training, government services, etc. There is evidence that SMEs are rapidly recognising the importance of the Internet as an important aspect of their day-to-day business. Even if all do not set up virtual storefronts, they are gearing up to compete in a more technologically advanced commercial environment. A survey conducted in the first quarter of 1998 by the Canadian Federation of Independent Business (CFIB) shows that 43 per cent of Canadian SME owners have access to the Internet, up from 31 per cent at the same period in 1997. SME Internet access has increased more than four-fold in the two and a half years that CFIB has conducted surveys on the issue (http://www.cfib.ca/english/research/reports/98internet.htm, 13 July 1998).

Given the paramount economic importance of SMEs and their intrinsic community value, the role of small businesses in emerging markets based on electronic commerce is a major policy issue for governments. Smaller companies can benefit disproportionately from the opportunities offered by information technologies and electronic commerce. The Internet can make size irrelevant, because it can level the competitive playing field by allowing small companies to extend their geographical reach and secure new customers in ways formerly restricted to much larger firms. On the other hand, it is conceivable that the dynamics of electronic markets could create conditions that might impede SME involvement, relating to access to networks and connectivity (see the discussion of access above), technical standards, or institutional arrangements that might have anti-competitive effects or pose barriers to entry. This means that both governments and the business community must remain attentive to developments in the electronic marketplace in order to prevent or remove barriers to full SME participation.[11]

Geo-political impacts

Access to telecommunications networks and the Internet is distinctly unequal, both in developed countries and between them and the developing world. OECD countries accounted for some 512.7 million (69.2 per cent) of the 741 million main telephone access lines in 1996 (ITU, 1997). While teledensities ranged from 45-65 per 100 population in the developed countries and averaged 47.1 for the OECD as a whole, the average was 5.2 in the major non-OECD economies; and only 4.5 in China and 1.5 in India. Visions of a global knowledge-based economy and universal electronic commerce characterised by the "death of distance" must be tempered by the reality that half the world's population has never made a telephone call, much less accessed the Internet.

The imbalance of access to communications networks translates easily into an equivalent or even greater disparity in the use of electronic commerce. Currently, 80 to 90 per cent of Web purchases are made in North America. Many online shopping and auction sites limit delivery to the United States. While it is possible to ignore borders in the case of intangibles that can be sent digitally, most goods that can be ordered via the Internet, such as books, CDs, flowers, groceries, and computer peripherals, still face the very real borders represented by international shipping costs, custom duties, and risk of theft or loss. The growth of transborder business-to-business extranets will likely play a strong role in lessening this bias. By 2002, IDC predicts that the North American share of Web purchases will have shrunk to 64 per cent of total sales.

In countries with extremely low teledensities, universal access must be defined in some way other than access from every home; the alternative is access at the level of community or institutions. Public access sites located in schools, post offices, community centres, public libraries or even franchised shops are likely to be the alternative of choice. Such sites have a role in both developing and developed countries, especially in rural/remote areas and poorer urban neighbourhoods. They can be provided with a higher bandwidth connection than the average home and provide access to a variety of electronically delivered government and public sector services. The telecentres concept pioneered in Scandinavian countries, Canada's Community Access Program (CAP), and UNCTAD's "Global Trading Point Network" are excellent models of ways to expand access. Once access is gained, e-commerce and the Internet offer certain opportunities to developing countries and regions, as previously inaccessible information becomes codified and internationally available (European Commission, 1997). For example, Bangladesh medical schools can now access medical journals on line for $2.50 a month. Previously, the main medical school (Dhaka Medical School) could only afford a few subscriptions to published journals (WTO, 1998).

POLICY IMPLICATIONS AND FUTURE WORK AGENDA

The speed with which information technology is transforming the economy and society makes it difficult to determine with absolute confidence the full range of social impacts and the net balance of social benefits and costs. It is clear, however, that fundamental changes are taking place at virtually every level of society, prompted by the growth of the Internet, electronic commerce and other applications of information networks.

- A *question for further investigation is whether the Internet and electronic commerce will contribute to existing distribution inequalities, whether it is essentially neutral or can help mitigate more general social inequalities.*

- *Since gaining access to the network is key for participating in the "Information Society", work should be conducted that analyses what factors help and hinder access to the Internet such as cost, language and skills and whether these factors can explain differences observed across countries.*

One of the hallmarks of electronic commerce is that, by drastically reducing transaction and search costs, it reduces the distance between buyer and seller, enabling businesses to target very small niches, develop individual customer profiles, and essentially provide a means of marketing on a one-to-one basis. The ability to realise this goal will largely hinge on the climate of confidence businesses are able to create in their relations with their business partners and customers. Assurances about protection of privacy and personal information play an important role in building that confidence. Both the public and private sectors need a fuller understanding of the requirements for fostering confidence in electronic markets, particularly among consumers.

- *Work is needed to better understand the economics associated with the use and protection of private information, and the means to evaluate the costs and benefits of various proposals to protect and expose private information. This might include firm- and industry-level benefits, and related costs of assuring the confidentiality and integrity of personal data; the relative impacts of firm-based, sectoral-based and economy-wide standards for safeguarding personal information; and the effects on trade and investment of divergent levels of privacy protection across economies and jurisdictions.*

E-commerce and other information and communication technologies reduce the importance of time as a factor that dictates the structure of economic and social activity. It both raises the potential of saving time as consumers shop more efficiently, but also could reduce leisure as the technology provides a continuous electronic link to work. Regardless, many find that the pressure to perform tasks quickly is increasing. Linked to this is the broader question of the ability of policy-making apparatuses to accommodate "Internet time".

- *Research is needed to determine the net impact of electronic commerce on working and leisure time and its broader effects on the economy and society. In particular, it is important to know whether reduced leisure time retards or spurs the demand for new information-based products and services, and under what conditions. Furthermore, the speed it enables should be evaluated in light of the capability of existing governing institutions to keep pace and for the potential volatility it may introduce into economic markets.*

NOTES

1. "In Cyberspace, Nobody Knows Who You Are", *Hamilton Spectator*, July 3 1998, p. E3.

2. "The Internet Economy", *Time*, July 20 1998, p. 19.

3. *Ibid.*

4. ITAA/Wirthlin Survey quoted in "New Electronic Commerce Survey Finds Internet Poised to Become Nation's Cash Register", *Business Wire* (DV), 23 June 1998.

5. "How Safe is the Net?", *Business Week*, 22 June 1998.

6. For example, "E-mail Brings Families Closer. A growing number of parents with children away at college are surprised at the frequency that their children are using e-mail to stay in touch. Parents also find their children are opening up to them via e-mail far more readily than if they were talking to them over the telephone or even face to face. Convenience is cited as a main reason for using e-mail, as well as cost savings and 24-hour contact availability without disrupting schedules. Of the 9 million students in college, 7 million use e-mail regularly.", *Washington Post*, 3 November 1997.

7. See, for example, Toronto *Globe and Mail*, 31 July 1996, p. A16.

8. US Department of Commerce (1998), "Falling Through the Net II," http://www.ntia.doc.gov/ntiahome/net2/falling.htm, 30 July 1998.

9. CommerceNet/Neilson study as cited in "Startling Increase in Internet Shopping", *Business Wire*, 3 December 1997.

10. Judy Balint, Senior Vice President, Global Marketing & Strategic Business Development, E*Trade, speaking at the IDC E-commerce Forum, 10-12 May 1998, Monaco.

11. "Cautious Ascent by the Smaller Companies", *Financial Times*, 1 July 1998.

REFERENCES

ActivMedia (1998),
"FutureScapes Executive Report", Peterborough, New Hampshire, http://www.activMedia.com, 15 March.

AEA/American University (1996),
"Internet Commerce: A Snapshot of the Marketplace", cited in "The Internet and Beyond", http://www.microsoft.com (28 July 1997).

Alzon Pierre (1998),
interview, OECD, 28 May.

Amano Takuma and Robert Blohm (1996),
"Calculation of Internet's Contribution to Income and Employment", http:/www.gip.org/GIP9E3.HTM.

American Electronics Association (1997),
Cybernation: The Importance of the High-Technology Industry to the American Economy.

Andersen Consulting (1998),
E-commerce: Our Future Today. A Review of E-commerce in Australia.

Anderson, Christopher (1997),
"In Search of the Perfect Market", *The Economist*, 10 May.

Ansoff, H. (1988),
The New Corporate Strategy, John Whiley, London.

Arthur, W.B., Y. Ermoliev, and Y. Kaniovski (1987),
"Path Dependent Processes and the Emergence of Macro-Structure", *European Journal of Operational Research*, No. 30.

Atkins, Ralph (1997),
"Deutsche Telekom in Internet Plan", *Financial Times*, 14 July.

Australian Department of Foreign Affairs and Trade (1997),
Putting Australia on the New Silk Road. The Role of Trade Policy in Advancing Electronic Commerce, Canberra.

Authers, John (1998),
"An Attempt to Cash in on Internet Commerce", *Financial Times*, 30 April.

Bailey, Jospeph P. and Yannis Bakos (1997),
"An Exploratory Study of the Emerging Role of Electronic Intermediaries", *International Journal of Electronic Commerce*, Vol. 1, No. 3, Spring, pp. 7-20.

Baker, George (1997),
"Greenspan Warns on Capital Flow Curbs", *Financial Times*, 15 October.

Bakos, Yannis and Erik Brynjolfsson (forthcoming),
"Aggregation and Disaggregation of Information Goods: Implications for Bundling, Site Licensing and Micropayment Systems", in D. Hurley, B. Kahin and H. Varian (eds.), *Internet Publishing and Beyond: The Economics of Digital Information and Intellectual Property*, MIT Press, Cambridge, Massachusetts.

Barboza, David (1998),
"Value of Seats on the Major Exchanges Declines", *New York Times*, 12 June.

Barr, Avron and Shirley Tessler (1998),
"How will the Software Talent Shortage End?", *American Programmer*, Vol. XI, No. 1, http://www.cutter.com/itjournal/itjtoc.htm#jan98, January.

Barras, Richard (1986),
"Towards a Theory of Innovation in Services", *Research Policy*, No. 15, pp. 161-173.

Beltz, Cynthia (1998),
"Internet Economics", *The World and I*, January.

BIAC (1997),
> "Business-Government Forum on Medical Information Networks and Technologies", Conference Report, 17-18 September.

Bloch, Michael, Yves Pigneur and Arie Segev (1996),
> "On the Road of Electronic Commerce – A Business Value Framework, Gaining Competitive Advantage and Some Research Issues", http://www.stern.nyu.edu/~bloch/docs/roadtoec/ec.htm#sec1, March.

Bollier, David (1996),
> *The Future of Electronic Commerce*, The Aspen Institute, Washington DC.

Booz-Allen & Hamilton (1997a),
> "On-line Services Market Benchmarking", report prepared for the Dutch Economics Ministry, December.

Booz-Allen & Hamilton (1997b),
> *Internet Banking: A Global Study of Potential*, April.

Borland, John (1997a),
> "Click Here and Get Paid for It", *Net Insider*, 13 October.

Borland, John (1997b),
> "Cisco CEO Eyes E-commerce Boom", http://www.techweb.com, 25 November.

Breault, Serge (1997),
> *Collective Reflections on the Changing Workplace*, The Advisory Committee on the Changing Workplace, Ottawa (LTT060-05-97E).

Brunker, Mike (1997),
> "Internet Casino Operator Raided by FBI", http://www.msnbc.com/news/76363.asp, 29 May.

Cairncross, Frances (1997),
> *The Death of Distance: How the Communications Revolution will Change Our Lives*, Harvard Business School Press, Boston, Massachusetts.

Cap Gemini (1997),
> "A Survey of European Retail Opinion", March.

Caruso, Denise (1998),
> "E-Ticket Wariness", *New York Times* , 11 May.

Cerf, Vin (1997),
> VON presentation, http://www/von.com.

Chandersekaran, Achamma C. (1998),
> "Education and Training Transformed by Internet-enabled Electronic Commerce", *Business America*, Vol. 119, No. 1, January, US Department of Commerce, Washington DC.

Chesbrough, Henry W. and David J. Teece (1996),
> "When is Virtual Virtuous? Organizing for Innovation", *Harvard Business Review*, January/February.

Childs, Kevin (1998),
> "Internet Threatens Postal Service", http://www.news.com, 30 April.

Chittum, J. Marc (1998),
> "Professional Services: Knowledge Transfer Redefined through Electronic Commerce", *Business America*, Vol. 119, No. 1, January, US Department of Commerce, Washington DC.

Coase, Ronald H. (1937),
> "The Nature of the Firm", *Econometrica*, Vol. 4, No. 4.

Cochrane and McIntosh (1998),
> *Reuters Business Briefing*, 21 July.

Cohen Robert B. (1997),
> "An Economic Model of Future Changes in the US Communications and Media Industries", *Communications & Strategies*, No. 28, 4th quarter.

Cohen, Bob (1998),
> "Business-to-Business E-commerce Market Poised for Rapid Growth", ITAA Press Release, 17 February.

CommerceNet (1997),
> CommerceNet/Nielsen Internet Demographic Survey, August 1995 and March 1996, http://www.commerce.net/work/pilot/nielsen_96/exec.html.

Confederation of Information Communication Industries (CICI) (1995),
> "Electronic Information or Professional Users in the UK: Supply and Use", London, December.

Conference Board of Canada (1997),
> *Jobs in the Knowledge-based Economy – Information Technology and the Impact on Employment"*, report prepared by Brenda Lafleur and Peter Lok, May.

Corrigan, Tracy and John Authers (1997),
> "Internet Use by Financial Services Group to Soar", *Financial Times*, http://www.ft.com, 6 June.

Cortese, Amy (1998),
> "E-commerce: Good-bye to Fixed Pricing", *Business Week*, 4 May.

Court, Randolph (1998),
> "Dell's Magic Formula", http://www.wired.com, 28 May.

Crane, Alan (1997),
> "Information Age will curb inflation", *Financial Times*, 17 March.

Crockett, Barton (1997),
> "The Risky Bottom Line of Cyber Casinos", http://www.msnbc.com, 28 July.

Cronin, Mary (1998),
> "Ford's Intranet Success", http://www.news.com, 17 March.

Cybersource (1998),
> "Credit Card Fraud Against Merchants", Document 22198, cybersource.com.

Data Analysis (1997),
> "Second Quarter 1997: Computer Industry Forecasts", http://www.sonic.net, 9 November.

Databank Consulting (1997),
> "Opportunities for Economic and Employment Growth in the Evolution towards the Information Society", FAIR *Working Paper* No. 29, March.

Databank Consulting (1998),
> "Preliminary Estimates of the Multiplier Effects of Electronic Commerce on the EU Economy and Employment", FAIR *Working Paper* No. 47, March.

David, Paul A. (1990),
> "The Dynamo and the Computer: A Historical Perspective on the Modern Productivity Paradox", *The American Economic Review*, May.

Davis, Beth (1998),
> "In Certificates We Trust", http://www.techweb.com, 25 March.

de Aenelle, Conrad (1997),
> "What's in the Cards? More Uses and Fraud", *International Herald Tribune*, 22-23 November, p. 17.

Denton, Nicholas (1997),
> "IBM Offers to Cut Prices in Return for Share of the Profits", *Financial Times*, 28 April, p. 18.

Dickinson, P. and G. Sciadas (1997),
> "Access to the Information Highway and The Sequel", Statistics Canada, *Canadian Economic Observer* and *Services Indicators*.

Direct Marketing Association (1998),
> "Economic Impact: US Direct Marketing", March.

Direct Newsline, Media Daily Archive (1998),
> Vol. 6, No. 7, http://www.mediacentral.com, 13 January.

Dyson, Esther (1997),
> *Release 2.0*, Broadway Books, New York.

E-land (1997),
> http://www.e-land.com/ e-stat_pages, 1 May.

Economist Incorporated (1996),
> "US Software Industry Trends, 1987-1994", report prepared by Stephen E. Siwek and Kent W. Mikkelsen for the Business Software Association.

Eichengreen, Barry, James Tobin and Charles Wyplosz (1995),
> "Two Cases for Sand in the Wheels of International Finance," *The Economic Journal*, 105, January, pp. 162-172.

Ernst & Young (1998),
> "Internet Shopping", http://www.ey.com, January.

Erwin, Blane, Mary A. Modahl, and Jesse Johnson (1997),
> "Sizing Intercompany Commerce", *Forrester Research*, Vol. 1, No. 1, July.

European Commission (1996),
> *The Markets for Electronic Information Services in the European Economic Area. European Report on the Member States' Study* (MSSTUDY), October.

European Commission (1997a),
> *Evolution of the Internet and the WWW in Europe, Telecommunication Infrastructures Study GI 2.2/96*, prepared by Databank Consulting, IDATE and TNO.

European Commission (1997b),
> *A European Initiative in Electronic Commerce*, http://www.ispo.cec.be/ecommerce.

European Commission (1997c),
> *Building the European Information Society for Us All*, April.

European Commission (1997d),
> *Strategic Developments for the European Publishing Industry Towards the Year 2000*, report prepared by Andersen Consulting with assistance from the Ienm (Institute for Information Economy and New Media at Techno-Z FH-Salzburg).

European Commission (1997e),
> *Panorama of EU Industry.*

European Commission (1997f),
> *Effects on Employment of the Liberalisation of the Telecommunications Sector*, report prepared by BIPE Conseil (France), IFO Institute (Munich) and the LENTIC Institute (Liège).

European Commission/High Level Group of Experts (HLEG) (1996),
> "Building the European Information Society for Us All", Interim Report, Brussels.

European Information Technology Observatory EITO (1997),
> *European Information Technology Observatory 1997*, Frankfurt.

European Information Technology Observatory (EITO) (1998),
> *Annual Report*, Frankfurt.

Evans, Philip B. and Thomas S. Wurster (1997),
> "Strategy and the New Economics of Information", *The Harvard Business Review*, September-October.

Faiola, Anthony and Steven Ginsberg (1998),
> "Those Who Surf Can Fly on the Cheap", *Washington Post*, 19 September.

Federation of European Direct Marketing and NTC Research Ltd. (1997),
> "Direct Marketing in Europe", report prepared for the European Commission DG XV, June.

Festa, Paul (1997),
> "E-trade Trading Commissions to Multiply", http://www.techweb.com, 20 August.

Fisher, Claude S. (1992),
> "America Calling: A Social History of the Telephone to 1940", University of California Press, Berkeley, California.

Forge, Simon (1995),
> "The Macro-economic Effects of Near-zero Tariff Telecommunications", CSMG Study prepared for the World Bank.

Forrester Research (1997),
> "On-line Ticket Sales to Reach $10 Billion by 2001", http://www.forrester.com, 16 July.

Forrester Research (1998a),
> "Report Predicts Strong Growth in Euro E-Business", http://www.internetnews.com, 7 April.

Forrester Research (1998b),
> "European New Media Strategies", *Forrester Research*, Vol. 1, No. 1, April.

Franson, Paul (1997),
> "The Market Research Shell Game", March, http://www.upside.com.

Franson, Paul (1998),
> "The Net's Dirty Little Secret: Sex Sells", http://www.upside.com, 31 March.

Frook, John E. (1998a),
> "Barnes & Noble Ups Ante For Amazon, Borders", http://www.techweb.com, 17 July.

Frook, John E. (1998b),
> "Automakers Hope Web Can Cut Costs", http://www.techweb.com, 16 June.

Frook, John E. (1998c),
> "Going Once – Sold? Packaged Apps Give Auctioneers Rich Options", http://www.techweb.com, 22 May.

Garcia, D.L. (1995),
> "Networking and the Rise of Electronic Commerce: The Challenge for Public Policy", *Business Economics*, Vol. 30, No. 4, October, pp. 7-14.

Ghosh, Shikhar (1998),
"Making Business Sense of the Internet", *Harvard Business Review*, March-April.

Gilder, George (1994),
"The Bandwidth Tidal Wave", Forbes ASAP, 5 December, http://www.seas.upenn.edu, 9 March.

Girishankar, Saroja (1997*a*),
"American Express Online Travel Service Flies High", http://www.techweb.com, 1 December.

Girishankar, Saroja (1997*b*),
"Feds Get Down to Business with Latest E-commerce Push", http://www.techweb.com, 3 November.

Girishankar, Saroja (1998*a*),
"CSX Reaps Java's Benefits," http://www.techweb.com, 23 March.

Girishankar, Saroja (1998*b*),
"Charles Schwab Trades Big in Online Business", http://www.techweb.com, 6 April.

Goff, Leslie (1998),
"Online Computer Store Forecasts Growth", http://www.techweb.com, 20 April.

Goldhaber, Michael H. (1997),
"The Attention Economy and the Net", http://www.harvard.edu/iip/econ, April.

Goldman Sachs (1997),
"Cyber Commerce: Internet Tsunami", 4 August.

Government of Canada (1972),
Privacy and Computers, Department of Communications/Department of Justice, Ottawa.

Grant, Linda (1997),
"Why FedEx is Flying High", *Fortune*, 10 November.

Griffith, Victoria (1998),
"Clinton Urges Computer Literacy Drive to End the Digital Divide", *Financial Times*, 6 June.

Griffiths, John (1998),
"Car Trade: Dealers Warned of Rise in Internet Sales", *Financial Times*, http://www.ft.com, 24 February.

Hagel, John and Arthur G. Armstrong (1997),
Net Gain, Harvard Business School Press, Boston, Massachusetts.

Hagel, John, III, and Jeffrey F. Rayport (1997),
"The Coming Battle for Customer Information", *The McKinsey Quarterly*, No. 3.

Havas (1998),
"Havas Voyage se prépare à une introduction en Bourse", www.affches-lyon.com, 28 May.

Hawkins Richard (1998),
"Creating a Positive Environment for Electronic Commerce in Europe", Working Paper No. 36, SPRU, University of Sussex, March.

Hawkins, Richard, Robin Mansell and W. Edward Steinmueller (1998),
"Towards 'Digital Intermediation' in the European Information Society", Fair Working Paper No. 50, SPRU, March.

Hays, Constance (1997),
"Hustler Loses Ground to Cable, Video and the Web", *New York Times*, 7 April.

Ho, James (1997),
"Evaluating the World Wide Web: A Global Study on Commercial Sites", *Journal of Computer-Mediated Communication*, No. 3(1), http://www.ascus.org/jcmc/vol3/issue1/ho.htm, June.

Hoffman, Donna L. and Thomas P. Novak (1998),
"Bridging the Digital Divide: The Impact of Race on Computer Access and Internet Use", *Science*, 17 April.

Hu, Jim (1998),
"Study: Net Use Eclipsing TV", http://www.CNET News.com, 30 March.

Iansiti, Marco and Alan MacCormack (1997),
"Developing Products on Internet Time", *Harvard Business Review*, September-October.

IDC (1997*a*),
"Cast a Wide Net", *The Gray Sheet*, August.

IDC (1997*b*),
"Directions 1997: Follow the Consumer", *The Gray Sheet*, May.

IDC (1997*c*),
"The 1997 Global IT Survey", *The Gray Sheet*, June.

IDC (1997*d*),
"The Web: Who, Where, When and Why?", *The Gray Sheet*, August.

IDC (1998),
"Internet Commerce Defined: Current State and Future Outlook", presentation material prepared for the Internet Commerce Breakfast, June.

Industry Canada (1997),
"Survey of Technology Diffusion in Service Industries", Ottawa.

Industry Canada (1998),
Sector Competitiveness Framework Series: Telehealth Industry, Sector Competitiveness Frameworks Series, Ottawa.

Information Highway Advisory Council, Canada (IHAC) (1995),
Connection, Community, Content: The Challenge of the Information Highway, Ottawa.

Information Highway Advisory Council, Canada (IHAC) (1997),
Preparing Canada for a Digital World, Ottawa.

Information Strategy (1998),
The Global Internet 100 Survey, 1998.

Information Technology Association of America (ITAA) (1998),
"Help Wanted: A Call for Collaborative Action for the New Millennium", Virginia Tech. (ed.), January.

INSEE (1997),
Les Entreprises des Services en 1995.

Institute for Technology Assessment (1997),
"Digital Money: Industry and Public Policy Issues", Washington DC, October.

Institute for the Future (1996),
The Coming Transformation of Mail, Menlo Park, California.

Internet Advertising Bureau (1998),
"Net Ad Sales Nearing $1 Billion", http://www.wired.com, 7 April.

International Telecommunications Union (ITU) (1997),
"Challenges to the Network: Telecommunications and the Internet", Geneva, Switzerland.

Jackson, Tim (1997a),
"The New Economics of AoL", *Financial Times*, 22 December.

Jackson, Tim (1997b),
"The $78M Grocery Store", *Financial Times*, 29 September.

Jackson, Tim (1998),
"E-commerce in Box", *Financial Times*, 14 April.

Janson, Emma and Robin Mansell (1998),
"A Case of Electronic Commerce. The On-line Music Industry – Content, Regulation and Barriers to Development", FAIR *Working Paper* No. 40, SPRU, University of Sussex, March.

Joachim, David (1998),
"AT&T Bundles E-commerce Hosting And Service Offerings", http://www.techweb.com, 31 March.

Jupiter (1997),
http://www.jupiter.com, 24 April.

Karpinski, Richard (1998),
"Web Merchants Offer Incentive to Affiliates", http://www.techweb.com, 17 February.

Katz, M.L. and C. Shapiro (1985),
"Network Externalities, Competition and Compatibility", *American Economic Review*, Vol. 75, No. 3.

Kavanagh, John (1998),
"Training Via the Internet", *Financial Times*, 7 May.

Kehoe, Louise (1998),
"High Street in Hyperspace", *Financial Times*, 18 April.

Kerstetter, Jim (1997),
"Cisco cites E-commerce Success of Web Site", PC *Week*, http://www8.zdnet.com/pcweek/news/0505/05ecis.html, 6 May.

KPMG (1998),
"e-Christmas: Achievements and Learning", http://www.kpmg.co.uk.

Krochmal, Mo (1998),
"E-commerce Takes a Backseat to Hardware Needs", http://www.techweb.com, 23 June.

Kujuba, Laura (1998),
"Can IP Answer AT&T's Call?", http://www.infoworld.com, 26 May.

LaTour Kadison, Maria, Blane Erwin and Michael Putnam (1998),
"Middlemen on the Net", *Forrester Research*, Vol. 1, No. 7, January

Lerman Robert I. (1998),
"Is There a Labour Shortage in the Information Technology Industry?", *Issues in Science and Technology*, Spring.

Lesk, Michael (1997),
"Projections for Making Money on the Web", paper presented at the Harvard University Infrastructure Conference, January.

Lipton, Beth (1997),
"Music Sales don't Sing Online", http://www.news.com, 4 December.

Lipton, Beth (1998),
"Digital Music hits Sour Note", http://www.news.com, 15 July.

Litan, Robert E. and William A. Niskanen (1997),
Going Digital!, The Brookings Institution and the Cato Institute, Washington DC.

Lorentz (1998),
"Electronic Commerce: A New Factor for Consumers, Companies, Citizens and Government", http://www.premier-ministre.gouv.fr/.

Macavinta, Courtney (1998),
"Playboy Pins hopes on Net", http://www.news.com, 19 March.

Magretta, Joan (1998),
"The Power of Virtual Integration: An Interview with Dell Computer's Michael Dell", *Harvard Business Review*, March-April.

Malone, T., J. Yates, R. Benjamin (1987),
"Electronic Markets and Electronic Hierarchies", *Communications* ACM, 6, pp. 485-497.

Manchester, Philip (1998),
"Employee Empowerment, Building Up the Skills Base", *Financial Times*, 7 May.

Mansell, Robin, David C. Neice and W. Edward Steinmueller (1998),
"Universal Access Policies for Knowledge-Intensive Societies", in L. Saint Clair-Harvey and L. Rapp (eds.), *Universal Service and Public Service: Interoperability Strategies and International Issues in the 21st Century Governance*, forthcoming, SERD, France.

Marable, Leslie (1997),
"$1.1B in Online Insurance Sales Predicted by 2001," http://www.techweb.com, 1 August.

Margherio, Lynn, Dave Henry, Sandra Cook, and Sabrina Montes (1998),
"The Emerging Digital Economy", US Department of Commerce, Washington DC, http://www.ecommerce.gov, April.

Margolis, Bud (1998),
"E-commerce and Retail Banking Review", http://ourworld.compuserve.com/homepages/budd_margolis, March.

Marsicano, James (1998),
"Online Travel: How is the Travel Sector Spearheading Online Retail Commerce?", paper presented at "New Media Shopping Conference", London, 4-6 March.

McKinsey Quarterly (1997),
"Retail Banking", No. 2.

Meeker, Mary (1997),
"Internet Retailing Report", Morgan Stanley, http://www.ms.com, 28 May.

Meeker, Mary and Chris DePuy (1996),
"The Internet Report", http://www/ms.com.

Ministry of International Trade and Industry (MITI), Japan (1997),
"Towards the Age of the Digital Economy", http://www.miti.go.jp, May.

Ministry of International Trade and Industry (MITI), Japan (1998),
"Interium report by the Study Group on the Impact of Informatisation on Industry", draft, July.

Ministry of Posts and Telecommunications (MPT) (1998),
"Report on the Current Situation in Communication", mimeo.

Moad, Jeff (1997),
"Toss the Boxes", PC*Week*, http://www.pcweek.com, 22 January.

Moltzen, Edward (1998),
"Is E-commerce Underestimated?", *Computer Reseller News*, http://www.techweb.com, 8 April.

Moozakis, Chuck (1998),
"Voice over IP takes First Steps", http://www.techweb.com, 10 June.

Morgan Stanley Dean Witter (1997),
"Internet Quarterly: The Business of the Web", http://www.ms.com, 23 September.

Morishita, Kaoru (1997),
"Internet Erasing Some Old Business Forms", *The Nikkei Weekly*, 20 October.

Murphy, Kathleen (1997),
"US Weighs Pulling Plug on Internet Gambling", http://www.webweek.com, 11 August.

Myhrvold, Nathan (1997),
"The Dawn of Technomania", *The New Yorker*, 20 October.

Nelson, Matthew (1998),
"Vendors Balk at Deploying SET", http://www.infoworld.com, 22 January.

Nelson R.R. and S. Winter (1982),
An Evolutionary Theory of Economic Change, Belknap Press, Cambridge, Massachusetts.

Newsedge (1998),
"On-line Trading Accounted for 17% of all Retail Trades in 1997", http://www.businessjournal.netscape.com, 26 February.

Noer, Michael (1998),
"GM Goes on Line", http://www.forbes.com, 9 April.

NTIA (US National Telecommunications and Information Agency) (1995),
Falling Through the Net.

Ody, Penelope (1996),
"Retailers Jump on the Loyalty Bandwagon", *Financial Times*, 2 October, p. FT-IT 7.

OECD (1996a),
Technology and Industrial Performance, Paris.

OECD (1996b),
Technology, Productivity and Job Creation, Paris.

OECD (1997a),
Communications Outlook 1997, Paris.

OECD (1997b),
"Internet Voice Telephony Developments", DSTI/ICCP/TISP(97)3/FINAL, http://www.oecd.org/dsti/sti/it/index.htm.

OECD (1997c),
Information Technology Outlook, Paris.

OECD (1997d),
"Webcasting and Convergence: Policy Implications", OCDE/GD(97)221, http://www.oecd.org/dsti/sti/it/index.htm.

OECD (1997e),
"Electronic Commerce: Opportunities and Challenges for Governments. The 'Sacher Report'", http://www.oecd.org/dsti/sti/it/index.htm.

OECD (1997f),
"Dismantling the Barriers to Global Electronic Commerce", DSTI/ICCP(98)13/FINAL, http://www.oecd.org/dsti/sti/it/index.htm.

OECD (1997g),
The OECD Report on Regulatory Reform, Volume II: *Thematic Studies*, Paris.

OECD (1997h),
"Global Information Infrastructure-Global Information Society (GII-GIS): Policy Requirements", OCDE/GD(97)139, Paris.

OECD (1998a),
"France's Experience with the Minitel: Lessons for Electronic Commerce" DSTI/ICCP/IE(97)10/FINAL.

OECD (1998b),
Technology, Productivity and Job Creation: Best Policy Practices, Paris.

OECD (1998c),
OECD *Economic Outlook*, June, Paris.

OECD (1998d),
"Measuring Electronic Commerce: International Trade in Software", DSTI/ICCP/IE(98)3/FINAL.

OECD (1999),
Communications Outlook, Paris, forthcoming.

OECD/ISO (1996),
The Economic Dimension of Electronic Data Interchange (EDI),
Geneva.

Oeler, Kurt (1998),
"Dell rejiggers site to boost sales", http://www.news.com, 22 May.

Ohlson, Kathleen (1998) "Small Business Grabbing Foothold on the Internet", http://www.infoworld.com, 16 July.

Page, Geoff (1998),
"How can ISP's Position Themselves in the Electronic Home Services Market?," UUNet UK, presentation made at "New Media Shopping Conference", London, 4-6 March.

Parliament of the Commonwealth of Australia (1998),
"Internet Commerce: To Buy or Not to Buy?", report 360, May.

Patrizio, Andy (1997),
"Multiplayer Gaming A$ 1.2B Market by 2001", http://www.techweb.com, 25 November.

Price Waterhouse (1998),
"Price Waterhouse Predicts Explosive E-commerce Growth," http://www.internetnews.com, 8 April.

Rafter, Michelle V. (1998),
"Pushing the Envelope", http://www.latimes.com, 9 February.

Rawsthorn, Alice (1997a),
"United States: Chain of Online Music Stores Planned", *Financial Times*, http://www.ft.com, 5 December.

Rawsthorn, Alice (1997b),
"Internet Music Retailers: Rapid Growth Expected", *Financial Times*, http://www.ft.com, 5 December.

Reeve, Simon (1998),
"Online but Off Target", *The European*, 23 March.

Reuters (1998),
"Net Telephony Grows", http://www.wired.com, 16 June.

Rouland, Odile (1998),
interview by the OECD, 28 May.

Saint Clair-Harvey, L. and L. Rapp (eds.) (1998),
Universal Service and Public Service: Interoperability Strategies and International Issues in the 21st century Governance, forthcoming, SERD, France.

Scannell, Ed (1998),
"Taming the Wild Web", http://www.inforoworld.com, 15 April.

Schavey, Aaron (1998),
"Publishing's Future in Electronic Commerce", *Business America*, Vol. 119, No. 1, January, US Department of Commerce, Washington DC.

Schwartz, Evan (1995),
"Wanna Bet?", *Wired*, October.

Scott, Allen J.(1998),
"Multimedia and Digital Visual Effects: An Emerging Local Labour Market", *Monthly Labour Review*, March.

Selingo, Jeffrey (1998),
"Small, Private Colleges Brace for Competition from Distance Learning", *The Chronicle of Higher Education*, 1 May.

SRI Consulting (1998),
"Report: Net to Dial up $9 Billion by 2002", http://www.internetnews.com, 17 April.

Standard and Poor's and US Department of Commerce (1998),
US Industry and Trade Outlook '98, McGraw-Hill, New York.

Statistics Canada (1998),
Work Arrangements in the 1990s, Ottawa.

Stentor (1997),
Reality Check 1997: An International Comparison of Telecommunications, Stentor Telecom Policy, Inc.

Stiglitz, Joseph E. (1998),
"Boats, Planes and Capital Flows", *Financial Times*, 25 March.

Stohr, Kate (1997),
"Surfing the Unfriendly Skies", netlynews, cgi.pathfinder.com, 30 April.

Strassel, Kimberley A. (1997a),
"E-commerce can be E-Lusive", *The Wall Street Journal – Europe, Convergence*, Autumn.

Strassel, Kimberly (1997*b*),
"Microsoft, UK Post Office Join to Set Up On-line Mail Service, *Wall Street Journal – Europe*, 6 April.

Sussman, Vic (1997),
"Sex Sites Hot on Web", USA *Today*, 19 August.

Tanaka, Jennifer (1998),
"From Soups to Lunch: Shop for Groceries without Leaving the Den", *Newsweek*, 16 March.

Tapscott, Don (1996),
The Digital Economy: Promise and Peril in the Age of Networked Intelligence, McGraw-Hill, New York.

Taylor, Paul (1997),
"Electronic Revolution in the Retailing World", *The Financial Times*, 3 September.

Telegeography 97-98,
Global Telecommunications Traffic Statistics & Commentary, Telegeography, Inc., October 1997, Washington DC.

Tchong, Michael (1997),
Iconoclast, 26 August.

Tommasi, Philippe (1997),
"Les services d'information financières et les réseaux électroniques", *L'Atelier*.

Travel & Tourism Intelligence (1998),
"The Impact of Electronic Distribution on Travel Agents", No. 2.

Triplett, Jack E. (1996) "High-tech Productivity and Hedonic Price Indices", in *Industry Productivity: International Comparison and Measurement Issues*, Paris.

Universal Postal Union (UPU) (1997),
"Post 2005: Core Business Scenarios", Bern.

US Department of Commerce (1998),
"Input-Output Commodity Composition of Personal Consumer Expenditure (PCE), in Producers' and Purchasers' Prices, 1992", Washington DC.

US Securities and Exchange Commission (SEC) (1998),
Edgar Database, http://www.sec.gov.

Varian, Hal (1996),
"Differential Pricing and Efficiency", First Monday, http://www.firstmonday.dk.

Varian, Hal (1998),
"Markets for Information Goods", draft, April.

Ward, Mark (1998),
"Wired for Mayhem", *New Scientist*, 4 July.

Weber, Thomas(1997),
"For Those Who Scoff at Internet Trade, Here's a Hot Market", *The Wall Street Journal*, 21 May.

Wigand, Rolf T. (1997),
"Electronic Commerce: Definition, Theory, and Context", *The Information Society*, Vol. 13.

Williamson, Oliver E. (1975),
Markets and Hierarchies: Analysis and Antitrust Implications, The Free Press, New York.

Wilson, Peter (1998),
"The Next Wave of E-commerce is More Sophisticated", The Edmonton Journal, 28 May, p. E9.

Wise, Monique (1998),
"Schwab Shares Fall as Online Trading hurts Earnings", Hoover's Company Profiles, 15 April.

World Bank (1993),
World Development Report 1993: Investing in Health, Oxford University Press, New York.

World Trade Organisation (WTO) (1998),
"Electronic Commerce and the Roles of the WTO," March, Geneva.

Yardeni, Edward (1996),
"Economic Consequences of the Internet", http://www.yardeni.com/yardeni, 22 October.

OECD PUBLICATIONS, 2, rue André-Pascal, 75775 PARIS CEDEX 16
PRINTED IN FRANCE
(93 1999 01 1 P) ISBN 92-64-16972-5 – No. 50441 1999